The Dynamics of Interstate Boundaries

The Dynamics of Interstate Boundaries explains why some borders deter insurgents, smugglers, bandits, and militants while most suffer from infiltration and crisis. Grappling with an issue at the core of the modern state and international security, George Gavrilis explores border control from the nineteenth-century Ottoman Empire to twenty-first-century Central Asia, China, and Afghanistan. Border control strategies emanate from core policies of state formation and the local design of border guard institutions. Secure and open borders depend on institutional design, not on military power. Based on research in numerous border regions, this book advances the study of the state, local security institutions, and conflict and cooperation over border control. It holds critical lessons for policy makers and international organizations working to enhance border security in dangerous regions.

George Gavrilis is Assistant Professor of Government at the University of Texas, Austin, and holds an International Affairs Fellowship with the Council on Foreign Relations (2008–09). He has previously held the positions of Director of Research for the Council on Foreign Relations Oral History Project, Columbia University; Associate Research Fellow at the Institute for Social and Economic Research and Policy, Columbia University; and National Security Postdoctoral Fellow, Olin Institute of Strategic Studies at Harvard University. His articles have appeared in *Foreign Affairs*, *The Washington Quarterly*, *American Behavioral Scientist*, and *New Perspectives on Turkey*, and he has conducted research in the Middle East, Central Asia, and Europe.

The Dynamics of Interstate Boundaries

GEORGE GAVRILIS

University of Texas, Austin

CAMBRIDGE
UNIVERSITY PRESS

CAMBRIDGE UNIVERSITY PRESS
Cambridge, New York, Melbourne, Madrid, Cape Town, Singapore, São Paulo, Delhi

Cambridge University Press
32 Avenue of the Americas, New York, NY 10013-2473, USA

www.cambridge.org
Information on this title: www.cambridge.org/9780521898997

First published 2008

Printed in the United States of America

A catalog record for this publication is available from the British Library.

Library of Congress Cataloging in Publication Data

Gavrilis, George, 1972–
The dynamics of interstate boundaries / George Gavrilis.
    p. cm. – (Cambridge studies in comparative politics)
Includes bibliographical references and index.
ISBN 978-0-521-89899-7 (hardback)
1. Boundaries. 2. Border security – History. 3. Security, International. I. Title.
II. Series.
JC323.G38   2008
320.1′2 – dc22   2008008424

ISBN   978-0-521-89899-7 hardback

To Constantine and Feridun

Contents

Tables, Figure, and Maps

Tables

Figure

Maps

Acknowledgments

From the very start of this project to its completion, I had the good fortune to travel to a dozen border regions around the world, work in a half-dozen archives, learn several languages, and speak to people from all walks of life whose daily existence borders affect. Because no two borders look or function alike at first glance, building a theory was a difficult task. If I have succeeded, even partially, it is thanks to the many wonderful people who have helped me every step of the way.

This project stands on the shoulders of three outstanding scholars at Columbia University. Karen Barkey brilliantly showed me how to turn the long-gone Ottoman Empire into a laboratory for social inquiry. Jack Snyder helped me balance method and theory and always demanded that I speak to real-world problems.

Then there is Charles Tilly. He graciously took an interest in my project even as our first conversation about borders turned me into a bumbling fool. His razor-sharp comments turned my interest into a workable project, and his advice and care over the years have taught me what it means to be a scholar.

I benefited from the wise suggestions of Rifa'at Abu-El-Haj, Vince Boudreau, Val Bunce, Alex Cooley, Colin Elman, Tanisha Fazal, Hein Goemans, Gary Goertz, Dimitris Gondicas, Tony Greenwood, Mike Hanagan, Pauline Jones Luong, Maria Kousis, Mary Ellen Lane, Roy Licklider, Charles Lipson, Heath Lowry, Elise Massicard, Michael Meeker, Joel Migdal, Victoria Murrillo, Katia Papagianni, Christine Philliou, Graeme Robertson, Philippos Savvides, Sid Tarrow, Wayne Te Brake, Alexander Wendt, İpek Yosmaoğlu, and Bill Zartman.

Many others offered up great suggestions at a number of workshops that include the Workshop on Contentious Politics at Columbia University, the Consortium on Qualitative Research Methods at Arizona State University, the PIPES Workshop in International Relations at the University of Chicago, the Workshop on Colonial Legacies at Cornell University, the Workshop on Interdisciplinarity in Middle East Studies at the Institute of the European University in Florence, and the Institut Français d'Etudes Anatoliennes in Istanbul. I also thank great discussants and audience members for their questions at conferences that include those of the International Studies Association, the American Political Science Association, and the American Historical Association, as well as an anthropology conference at the University of California at Berkeley and the Lineae Terrarum Borders Conference in El Paso and Ciudad Juárez.

The Social Sciences Research Council gave this project a start with a generous grant whose funds were provided by the Ford Foundation. The grant sponsored my education in Ottoman Turkish and allowed me to spend an idyllic semester studying Ottoman history in the Department of Near Eastern Studies at Princeton. The American Research Institute in Turkey and the Institute for Turkish Studies generously supported my archival work. The Dean's Office at the University of Texas funded my research in Central Asia.

In the field I amassed huge debts of gratitude left and right. The knowledgeable staff of the Archives of the Prime Ministry in Istanbul, especially Berrin Başbuğ and İlhan Ovalıoğlu, made working there a pleasure. Thanks go to Koç University and Atilla Aşkar for logistical support. In Istanbul, Neşe Evliyaoğlu and the Özgür, Hacıevliyagil, and Yosmaoğlu families made me feel very much at home. Feridun Özgür was an outstanding language teacher. In Athens, Greece, at the Historical Archives of the Foreign Ministry I am grateful to all the staff and, above all, to Ioannis Mpegos. In London, many thanks go to Shelley Deanne. At NATO headquarters in Belgium, Ino Afentouli organized an outstanding briefing and initiated invaluable interviews. In Kyrgyzstan, I was once again surrounded by wonderful, generous individuals such as Nana Canter, Amanda Wooden at the OSCE field office in Osh, and, most of all, Ernist Jumagulov and his entire family. There are a number of people in Uzbekistan who deserve thanks, but given the political situation there, I would rather not identify them. They know the extent of my gratitude.

In 2003–04 I was a postdoctoral Fellow at the Olin Institute for Strategic Studies. There, thanks go to Steven Rosen, Monica Toft, and especially to Ann Townes. A fellow post-doc, Taylor Fravel, gave me brilliant comments more than once. My office mate, Ron Hassner, made me laugh constantly except when he referred to one of my early chapter drafts as a "two-story house with three elevators." I hope I have made the most of their thoughtfulness.

More recently, I have found a supportive environment at the University of Texas at Austin and with my colleagues there: Zoltan Barany, Catherine Boone, Gary Freeman, John Higley, Wendy Hunter, Ian Manners, Nancy Moses, Shylashri Shankar, Peter Trubowitz, and Harrison Wagner. Kaushlesh Biyani provided great technical and research assistance. Our dean at the time, Richard Lariviere, graciously encouraged my research.

I should add that this project owes a great deal to the Institute for Social and Economic Research and Policy (ISERP) at Columbia University, which made for a wonderful sabbatical. Most of all, endless thanks must go to William McAllister at ISERP for his intellectual support and friendship.

At Cambridge University Press, I thank Lew Bateman, Jack Goldstone, Libby Wood, and the two anonymous reviewers. Lew has published many authors who have inspired me, and so I am honored to have received his vote of confidence.

Dear friends made this project viable, and a passing acknowledgment cannot do them justice. Ioannis Armakolas, Chares Demetriou, Viki Kotsikopoulou, and Tammy Smith are marvelous friends and a tremendous source of support. Yonca Köksal is a brilliant sociologist, and her outstanding knowledge of Ottoman Turkish helped me decipher my most difficult documents. Jennifer Mitzen, a truly philosophical and thorough mind, gave my work a critical eye whenever I asked. Patrick McDonald and Ami Pedazhur combine the best of friendship and collegiality at UT-Austin. Mona El-Ghobashy delivered incredibly constructive comments and a good dose of humor in the final stretch. Antonio Borrelli guided me and suffered through much of this project.

My two sets of parents, Irini and Nick, Dimitri and Jane, extended unconditional love, support, and minimal grief for my long international absences. My sister, Antonia, was my best friend through and through. But most of all, my accomplishments are a credit to my mom, Irini, and her parents, Antonia and Constantine.

1

The Trouble with Borders

Debates on interstate boundaries focus on where a boundary ought to lie. Scholars study disputed boundaries in places such as Kashmir and the Golan Heights to account for the persistence of these disputes and their potential to escalate. Other scholars focus on secession, ethnic conflict, and attempts by well-armed ethnic groups to carve out their own ethnically homogeneous states. Others advocate redrawing boundaries and partition; Bosnia, Jerusalem, and Iraq are prominent examples of whether and how to redraw interstate borders in order to keep peace. The study of borders in the social sciences is largely concerned with location.

This book is about none of those debates. Historically and in the present, states and their outlying populations have faced tremendous security challenges along boundaries that are in fact not disputed. Nineteenth-century European states struggled to prevent bandits and mercenaries from committing violent acts and fleeing to neighboring states across stable but poorly defended borders. Currently, Iran is struggling to contain smugglers and bandits along its shared boundary with Afghanistan and – much like the United States and Israel – is constructing expensive barriers to deter infiltrators into its frontier territories.[1] Zimbabwe's attempt to monitor and regulate the flow of goods and people is so irregular that government statistics register annual population losses of nearly one million people. Rebels smuggle weapons back and forth across the poorly administered boundaries

---

[1] On the United States, see Marek (2005) and the Secure Fence Act of 2006, H.R. 6061. On Iran, see Walsh (2006); AFX News, March 17, 2006, "Afghan Bandits Kill 22 in Iran"; and Agence France Press, May 4, 2006, "Iran Arrests Rebels in Restive Border Regions." On Israel, see Gavrilis (2004, 2006).

of the D.R. Congo, launching rebellions in a well-organized rotation. In most of these cases borders are not disputed; rather, borders are sites of extreme instability and mismanagement.

One way to explain this cross-border insecurity is to investigate state strength. Many states are too poor or too weak to respond to challenges to their authority in outlying territories (Fearon and Laitin 2003). The weaker the state, the less secure its boundary against threats posed by smugglers, insurgents, and bandits. This book argues that this seemingly plausible explanation is misconceived. The difference between an insecure border and one that is well administered has much more to do with how states organize their institutions at the boundary than with how strong they are. Institutional design trumps state strength. A state with powerful coercive institutions and a capable military can easily intervene to manage borders, but such intervention may produce perverse effects, such as minor border skirmishes escalating into major incidents and a counterproductive micromanagement of the actions of border guards. By contrast, a state that delegates and surrenders authority to its boundary administrators has a better chance of achieving a secure border. Its guards are more likely to cooperate with their counterparts along the other side, pool resources to secure the border, and adopt innovative policing methods to cope with emerging security problems. I dub such a locally embedded, bilateral institution a "boundary regime."

The pages that follow will explain that boundary regimes, despite their durability and effectiveness in providing security for states and outlying populations, exist as exceptions rather than the rule. The reason for this presents a paradox: states often attempt to micromanage their borders in order to enhance their security, yet the delegation and surrender of authority to boundary administrators ultimately leaves states more secure. Put another way, if strong states have been lacking in much of the world, even fewer states have been able to manage their borders efficiently.

Throughout this project, I pursue three objectives that relate to the institutional dynamics of borders: (a) to understand the relationship of a state to its border security institutions, (b) to account for variation in institutions of border control, and (c) to model how different ways of organizing border administration at the local level have variable outputs on security. A few words on each of the three are in order.

Security studies approaches within international relations typically treat the relationship of states to their borders as static. They assume an instinctual state drive to use a border as a line of defense against aggressors and in particular against enemy states.[2] All states have a vital interest in maintaining well-patrolled borders. What varies is their capacity to defend them. Mearsheimer argues that common borders between great powers provide direct and easy access for putting military pressure on a common foe (2001: 271). Others find that borderland terrain and the proximity of a capital city, roads, and rail to a boundary affect the incidence of conflict (Siverson and Starr 1990; Starr and Thomas 2002; Buhaug and Gleditsch 2006). Fazal (2007) argues that borders and geography hold the key to why some states die while others survive. She explains that before 1945 buffer states, whose borders placed them between two stronger rivals, had a high likelihood of being aggrandized into nonexistence. After 1945, norms against territorial conquest ensured that relatively weak buffer states with easily violable borders would survive. These accounts treat borders as tools of brinkmanship and proxies for strategic geographic variables. While appealing in their parsimony, they do not account for variation in how states design and organize their borders to provide security for themselves and for their outlying territories.

Taking a cue from Prescott's *Political Frontiers and Boundaries* (1987), we can divide the function of boundaries into positional and administrative tasks. Positional tasks include the actual delimitation and demarcation of the boundary on the ground and the creation of neutral zones or grey areas along that boundary. Administrative tasks include prevention of border jumping, suppression of smuggling and contraband, extraction of customs duties, and the regulation and facilitation of legal crossing of goods and people.

Not all states perform these functions equally well, nor do they value them equally. Some states pursue the delimitation of their borders immediately after independence, while other states age inside poorly delineated boundaries.[3] Other states deploy customs officials but not border guards. Still others use military units, while others use irregular or civilian police forces. Some states police their borders unilaterally, while others cooperate

---

[2] This Hobbesian account shares some commonalities with studies of how other groups – from primate societies to ethnic groups – create defensible and distinguishable borders. For general discussions, see Malmberg (1980), Sack (1986), and Hechter (2000).

[3] Territorial disputes are altogether different from delimitation and demarcation disputes. Delimitation refers to the affixing of a border in a treaty or on a map. Demarcation refers to the placement of on-the-ground markings to identify the route of the border. States may have undelimited and nondemarcated borders without necessarily making overlapping claims to the territory of their neighbors (Gavrilis 2009).

with neighbors to address common security problems. On the African continent, some states do not bother to police their borders at all; others attempt to fence their borders; and still others experiment with joint patrols involving their neighbors' border guards (Asiwaju and Adeniyi 1989; Anderson 1997; International Crisis Group 2004b). Consider also the example of post-Taliban Afghanistan, where cross-border drug and weapons smuggling has drastically increased. The state-capacity explanation might lead us to conclude that the Afghan state simply cannot control its borders. A closer look, however, suggests that the government in Kabul has little interest in controlling its borders; open borders permit the drug trade to continue and generate revenues that keep provincial warlords content and the state afloat. State capacity is irrelevant; state preferences for an open border are critical.

The second analytical goal is to explore variation in states' strategies toward their borders. A cluster of excellent studies in history and the social sciences has demonstrated a link between domestic political processes and states' attempts to control their borders. In an influential study of the United States–Mexico border, Andreas (2000) argues that the intensification of border policing and attempts to fence off the boundary are not the result of increasing illegal activities such as drug smuggling. Instead, more aggressive policing occurs at times that are opportune for political elites and the media. In his work on African borders, Herbst (2000) explains how international and domestic processes combine to prevent African states from policing their outlying borders. The states have inherited vast territories whose borders are perceived as legitimate by the international community but are nonetheless far beyond the coercive reach of their respective authorities. In such a benign international environment, states have little incentive to institute border control. In his sweeping historical study of the Spanish-French frontier, Sahlins (1991) shows how centuries-long modernizing and centralizing state-building processes on each side of the frontier created an increasingly regulated and militarized line. While the sum total of all of this scholarship indicates that strategies for border control vary in nature and intensity, it has not resulted in a singular framework that links domestic politics to state building. Here, I develop a framework that spans both continents and centuries.

The third goal of this book is to model how different organizations of border control at the local level have variable outputs on security. This area has received the least sustained attention from social scientists. Yet studying the behavior of border guards and customs officials is essential for understanding how local state agents implement centrally devised directives. Organizations and personnel deployed at borders are vested with authority to implement and enforce binding rules for crossing and accessing the border. Passports are checked, customs taxes are collected from lorries laden with goods, and insurgents are chased down by military units on patrol as they attempt to infiltrate the border. Understanding how border personnel carry out these duties, improvise solutions to emergent threats, and interact with their counterparts on the other side is essential to understanding why some border zones are more porous, more dangerous, and more corrupt than others.

The Argument

Borders are institutional zones, not lines of separation between states. Borders regularize and structure contact and interaction between states (Luhman 1982; Kratochwil 1986; Sahlins 1991; Ron 2000a, 2000b; Newman 2006; Simmons 2006). Andreas (2003) underscores this point cogently in a study that examines changes affecting the borders of postindustrial states in the twenty-first century. He argues that while many boundaries are becoming demilitarized and more open to trade, other cross-border activities, such as immigration, are becoming more regulated.[4] This view contains both a macro- and a micro-level dynamic. On a macro level, states make choices about what they will attempt to police and regulate along their borders and about who they will vest with the task of policing. At the micro level, the local organization of border authority is responsible for managing and policing the boundary.

The macro level argues that borders are institutions that directly contribute to state formation and state authority. Passport controls at official crossings and policing of unofficial crossings can deter the entry or exit of individuals who challenge authority or attempt to evade capture.[5] The restriction of the import or export of certain goods across borders

---

[4] He refers to this latter process as "criminalization." He also notes that when states deregulate controls on the flow of goods and cooperate to criminalize certain activities, they are effectively pooling their sovereignty. The implication of his point is that frontiers have more in common with modern boundaries than has previously been thought. I agree with this definition, although I tend to limit myself to the terms "boundaries" and "borders."

[5] The area that lies along the length of a border between official crossings is called the "green border." This should not be confused with "grey areas" or "neutral zones," terms that refer to unclear sovereignty over small pieces of land along boundaries.

protects domestic markets. The collection of customs duties adds to precious revenues that governments require in order to rule. The delimitation of a border signals the point at which a state's authority ends and provides officials and populations with a point of reference beyond which their activities are not authorized. Borders, in short, are local manifestations of the claims of a state's authority. They enable coercion and extraction and signal ownership.

However, no two paths of state formation are exactly alike. As work on state formation demonstrates, state leaders practice a wide array of combinations of extraction, co-optation, coercion, and legitimation to enable rule and ensure compliance (Ardant 1972; Hirschman 1978; Levi 1988; Tilly 1992; Herbst 2000; Migdal 2001; Boone 2003; Thies 2004; Hui 2005). There are many variations on these general practices. In a sweeping study of how states generate revenue, Levi (1988) finds that the types of revenues collected and methods of collection change across time and place due to a number of constraints that include the bargaining power of state authorities, the cost of extracting such revenues, and the emphasis that authorities place on short- versus long-term gains. For our purposes, the details of these arguments are less important than their implication: state-building strategies vary.

This variation in state-building strategies, consequently, should explain the variation in how states perceive their borders and intervene at them. Borders are potentially sites of coercion, extraction, and demarcation of territory, yet all states do not maximize these practices at their boundaries. I argue that state-building processes explain several counterintuitive puzzles: why states differ in how they value demarcation procedures, customs agents, and border guards; why there is tremendous variation in the local organization of border authorities; why neighboring states fail to coordinate their border policing even as they face seemingly mutual threats; and why states and border authorities do not react uniformly to what scholars or analysts may see as an objectively grave threat.

This variation also has a micro-level component. At the micro level, I argue that border authorities vested with administrative autonomy and the ability to interact with their counterparts on the other side will tend toward cooperation in order to manage the shared boundary. Border guards who have the ability to regularly interact and communicate with their counterparts along the other side of the border will use those arenas of interaction to pool their efforts, propose solutions to common problems of administering the border, and locally resolve disputes before they escalate.

The Trouble with Borders

My argument runs counter to a large body of work in the social sciences that insists that effective governance and policy implementation require states to monitor and directly enforce the actions of their agents in the field (Solnick 1998; see also Hardin 1968; Migdal 2001; Fearon and Laitin 2003). The unifying strain in this literature is that agents vested with authority will shirk work, abuse their power, and derail the implementation of state policies unless they are monitored adequately from above. This literature warns against giving local agents broad discretion. Such discretion may tempt border authorities to skip patrol duty, seek bribes to let unauthorized goods through, and collude with weapons smugglers and militants. In the case of interstate borders, this literature has limited applicability.

I do not argue that local officials will not abuse their authority. To some degree, this is inevitable along any border. However, intervention from above is no panacea for the problems of border security. Central states are located far from their borders. This distance is not necessarily geographic; it is conceptual and hierarchical. If high-level authorities broadly tailor border administration to fulfill selective and particular policies of top-down state-building, they may very well ignore security problems along their borders that do not affect their preferred policies. Under the right conditions, the local organization of border administration may resolve the countervailing tendencies between the broad strategies of states and the particular needs of border zones.

This project stands on the shoulders of the literatures on institutions and cooperation. Institutions are the rules of the game (North 1990). They are chosen strategically and deliberately by constrained but goal-minded actors (Levi 1988; Ostrom 1990; March and Olsen 1998; Boone 2003). I argue that states deploy institutions to their borders that best match their preferred state-building policies. At the local level, I rely on the literature on the evolution of cooperation, which models how actors may self-organize and develop durable cooperation in order to solve social dilemmas (Ostrom 1990; Ostrom, Walker, and Gardner 1992; Axelrod 1997). Local authorities have traditionally policed long stretches of boundaries with meager resources and under dangerous conditions. Given this, it is important to understand the conditions under which guards cooperate with the other side to innovate policing strategies.

This study has substantive and theoretical motivations. All states have borders, and few, if any, can credibly claim to have resolved the dilemmas of policing, extracting resources at their borders, and delimiting their boundaries. At the same time, social scientists have paid scant attention to

7

the dynamics of border security even as the number of new states in the international system has multiplied.[6] In 1900, there were forty-two states. In 2006, there were 192 (Carter and Goemans 2007; Fazal 2007). The mileage of violable borderlines has drastically increased. Yet a substantial body of work implies that boundaries are increasingly irrelevant (Rosecrance 1996; Adler and Barnett 1998) or that the forces of globalization are unleashing illicit flows the likes of which states cannot hope to contain.[7] As one prominent globalization scholar put it, "If a paranoid state such as North Korea is incapable of controlling its borders and deterring illicit trade, there seems to be little hope for open, democratic, and technologically advanced nations seeking to uphold their common borders" (Naim 2006). Such a pessimistic view neglects institutional design. Moreover, the focus on globalization, with its high-technology, virtual flows across borders, obscures the fact that for most states the dilemmas of border policy remain much the same as in the past: preventing challenges to state authority by rival groups in remote regions, suppressing the flow of weapons, and deterring bandits and extremists.

My theoretical motives are twofold. The first is to explain state behavior. The second is to demonstrate that local institutions matter. These objectives require linking the macro and micro levels. At the macro level, I use theories of state building to explain the institutions deployed by states to their borders. At the micro level, I specify the constraints and conditions that these institutions face at the local level.

Connecting the two levels allows me to bridge the large gaps between international relations, comparative politics, and sociology even as it may seem that my approach condemns international relations approaches for their conspicuous lack of a theoretical perspective on boundaries. Strategic approaches that study state-to-state interactions have yielded tremendously valuable conclusions on the limits and successes of international cooperation (e.g., Snidal 1985; Wendt 1999; Mitzen 2005). However, it would be wrong to model a theory of boundaries by focusing on the interactions that occur across central states. This is effectively how such approaches model behavior and outcomes. They either personify the state as an actor

---

[6] Studies in the social sciences that prominently feature the word "borders" or "boundaries" are rarely about interstate boundaries. Rather, they typically concern social boundaries (Abbott 1995; Lamont and Molnar 2002; Gibson 2005; Tilly 2005a).

[7] On different positions and views regarding these debates, see Kahler and Walters (2006) and Adamson (2006).

or measure its interactions with other states via its diplomatic agencies. This is a valid enterprise. However, in the case of interstate borders, the most dense and formative interactions occur at the micro level and across borders. Taking interactions seriously would mean that a research agenda on the institutional dynamics of interstate boundaries would necessarily have to shift the scale of observation down to the level of the border.

The approach in these pages benefits audiences beyond those interested in boundaries, institutions, or international relations. This work also expands the boundaries of contentious politics. It explains the origins of political claims that states make via their borders and the variations in these claims across time and place. It also shifts the usual focus from contention against governments (McAdam, Tarrow, and Tilly 2001; Tilly and Tarrow 2007) to contention *within* and *across* the institutions of states. Such contention occurs when border guards find their preferred way of administering a boundary to be in conflict with the aims of their superiors in the capital. Contention also occurs when border guards alternately communicate, cooperate, collude, monitor, and sanction their counterparts.

This project will also interest scholars who study territoriality and territorial disputes (Kapil 1966; Mandel 1980; Goertz and Diehl 1992; Hensel 2001; Fravel 2005; Diez, Stetter, and Albert 2006; Kahler and Walter 2006; Fazal 2007). The cases in this project demonstrate that cross-border cooperation can occur even in the context of a territorial dispute, despite arguments that territorial disputes lead to belligerence, tension, and escalation (Vasquez 1993; Huth 1996; Hassner 2006).

The Cases

This book focuses on successful and failed boundary regimes in new states. As the next chapter explains, new states allow the researcher to isolate the effects of state building on borders. Cases span region and time to include the nineteenth-century Ottoman-Greek boundary as well as the present-day borders of newly independent states in Central Asia. At first glance, such cases would seem to lead to incongruous comparisons. Following a protracted rebellion, the Greek state emerged from the Ottoman Empire in the 1820s with scant political institutions and makeshift governments seated in different towns. A new nation-state faced a declining multiethnic Empire. In Central Asia, five new republics emerged from Soviet collapse without a shot being fired and with old Soviet borders and capital cities intact. What can a nineteenth-century beleaguered imperial border share with the twenty-first-century borders of nation-states that are relatively more modern and technologically advanced?

The security threats that new states face today are strikingly similar to those that confronted nineteenth-century states and empires. The Ottoman Empire and the Greek state commissioned a ragtag force of former bandits, toll collectors, and provincial police to take up positions along the boundary and guard against bandits, weapons smugglers, and insurgents. Central Asian states became collectively independent in 1991 and had to confront mutual problems of militant insurgencies and weapons and drug smuggling. In both regions and times, states had to make decisions about whether and how to demarcate their borders, how much to regulate access to boundary zones, where to open crossings, whether to deploy border guards and/or customs officials, and how much to police the areas that fell between official crossings.

The similarities end there. In the Ottoman-Greek case, foreign policy makers of the time warned that the ex-bandits would do little to prevent violence along the newly established border. British and French diplomats predicted that the former bandits would shirk policing duties and opportunistically participate in banditry and insurgency in frontier regions. Nonetheless, the Ottoman and Greek guards proved to be effective managers of the boundary, mainly because their respective governments granted them substantial autonomy and allowed them to establish posts that facilitated communication and monitoring across the boundary. In Central Asia, the new states faced mutual threats, pledged cooperation from the moment of independence, and hosted international organizations that attempted to foster cross-border cooperation. Yet most Central Asian state borders became dysfunctional. Instead of cooperating and pooling their efforts against smugglers and militants, most states resorted to escalation and closure even as these policies did little to provide security to outlying territories.

The goal in these cases is to identify and explain consistent patterns in the dynamics of interstate boundaries and to show that my explanation is stronger than alternatives. Along the Ottoman-Greek boundary, I search for cooperation where diplomats predicted conflict and closure. Along Central Asian borders, I search for conflict and unilateral management where plausible alternatives suggest that pooling of resources and cooperation would have been the standard, given common interests.

The Ottoman-Greek border offers a particularly rich account of the evolution of a boundary regime. I study the boundary over its fifty-year life span (1832–82). This allows me to trace how border guards used their administrative autonomy and interactive posts to devise new procedures to police the boundary. The case study also presents an opportunity to study how policing varied along the border. I split the border into segments and study particular posts. Each of the posts demonstrates a different scale and type of cooperation among Ottoman and Greek border guards. As a result, I am able to demonstrate how differences in the ability of border guards to interact with one another had different outcomes for cooperation at particular posts.

In a second chapter on the Ottoman-Greek boundary, I shift the focus from local border guard institutions to the high state. I contend that the cooperative boundary regime collapsed due to external interference on the part of high-level state officials. Their attempt to centralize and streamline state institutions led them to strip the boundary regime of its autonomy and to micromanage its day-to-day affairs with disastrous results. Rather than allowing their border guards to devise policing procedures, exchange information on security and suspects, and cross the boundary while in pursuit of bandits, officials forced their guards to justify and document cross-border cooperation. Eventually, guards had to seek permission from distant administrators before responding to infiltration and banditry. Cooperation between Ottoman and Greek local authorities was restricted from above, and infiltrators became adept in evading state-sanctioned policing tactics.

The chapters on new Central Asian state boundaries examine both levels of the theory in a broader context. The first set of cases focuses on the state-building trajectories Central Asian states pursued in the wake of independence. I identify the emergence of distinct strategies state builders used to extend authority and extract revenues from new national territories. State building triggered unique preferences and outlooks on border control strategies, which proved incompatible with those handed down on the other side of the boundary. States raced to implement their preferred policies, preventing their neighbors from implementing their own policies. Conflict and diplomatic crises followed.

The empirical work here is based on a large number of primary sources. To reconstruct events along the Ottoman-Greek boundary, I consulted the Ottoman Archives, the Archives of the Greek Foreign Ministry, British consular sources at the Public Record Office, and a variety of provincial newspapers from frontier towns. I read documents in Ottoman-Turkish, Greek, French, and English representing different sides of the boundary and penned by actors at different levels. For the Central Asian cases, I consulted news sources, traveled to a number of border regions in

Kyrgyzstan and Uzbekistan to observe the borderlands and their functioning, and conducted a score of interviews with officials belonging to government ministries, the border guard, and international organizations. I read newspaper accounts in Uzbek but relied on an interpreter for Russian- and Kyrgyz-language interviews.

Selection bias may affect scholars using primary sources, so a few words on the subject are necessary. Lustick (1996) cautions against overreliance on published historical work in conducting case studies as such work may contain an underlying perspective that is sympathetic to the author's framework. A partial solution to this lies in going directly to primary sources. However, it is necessary to guard against selectively using archival records to fit a preferred theory. I searched documents for evidence both to back my theory and to evaluate alternative arguments. Moreover, when I read documents, I tried to gauge the writer's perspective and considered the overall social and political context of the document. Perhaps a document written by a local border captain was intended to impress a central state office. I took similar precautions when conducting interviews for my contemporary case studies. Perhaps the interviewee was a Kyrgyz nationalist whose interpretations were motivated by dislike for Uzbeks. There are limits to such analysis, particularly because – as I will argue in the next chapter – an actor's intentionality is elusive and deciphering it may be a waste of time (Tilly 1998; Kalyvas 1999; Manski 2000; Ostrom 2000; McAdam, Tarrow, and Tilly 2001; Schwedler 2006; Tilly and Tarrow 2007).[8] Thus I focused on actions and outcomes and tried to confirm them as best I could using documents from the other side of the boundary.

In using documents and primary sources, I hope to have accomplished a useful fusion of international relations theory, comparative politics, and history (Elman and Elman 2001; Thies 2003). It was also my intent that the plurality of languages and sources used in the project would reveal new empirical data and untold narratives. The empirical information in this project – be it from Ottoman documents or Central Asian state officials – should be of great interest to those who are interested in Ottoman history, the Middle East, and the post-Soviet world.

---

[8] In an outstanding study of the Boxer Rebellion in China, Cohen (1997) resolves this problem in a unique way. He shows how the experience of participants in historical events and their accounts of the experience differ from the subsequent analysis and explanation of scholars. Cohen achieves this by splitting his book into three sections: how historians write about the event, how individuals who experienced it talked about the Boxer Rebellion, and how different myths about the events and meaning of the rebellion subsequently developed.

Outline of the Book

The following chapters are an attempt to explain the dynamics of interstate borders. Chapter 2 is the theoretical staging ground of the book. It unifies the macro- and micro-level dynamics via a series of four theoretical claims. It elaborates and defends each claim and gives a series of indicators for supporting or disproving it. Chapter 3 studies border guard institutions and the evolution of administration along the nineteenth-century Ottoman-Greek boundary. It uses archival data to show how Ottoman and Greek guards used their administrative autonomy and arenas of interaction to innovate security policy and devise increasingly complex systems of boundary policing. Chapter 4 shifts the focus upward to the pinnacles of the Ottoman and Greek states to show that the boundary regime collapsed over time because of external interference by state officials. Their attempts to centralize and streamline state institutions led them to strip the boundary regime of its autonomy and to micromanage its day-to-day affairs with disastrous results for local security and diplomatic relations.

Chapter 5 moves to the dangerous peripheries of contemporary Central Asian states, where cross-border militants and weapons and drug smugglers have the capacity to foment conflict and challenge state authority. It examines the different state-building trajectories of Central Asian states and the consequent divergent forms of border control along two sides of the same border. Chapter 6 moves back down to the micro level. It studies the organization of border guards along a series of paired Central Asian borders and explains why this configuration has varying effects on security, corruption, and relations with local populations. The Central Asian cases do not merely provide further illustrations of the general argument; rather, they clinch and clarify crucial points left unsettled in the Ottoman-Greek analysis. Chapter 7 concludes the argument by extending it. It applies the theory to states recovering from collapse, particularly present-day Afghanistan. Finally, it examines contemporary interventions along borders, explains the limits of such interventions, and suggests alternative avenues for designing borders that are open and secure.

2

Four Claims about Interstate Boundaries

On maps, boundaries appear as static legal divisions between sovereign states. In reality, they are complex institutions that make political claims about who and what may cross the line. Consequently, when constructing a theory of boundaries and border control, it is important to begin with two premises. First, boundaries are inherently shared. Any given point along a land boundary is shared by at least two states. Two different sets of political claims may be made along that boundary governing border control, and those claims may or may not be complementary. Second, borders are institutions all the way down to the local level. As Newman (2006) argues, borders are defined not only by the central governments that attempt to assert control over them, but also by bottom-up processes of change and local dynamics. Indeed, borders are institutions staffed by individuals, who may include border guards, police agents, military officers, immigration officials, and customs officers. Though they are part of the state, these officials may or may not enforce the claims of capital cities at the border. With these minimal premises in hand, this chapter offers up a theory to account for variation in border control strategies and to explain the macro- and micro-level dynamics of border-security institutions.

The chapter proceeds by presenting a basic typology of border-security strategies, which I contrast with a plausible yet incorrect alternative typology. Four claims are then advanced about interstate borders. These claims explain the various strategies that states adopt to secure their borders and outlying territories as well as the variable success of those strategies.

I classify border control strategies into four principal categories: boundary regimes, unilateral policing, conflictual unilateral policing, and ad hoc strategies. These categories run the gamut of how states police their borders. A boundary regime, as defined in the previous chapter, refers to locally cooperative methods of border control. In such boundary regimes, border authorities have substantial administrative autonomy and manage the frontier locally and jointly with their counterparts on the other side. In unilateral policing, a state manages its side of the boundary exclusively. Unilateral policing tends to be centralized; states hand down restrictive parameters on how guards and boundary officials are to police and manage the border. Two neighboring states may benefit from good relations, agree on the stakes and objectives of border control, and yet administer their respective sides of the boundary via unilateral methods with limited coordination of policing. Conflictual unilateral policing refers to situations where contiguous states manage their border directly with conflicting or mutually exclusive objectives of border security. One state's policing strategies adversely affect its neighbor's border control strategies or security. Finally, states may engage in minimal, ad hoc policing. Here, the state and its representatives are usually absent from the border with the exception of rare interventions to provide security. These four categories represent the spectrum of how states administer their borders.

This book aims to show that while boundary regimes are optimal institutions for securing frontier areas against insurgents, smugglers, bandits, and cross-border terrorists, they are rare compared to the other three categories. Conditions for boundary regimes are severe. These conditions are advanced in this chapter in the form of four claims: (1) new states design their borders as an extension of their preferred state-building strategies (rather than as a response to threats at their border); (2) neighboring states with divergent trajectories of state formation will adopt incompatible and conflict-prone strategies of securing their borders; (3) the greater the degree of state intervention, the lower the ability of border authorities to cooperate across a boundary (even when state-building strategies converge); (4) border guards vested with the ability to interact with their foreign counterparts will pool their efforts and jointly police the boundary.

The framework of this chapter and the categories of border control are expressed in Table 2.1. This table represents the paradox discussed in the introduction: states attain superior levels of cross-border cooperation and security against mutual threats in their outlying territories when they devolve authority to local border administrators and allow them to interact with their foreign counterparts. The more states intervene and micromanage their borders, the more likely they are to forgo beneficial cooperation with neighbors, misidentify threats at their borders, and promote escalation. The reader may usefully refer to this table while reading the remainder

Table 2.1. *Typology of border security strategies*

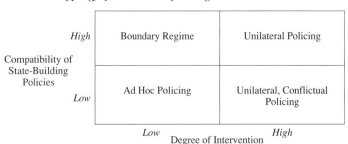

High	Boundary Regime	Unilateral Policing
Compatibility of State-Building Policies Low	Ad Hoc Policing	Unilateral, Conflictual Policing
	Low	High

Degree of Intervention

of the chapter. For now, it is important to discuss implications and make crucial clarifications about this typology.

I coined the term "boundary regimes" to describe locally cooperative forms of border control. Admittedly, the term is not a perfect one. After all, all boundaries involve some sort of regime, rules, and practices that are more or less conflictual and more or less dictated by the center. Still, I employ the term "boundary regime" for locally cooperative forms of border control because the concept reflects the bilateral origin of rules, regulations, and institutions of policing.

This typology is in contrast to plausible alternative arguments. My argument claims that border control strategies depend on the degree of state intervention and the extent to which the state-building policies of bordering states are compatible. An alternative to my argument would be to posit that border control strategies and the resulting level of border security depend on a given state's strength and the quality of its diplomatic relations with its neighbor. This alternative is expressed in Table 2.2. Where contiguous states suffer from poor relations, strong states are likely to secure their borders against infiltration and illegal activities by means of militarization, aggressive policing, and general closure (Martinez 1994; Mearsheimer 2001). Where states are weak and lack the capacity to effectively police their borders, frontier territories are likely to be rife with spillover activity, such as cross-border rebellions, insurgent activities, and arms smuggling, irrespective of diplomatic relations (Herbst 2000; Atzili 2007).

While appealing in its simplicity, this alternative conceptualization is limiting. It implies that only strong states can benefit from adequate levels of border control. My claims and the cases that follow demonstrate that all states – weak or strong – can benefit from secure boundaries if border control institutions are designed well. Moreover, arguments that rely on

Table 2.2. *Counterargument*

Cooperative	Frontier Lawlessness, Ad Hoc Policing	Borders Secure and Open
Diplomatic Relations		
Conflictual	Frontier Lawlessness, Ad Hoc Militarization	Borders Militarized and Closed
	Low	*High*
	State Strength	

diplomatic relations to explain border security assume that borders are fated to be tools of statecraft and front lines of hostility. My argument provides a theoretically reasoned explanation as to why border control may be isolated from high-level diplomatic disputes. Neighboring states may suffer from shattered diplomatic relations but may simultaneously benefit from well-functioning border control organizations.

This last point highlights a crucial implication in my argument: the local organization of border control and high-level state politics may feature countervailing tendencies. Borders are institutions all the way down, and no theory of borders can be considered complete unless it accounts for the local organization of security. To this end, the subsequent sections of this chapter outline and explain the four major claims and related counterarguments that define this book and its case studies.

State Building via Boundaries

Claim 1: New states design their borders as an extension of their state-building strategies. This claim implies a connection between states' attempts to extend their authority across outlying territories and the resulting strategies and organizations that states adopt to police their new borders. Defending such a claim requires (a) outlining the unique security dilemma that new states face, (b) explaining the relationship between border organization and types of state-building strategies, and (c) specifying the observations that should be made if this claim is correct.

Social scientists have long recognized that states organize their borders in order to enforce their particular claims of authority. The delimitation and demarcation of a boundary outlines the limits of sovereignty and makes a succinct claim regarding where the authority of one state begins and another ends (Jones 1945; Kristof 1959; Johansson 1982; Kratochwil 1986;

Griffiths 1996; Black 1997; Goemans 2006; Carter and Goemans 2007).[1] Border controls represent a series of political claims about who and what can exit and enter national territory (Martinez 1994; Andreas 2003; Simmons 2006). Control of territorial borders promotes a state's interests and ruling strategies to the extent that the state's agents are engaged in extraction of resources, control over enemies, reward and protection of friends, and provision of collective goods throughout a contiguous territory but not beyond it. Defense of static boundaries hardly mattered to Mongol Khans, African nomadic tribes, or even to modern Monaco, which depends heavily on flows of goods, but it matters crucially to states that are interested in coordinating the activities just mentioned. In this respect, China's imperial Qing rulers and Soviet leaders in Moscow had similar interests vis-à-vis their agents at their respective borders. The Qing walled off their territory to prevent trade, to stop the exit of taxable agricultural stocks, and to end nomadic incursions (Lattimore 1962; Waldron 1990). The Soviet Union practiced aggressive border controls to seal off its command economy from foreign goods, to prevent the exit of subjects unwilling to submit to its rule, and to suppress the entry of seditious literature (Chandler 1998). Other states fall somewhere in the middle in their coordination of such activities. Along the nineteenth-century borders of the United States, customs and currency controls lagged compared to the control of people. The United States government tried to stop the flow of individuals and settlers across its borders at various times (Hoover 1930), yet it allowed the Mexican gold peso to circulate widely throughout its territory for much of the nineteenth century (Helleiner 2003).

But what does all this mean for the chapter's first claim? As scholarship indicates, boundaries are about policing membership, preventing exit, and maintaining internal control – not about keeping invading armies at bay (Hirschman 1978; Thomson 1994; Herbst 2000; Squatriti 2002). For instance, Ron sees borders as "institutional mechanisms patterning state activities and generating notions of appropriate behavior thought tacit norms and explicit rules" (Ron 2000a: 610). In their core territories, states coerce their populations through policing tactics. In frontier territories, located on the other side of a core territory, states are more likely to deploy

---

[1] For approaches on the subject from constructivist, postmodernist, and critical theory perspectives, see Diez, Stetter, and Albert (2006), Walters (2002), Goff (2000), Albert (1998), Paasi (1996, 1998), Weber (1995), Ruggie (1993), and Walker (1993). Also see Caporaso (2000) for an outstanding overview of the literature on sovereignty and borders.

extreme forms of coercion that include indiscriminate violence and ethnic cleansing. While Ron's work is not about border control per se, it serves as an example of how states use borders to shore up state-building practices.[2] Later I will demonstrate how the types of institutions states deploy affect cooperation and security along an interstate border. Here I proceed to show how it is possible to predict border control strategies by identifying state-building practices immediately following independence.

Classic work on state formation demonstrates that states practice a combination of at least two strategies to expand authority: coercion and extraction. Coercion refers to the application or threat of application of actions that cause harm or damage to populations. Traditional forms of coercion include incarceration, expropriation, humiliation, and the public issuance of threats (Tilly 1992). Extraction, on the other hand, refers to the processes by which states draw revenues from subject populations in order to perpetuate the survival of the state (Barnett 1992).

Each of these indicators affects state claims and practices at borders. Consider coercion, which all states use to one extent or another in order to enhance their rule over territory and ensure compliance over subjects.[3] I gauge coercion in two ways. The first is a state's willingness to limit particular challenges to its authority, and the second is the state's ability to restrict those challenges. Willingness in the cases examined here appears in the form of the statements and actions of central state leaders and high-level coercive agencies.[4] Ability can be measured using a variety of indicators, such as the size of a state's police forces. If state leaders identify a particular armed group as an impediment to the expansion of their authority, security strategies along the border will adopt coercive measures to prevent the flight of its members and to monitor the flow of weapons.

---

[2] Ron tests his argument by investigating the cases of Serbia and Israel. In the case of Serbia, he notes that officials prevented indiscriminate violence against Muslims on the Serbian side of the border but allowed Serb paramilitaries to practice ethnic cleansing in Bosnian "frontier" territories just beyond the core land of the Serbian state. Similarly, Ron shows that Israeli leaders and military commanders practiced coercion and policing in the West Bank by innovating nonlethal methods of punishment while engaging in much heavier violence along the Lebanese frontier (Ron 2000a, 2000b, 2003).

[3] Legitimacy and quasi-compliance are alternatives to coercion (Levi 1988; see also Jackson and Rosberg 1986).

[4] I do not confine myself in the cases solely to the investigation of official statements. The reason for this is that talk may be cheap. For instance, in one of the cases I demonstrate that the Kyrgyz state pledged to use coercion to enhance authority in outlying areas. Yet the actions of its high-level agencies betrayed an unwillingness to use coercion.

Extraction is the other primary strategy of state formation. Revenue, as Levi elegantly argues, is a major limit to rule (1988: 2). The greater the revenue of the state, the more possible it is to extend rule. Levi argues that rulers are revenue maximizers; they attempt to extract as much as they can while being constrained by agents, constituents, transaction costs, and discount rates. Levi's work explains a poorly understood empirical fact – the tremendous variation across time and space of rulers' extractive policies and the organizations designed to generate revenue. Following Levi's lead, I anticipate that extractive strategies will vary across new states and that it is possible to identify predominant economic orientations in new states. I measure extraction as the state's preferred mode for generating revenue in national territory and the degree of intervention in the economy that this entails.[5] My hypothesis is that the dominant extractive strategy should have a major impact on the design of a state's border. For example, states that rely on revenues from trade flows will design boundaries in order to enhance the flow of goods. States that rely on price controls and the regulation of internal markets will design borders in order to prevent the leaking of state goods abroad and will assess large customs duties at their borders.

It is important to note at this point the assumptions that I make about state formation. States operate with limited resources and tremendous challenges to extending their authority.[6] Some states become sovereign retaining the borders and regional capitals that they held as colonial possessions or internal republics, while others find themselves building capital cities and governing institutions from scratch.[7] Some start independent life with healthy economies, while others are strapped for revenues and resources. Still others may find themselves facing multiple challenges from insurgents, warlords, and ethnic rebellions throughout their territory, while others may find such challenges localized to a single region or area. Taking this assumption seriously means softening and qualifying the usual way

---

[5] The dominant strategy will not necessarily bring in the most money at the border. For example, a state may receive more revenue in the form of foreign direct investment, grants, and credit from foreign agencies such as the International Monetary Fund or the World Bank in exchange for reducing customs tariffs at its borders.

[6] On these constraints, see Levi (1988), Migdal (2000), and Boone (2003). Gilpin (1981) demonstrates a similar constraining logic governing states and the international environment. David (1991) specifically argues that internal threats in postcolonial and young developing states far outweigh external threats.

[7] Laitin (1986) and Herbst (2000) argue that post-independence African states borrowed liberally from colonial administrative traditions and institutions.

the social science literature defines states. Wagner's study of state formation and war notes the bundles of functions that make up the ideal modern state: an organized ruling group or government that can successfully use the threat of force to compel individuals within a defined territory to surrender economic resources that are in turn channeled to the perpetuation of the state, its defense, and the regulation of the population from which the resources come (2007). Yet Wagner, like many others before him, notes that states rarely perform such functions evenly or equally (Tilly 1992; Migdal 1994; 2001).[8] States, as Moravcsik argues (1997: 519), are functionally differentiated and pursue particular combinations of security, welfare, and sovereignty.

On the whole, the challenges that new states face are likely to be internal rather than external. State builders face greater threats from challenges to their authority inside inherited territory than from the armies of neighboring states. The literature on state formation sees the lack of external threat as an impediment to effective state building. Leaders of new or developing states have little incentive to build strong state institutions in their outlying territories if they are guaranteed to retain those territories owing to the lack of an external military threat. The inability of neighboring states to take over those territories means that there is little reason for state builders to expand extractive and coercive institutions aggressively into frontier regions. While scholars elaborate different arguments on the types of wars necessary to cajole state builders into creating strong state institutions, the absence of external threat is generally seen as a liability (Desch 1996; Herbst 2000; Thies 2004; Atzili 2007; Fazal 2007).

The absence of war and external threats may certainly be associated with weakness in the developing world, but such weakness does not prevent new states from pursuing an array of state-building strategies. Nor does it determine the types of border control arrangements states choose. States, weak or otherwise, will pursue different styles and combinations of coercive and extractive strategies. It is these particular state-building preferences that determine the border control strategies that states implement in the years following their independence.

If the argument linking paths of state formation to distinct strategies of border security is correct, it should explain both the type and timing

---

[8] Also, on the European context, see Tilly (1992). On the economic trajectories of post-Soviet states, see Darden (2008). On sub-Saharan Africa, see Herbst (2000). On China, see Hui (2005). On Latin America, see Thies (2004, 2006).

of organizations that new states deploy to their borders. States that prioritize extractive strategies of state building are likely to deploy customs officials at the border before police forces. Police forces, when deployed, are likely to be subordinated to the task of regulating the flow of goods. Conversely, states that are concerned with coercing target populations will make policing the focus of the border administration at the expense of extracting revenues. The interaction between extractive and coercive functions at new borders may not necessarily be zero-sum. However, I expect to find that the dominant path of state building generates border security strategies that enable that path.

I do not argue that a state's strength determines its orientation to border security. In his research on fixed borders and weak states, Atzili (2007) argues that weak states generate unpleasant security externalities for their neighbors. Because weak states are unable to control their outlying territories, their border zones become sites of refugee flows and insurgencies, creating more insecurity and drawing their neighbors into cross-border wars and interventions. Atzili finds that state weakness is related to international norms that resist altering state borders; states are allowed to keep their borders intact even as they fail to control their outlying territories. The implication is that very low levels of state strength mean that states fail to control and police their core territories, let alone their border areas.

Such capacity-driven arguments are very different than the one I am proposing. Such arguments insist that weak states cannot effectively police their boundaries. The point I make, by contrast, is that particular combinations of coercion and extraction determine how states perceive threats and the manner in which they intervene at their borders. The kinds of institutions deployed at the boundary are more important than their relative strength. Consider the borders of Central Asia's newly independent states that I discuss in subsequent chapters. Uzbekistan and Kyrgyzstan adopted extractive strategies as the primary mode of state building following independence in 1991. Consequently, each deployed customs officials to its borders (respectively to repress and to promote trade), delayed the deployment of border guards, and subordinated the task of policing against militants to that of regulating the flow of goods. An argument hinging on military or coercive strength would have predicted that Uzbekistan would have deployed its extant and superior military forces to police its borders, especially following early instances of ethnic conflict, militant activity, and refugee crises along its neighbor's borders.

Another example from my cases shows a similar link between state building and border control. Officials of the newly independent Greek state in the 1830s identified banditry as the primary impediment to extending authority to outlying territories. They organized their agents along the shared border with the Ottoman Empire to suppress banditry. Coercion was the order of the day, and boundary officials did little to extract customs duties despite the sad state of the new government's finances.

Boundary management is an endogenous process derivative of state-building strategies. The government of the newly independent African state of Eritrea aggressively militarized its borders and coasts after its independence in 1992 and used them as sites to train military conscripts and forge a national army in an otherwise divided, multiethnic state (Tronvoll 1999). In the process, the deployments triggered escalation and violence along all of Eritrea's borders, including the maritime boundaries with Yemen (Kwiatkowska 2000).

I examine my claim against a set of alternatives that focus on external determinants of border security policies. My claims will be weakened if external actors, such as international organizations and intervening states, are easily able to alter the border security strategies of new states. The logic behind this is that if state actions at their borders are part and parcel of state-building imperatives, then a broad change in state formation will be necessary to change the substance of border policy. Unless it is in line with their state-building strategies, governments will resist the advice and input of foreign diplomats and international organizations on how to police their boundaries.

It may appear that this project views borders as stubbornly inefficient – slow to adapt to the environment, unable to multitask, inflexible in the face of new challenges. The former bandits who policed the Ottoman-Greek boundary, for instance, collected few customs duties even though such revenues would surely have benefited the miserable finances of the Greek state. More recently, Kyrgyzstan tried to maintain open borders in order to profit from trade and customs revenues, yet left its guards in their barracks when militants infiltrated and attacked its border regions. Such policing strategies make sense when viewed from the perspective of the state-building imperatives of each capital.

However, the border-control policies that states unilaterally implement necessarily interact with those of neighboring states. The next claim examines the interactive dynamics of these policies and their effect on conflict, cooperation, and security.

Mediating the Micro and Macro Levels

Claim 2: Divergent state-building trajectories will cause conflict and escalation along interstate boundaries. Why should one state's attempt to expand its authority to, but not beyond, its boundaries cause conflict with neighboring states? An obvious answer to this question would be that one state's internal policies create externalities for its neighbors.[9] Sudan's genocide in Darfur has sent countless refugees across the border into Chad. International relations scholars would explain the lack of cooperation and conflict simply as a function of the security threats created by the practices of a neighboring state. These are not the cases investigated here.

The goal here is to demonstrate that a significant divergence in the coercive and extractive paths of two neighboring states will trigger conflict over border control under three conditions that would predict cooperation: (a) otherwise good diplomatic relations, (b) absence of a territorial dispute, and (c) presence of a mutual cross-border threat. I chose cases involving one or more of these conditions because they offer a good setting in which to investigate my state-building argument. The cases allow me to debate related arguments in international relations.

For example, scholars who study territorial disputes argue that such disputes exert a host of destabilizing influences on states that are party to the conflict. These include a higher likelihood of war (Goertz and Diehl 1992; Vasquez 1993, 1995), the improbability of resolving the dispute as time passes (Hassner 2006), as well as a willingness to foment instability in the neighboring territory through infiltration and proirredentist policies (Kapil 1966; Wiener 1971; Mandel 1980). This literature considers multiple variables that affect the initiation and resolution of territorial disputes. Huth (1996), for example, argues that domestic politics and ethnic ties across a disputed border have more to do with initiating the dispute than the relative military strength of the neighboring states. However, military strength, alliance commitments, and the strategic value of territory have much to do with the intensity of the conflict and whether or not it is peacefully resolved. While this literature is relatively silent on matters of border security, it

---

[9] Rothchild (2002) argues that the failure of authority in Africa allows rebellions and refugee flows to spill across borders. Wiener's (1971) seminal article on competitive cross-border ethnic mobilization coined the phrase "Macedonian Syndrome," which would subsequently be used to describe troubled multiethnic border areas in other parts of the world.

implies that conflict, escalation, and militarization over territory will spill over into matters of border control. Where a territorial dispute exists, borders are likely to be militarized and closed. The Golan Heights and Kashmir are two prominent cases where boundary disputes have resulted in hypermilitarized boundaries that are prone to severe escalation, tightly regulated by each side, and difficult to cross even via legal channels. In a territorial dispute, each state may be expected to unilaterally and exclusively police its side of the border. Simmons (2006) comes closest to establishing this connection in her research on disputed borders and trade relations. She finds that territorial disputes coincide with closed, militarized borders, which in turn represent lost opportunities for trade between neighboring states.

Some of my cases will investigate border control practices in the context of territorial disputes. I argue that territorial disputes do not necessarily spill over into issues of border control. Along borders where state-building policies converge, cooperation in matters of border control and policing should be observed even in the context of a territorial dispute. This is because border control institutions are consistently generated by state-building preferences and not by military strength or the ebb and flow of nationalist politics inside states that are claimants to the dispute. Indeed, Fravel's (2008) recent work on territorial disputes indicates that states may choose to resolve some border disputes when neighboring states pledge cooperation in vital security matters that involve separatism and terrorism. While Fravel does not use the language of state building, he shows how territorial disputes can be springboards for state-to-state cooperation. My approach argues that the deleterious effects of territorial disputes on border control are overridden when state-building policies converge. Such convergence permits states to coordinate their border security strategies.

One way of explaining cross-border cooperation may be to model these cases as coordination games in which two actors must match their policies to achieve an outcome that is individually and collectively optimal.[10] But what does this mean? Consider a hypothetical coordination dilemma between two new states, A and B. States A and B become independent at the same time. Their leaders make claims about the amicable state of diplomatic relations but also note that they both face a threat from insurgents along

---

[10] On the coordination problem in international relations, see Stein (1982), Snidal (1985), Goemans (2006), and Wagner (2007). On applications outside of international relations, see Kreps (1990).

the border who are targeting both states equally. States A and B have not yet delimited their border, nor have they deployed organizations to guard and police the border. States A and B are in a coordination dilemma, or what we may alternatively refer to as a problem of common aversions. They both want to avoid losing control of their peripheries to cross-border insurgents, but first they must coordinate their preferences on delimiting the border and deploying guards to it. There may be many paths by which they can delimit the border and fortify it, but their preferred outcome is to act jointly to suppress the nonstate threat to their security.

The constraints on coordination are much greater than this stylized example suggests, and a distinguished tradition in international relations demonstrates that pure coordination problems are few and far between in the empirical world (Stein 1982). Thus I complicate the game: I assume that States A and B have a truly mutual conception of the insurgent threat and an equal capacity to pursue joint action to avert that threat. To focus on their preference for the mutual outcome may obscure the possibility that A and B have nonmatching and inflexible preferences about how to address that mutual threat. State A may insist that the border be delimited before guards can be deployed to it, while State B may insist that both sides deploy units to the border and coordinate policing before delimitation talks can start.

The amended example demonstrates that dependence and conflict may exist in what initially seems to be a simple game of coordinating activities toward a mutually desired outcome. I argue that divergent state-building policies along a common border make cooperation and coordination across an international border improbable.

If I am correct, then I should observe that neighboring states with divergent state-building trajectories will have an exceedingly difficult time coordinating policy in order to secure their common border. Skeptics may argue that, given the ability to interact with their neighbors across a common border over a long period, policy convergence is likely.[11] I argue the opposite is the dominant tendency. Early escalation and conflict over policy may disrupt diplomatic relations, foster mistrust, and prevent coordination. Indeed, such escalation may convert the dispute from one of coordinating policy to one of state-to-state brinkmanship. Worse yet, along a common border

---

[11] This is also known as the shadow of the future (Oye 1986). On other approaches to interaction, see Wagner (2007), Gartzke (2007), Fearon (1995, 1997), Kydd (1997), Kier (1997), Legro (1996), Fierke (2000), and Mitzen (2001, 2005).

where two states deploy their organizations, there is the possibility that the policy implemented by one side will necessarily prevent the other side from securing its preferred strategy.

Moravcsik (1997) argues that international relations scholars may better explain cooperation and conflict across states if they focus on the processes that give rise to state preferences before the stage of interaction. In a variation on this theme, I argue that the interests and policies states deploy to their boundaries are determined through the slow-moving trajectories of state formation. International relations scholarship tends to ignore the effects of state building to its detriment.

The next chapter demonstrates that the Ottoman Empire and Greece cooperated broadly for a number of decades to manage their common border in part because of the compatibility of their state-building policies and their mutual desire to suppress the greatest challenge to their coercive authority – banditry. An examination focusing solely on their hostile diplomatic dialogue and Greece's residual territorial dispute against Ottoman lands would have predicted only escalation and brinkmanship at the border.

While compatibility of objectives is a necessary condition for cooperation, it is not a sufficient one. The next two claims thus explain the conditions under which states with highly compatible preferences on managing their borders will forgo or achieve cross-border cooperation.

Claim 3: The greater the degree of direct state intervention, the lower the ability of border authorities to cooperate across a border (even if state-building strategies converge). There are two reasons to expect a trade-off between the ability of border agencies to cooperate across the boundary and the degree of top-down intervention. First, higher degrees of intervention entail levels of micromanagement that reduce the latitude given to agents at the border to determine and alter administrative and security practices. This problem is not specific to borders. Social scientists have observed it in a variety of interactions that involve the state and local actors. In an outstanding study of forest rangers across five dispersed forest districts in the United States, Kaufman (1960) discovered that the decentralization of the Forest Service allowed the rangers to cooperate more effectively with their counterparts, to develop symbiotic relations with local communities in managing forestland, and to craft specific repertoires of management optimally tailored to local needs. Likewise, in a study of public services in South Asia and West Africa, Agrawal and Ribot (1999) find that decentralization allows for better governance and policy implementation because actors become accountable at the local level to their fellow citizens and counterparts.[12]

A similar dynamic occurs with respect to the state and its agents at the border. The greater the degree of intervention, the more the central state tends to issue sets of authorizations, directives, and prohibitions in order to determine the behavior of its officials at the level of the border.[13] This means that cooperation with the other side's authority in policing a boundary is greatly proscribed, rigid, and inflexible even as new threats emerge. An interventionist state may, in theory, broker cooperation with the border guards of its neighbor via high-level diplomatic channels. In practice, diplomatic caution is likely to limit such cooperation and to prevent the adoption of new or innovative methods of administering the border.

Second, high degrees of top-down intervention require deep monitoring. These channels tend to shift the scale of incidents at a border to the national and international levels and further limit the ability of border guards to cooperate with their foreign counterparts. This argument may seem unpersausive given the literature in political science and economics that argues that effective monitoring and enforcement are essential to the local implementation of policy and effective governance (Hardin 1968; Solnick 1996, 1998). It is not my intention here to challenge the validity of studies of the principal-agent dilemma; instead, I want to demonstrate that conventional solutions to the dilemma along an international border may have unintended and violent consequences.

Studies of the principal-agent problem in institutions tend to see monitoring as holding the balance between effective governance and institutional failure (Solnick 1996, 1998). If agents can control and exploit

---

[12] Varshney finds a similar dynamic in ethnic conflict in Indian cities. He finds that cities with dense intraethnic associational networks tended to cooperate and maintain stable, conflict-free relations. The lack of such networks coincided with top-down manipulation and higher levels of ethnic conflict. He explains, "the more dense associational networks cut across ethnic boundaries, the harder it is for politicians to polarize communities" (2001: 363).

[13] Political geographers have generated outstanding typologies of border control and rich empirical studies of border regions. The sum total of the studies indicates that state control in border areas is highly variable (e.g., Rumley and Minghi 1991; Martinez 1994; Henrikson 2000). However, they focus on the effects such control has on local populations and do not explain the sources of such variation. Moreover, there is a curious lack of work on border guard organizations in political geography. This may be, in part, because of the emphasis on de-bordering among some scholars. Newman (1999, 2006) criticizes such predictions as premature and wrong.

the information that reaches their supervisors, this will allow them to shirk their duties and engage in corrupt activities. Implementation of high-level policies can be compromised, and state institutions may collapse if monitoring failures reach critical proportions.

Applying such frameworks to the study of interstate borders would lead to the conclusion that aggressive monitoring from above is necessary to cajole border guards to perform their duties, to punish those who engage in corrupt practices, and to evaluate the effectiveness of the border administration against the daily requirements of a frontier zone. Otherwise, the organizations charged with securing a state border may suffer incremental increases in dereliction of duty and corruption. As a case in point, the recent public scrutiny of border control in the United States and the politicized description of the border as "broken" highlight the belief that tight monitoring and control are necessary for a well-functioning border.

Yet states that create rigid and tight monitoring channels from their borders to their capital cities suffer a host of unintended consequences. An effective monitoring channel from the border to the capital means that events and incidents that occur along an international boundary get reported to high-level security agencies and executives in the capital. The reporting of incidents is heavily biased toward violent events. Border authorities who are upwardly accountable and who must regularly report to supervisors will have an incentive to blame the administrative practices of the other side as permitting or causing border incidents. Such feedback will negatively affect diplomatic relations and further promote intervention along the state border.

In order to properly examine the claim that directness of state intervention prevents cross-border cooperation, it is necessary to outline how directness may best be measured. I propose to measure directness of state intervention in two ways in my cases. One way is by measuring monitoring mechanisms that are part of the organizational hierarchy of border control. This can be done by investigating the border control headquarters in capital cities. If monitoring is rigorous and if performance targets relating to border control are strictly specified, then there is a high degree of direct intervention. If agents at the border are less rigorously monitored or have flexible performance targets and broadly defined goals, then there is a low degree of direct intervention. By paying such attention to the hierarchy of border guard institutions, it becomes possible to determine whether it is the organizational hierarchy itself that causes events to escalate.

Another way to measure the degree of state intervention is by investigating the depth and scope of monitoring and oversight of the administration of the border by third party, high-level political actors. It is plausible that macro-level intervention in matters of border control may emanate from parts of the state other than the border guard or military hierarchy. For example, monitoring and oversight may come from another state agency that has formally or informally been tasked with observing the administration of the border. This is fulfilled when a parliament commissions reports on border affairs, conducts hearings on border security, and passes laws that alter or restrict the administration of the boundary. Likewise, this condition is fulfilled when a border guard agency is made accountable to another high-level state agency. This may be an executive cabinet or a high-level national security agency. Such forms of intervention are not as direct as the prior form of internal intervention. However, they may restrict the autonomy previously granted to local border authorities. When high-level state agencies hastily intervene, they give little opportunity for local resolution of disputes. This was the dilemma a provincial police chief in a Cambodian border province had in mind when he criticized the interference of state officials, including the prime minister, in the administration of the boundary (Amer 1997). Some of the cases at hand will involve one or both of these forms of high-level intervention. Whenever possible, the cases will explain substantive differences in the effects of these types of interventions on border control.

Boundary Regimes

Claim 4: Border guards vested with the ability to interact with their counterparts on the other side will pool their efforts and jointly police the boundary. This project argues that locally embedded, cross-border organizations are the key to security along peripheral regions. I refer to such organizations as boundary regimes. Specifically, I define a boundary regime as the institutionalized and routinized process of regulating access to boundary zones and policing borders in a manner that bilaterally enhances border security without unduly restricting lucrative economic flows or movements that are not threatening to territorial security. This is not meant to imply that a boundary regime is free of disputes and crises. Rather, in a boundary regime a set of norms and routines will be in place along both sides to deal with violations as they arise.

Four Claims about Interstate Boundaries

An essential feature of boundary regimes is the durability and evolution of cooperation across the authorities of the two states. Border guards on the two sides may coordinate patrols to maximize their resources to police a long border; they may jointly regulate access to grey areas to prevent conflict among local populations; and they may agree on how to manage incidents locally without escalating. This will be discussed in detail later. However, it is important to note an implication of the prior three claims for boundary regimes. Boundary regimes are conceived when two contiguous states bilaterally and simultaneously hand down to the local level parameters that involve a substantial amount of discretion. These parameters must include some tolerance for evasion and imperfection in border control matters, and the two sides' parameters must be compatible with each other. Boundary regimes are prevented from forming when state-building practices diverge and states directly intervene in the functioning of the border.

Consider the nature of the game along a given international boundary (for the time being, we are agnostic about the role of central state agencies or the actual content of diplomatic relations of the states sharing the boundary). Border guards are stationed on both sides of the boundary along various points such as roads, mountain passes, and near border towns. A boundary in a remote region might be the site of smuggling, banditry, or cross-border rebellion. Border guards along both sides of the boundary face a common dilemma. A given post can patrol its stretch of the boundary against smugglers, bandits, and other third parties that would violate its territorial jurisdiction. If the post on the other side is lax in its duties, takes bribes from those who wish to carry out illegal activities across the border, or is sloppy in its patrols, then its paired post suffers the costs disproportionately. Those border guards must now work harder and more vigilantly to police the border against flows from the other side. If they decide to respond in kind, then both sides are negligent in their duties, the border attracts more illegal activities, and violations reach a destabilizing critical mass.

If border posts along both sides of the boundary can pool their resources and coordinate their actions, then it is likely that smaller and incremental cooperative efforts will have exponential success in stabilizing the boundary and in implementing effective border controls. But this statement is only the most basic part of the cooperative dilemma, and it is necessary to explain why this tit-for-tat cooperation turns into a durable and self-enforcing boundary regime over time.

Ostrom's work on the evolution of cooperation and self-governing institutions is essential here. Ostrom (1990) finds that individuals have the capacity to organize internally and design efficient institutions in order to manage their resources. She argues that actors facing social dilemmas can develop credible ex ante commitments without relying on external authorities. These commitments are secured when individuals have the capacity to communicate in order to pose solutions to cooperative dilemmas, to monitor each others' behavior, and to impose sanctions on those who break their commitments. Ostrom argues that individuals who expect to confront one another in repeated social dilemmas will devote substantial effort and time to monitoring one another and imposing sanctions. Monitoring mechanisms and graduated sanctions are likely to lead to efficient management of the given dilemma. However, in order for monitoring and enforcement to be adopted, individuals must have sufficient information to pose and solve the allocation problems they face and an arena in which to discuss joint strategies and to implement monitoring and sanctioning.

An implication of this model is that successful monitoring must be internal to the actors involved in cooperation or competition. External actors, especially high-level central agencies, have a tendency to mis-sanction; they lack access to full information, and this lack often leads to sanctioning the innocent or a failure to sanction the guilty.[14]

Taking a cue from Ostrom's work, this project examines three conditions that allow border guards along both sides of an international boundary to become cooperative and professional managers. These conditions are (a) an arena for communication, (b) the ability to monitor behavior, and (c) shared parameters of administrative tasks.

Arena for communication: In order to communicate intent and pose solutions to border problems, guards need communicative access with the other side. This condition is fulfilled when posts on the two sides of a given border are within visual and communicative range. A boundary where border guards are separated by dead zones or electric fences, or where only one side has stationed guards, does not fulfill this condition. In order for this condition to be fulfilled, border guard posts must be located within visual

---

[14] See Ostrom (1990: 17). Similar approaches have been used to explain institutional solutions to collective action problems in other settings. These range from studies of cooperation among rival entrepreneurs in the tourism business (Ingram 1996) to studies of cooperation and in-group policing that moderate conflict among ethnic groups (Fearon and Laitin 1996).

range along the length of their border, and border guards must be able to communicate with their foreign counterparts. A border where pairing occurs only at official crossings does not fulfill this condition. The emphasis on visual contact may strike the reader as archaic, as relevant only to historical cases of border control before the advent electronic communications. However, my cases will demonstrate that the evolution of a boundary regime requires that guards have face-to-face communication. Communication via technologies such as wireless devices is not sufficient to trigger cross-border cooperation. While useful for communicating vital information, it provides a truncated form of discussion and does not allow border guards to have an extended and communal discussion of border security problems.

Monitoring capacity: The ability to monitor behavior follows from the first condition. Monitoring capacity here is defined as the ability to confirm the other side's implementation of agreed-upon solutions or procedures. This is fulfilled when border guards have sustained visual or communicative confirmation that the other side's border guards are implementing patrols, fulfilling security tasks, and so on.

Shared parameters: Border guards must view one another as legitimate actors with the right to administer the border and the right to organize to discuss border administration. These parameters must also include a shared understanding of the cooperative dilemma. This parameter condition is fulfilled when border guards along both sides share an understanding of the general goals of border management (e.g., stop bandits, prevent smuggling, don't allow territory to be violated). This understanding may be broad, as long as it is shared. When border guards' perceptions of the objectives of boundary management diverge, this condition is not fulfilled. This is the case when border guards along the two sides of a boundary have been given management tasks or administrative instructions that are mutually exclusive or do not imply the same goals of border management.

It should be clear from the conditions just enumerated that this level of the argument does not delve into issues of actor intentionality, consciousness, or personal interests.[15] The conditions instead constitute interactions and relations among border guards. Where hundreds or thousands of border guards patrol a border, it is not feasible to try to understand each

---

[15] In a study of a Parisian communal revolt in the nineteenth century, Gould finds that group boundaries and a perception of common social ties are much more important to high-risk collective action than convergent interests (1995: 19).

individual's motives and intentions. Even if feasible, such a venture may not be worth the trouble. In an experiment that studies how individuals play strategic games, Ostrom (2000) undermines the assumption that the standard individual is a rational egoist. She discovers that the strategic world contains multiple types of players. The rational egoist is joined by altruists, conditional cooperators, and willing punishers. Gould (1993) likewise casts doubt on the belief that individuals are pure rational egoists and instead underscores the effects of group boundaries and the individual's desire to avoid making contributions to collective action that will be wasted.[16] It is more beneficial to explain outcomes via a focus on arenas and scopes of interaction (Tilly 1998). The conditions enumerated here thus allow for a boundary regime to form even if ranks of local officials include border guards that are underhanded, corrupt, or lazy.

But how do we identify a boundary regime without slipping into tautologies? I search for evidence of cross-border cooperation along three indicators: escalation, innovation, and corruption. By searching for evidence of these three phenomena along the boundaries examined, I gauge the extent to which a boundary regime operates autonomously at the local level, the degree to which it crafts new policies to meet emerging security challenges, and the extent to which collusion, bribery, and rent seeking underlie cross-border cooperation. I discuss each indicator in turn.

Escalation is a process whereby actors signal willingness to fight over a given dispute. This signaling can happen when actors bring the dispute to the attention of higher levels of authority or mobilize more resources to back conflicting claims. Scholars use escalation to model state-to-state conflict in the international system (Fearon 1995). In these models, escalation is usually defined as the opposite of restraint (Legro 1996; Kydd 1997). I apply the concept of escalation both to the micro level (border guard to border guard) and to the interstate level. If a boundary regime is durable, I expect that border authorities will avoid escalating disputes that they can resolve at the local level. I expect that border guards will exhaust all local forms of dispute resolution before requesting the intervention of higher authorities.

The second indicator, innovation, measures the extent to which a boundary regime evolves and adapts to new security challenges. This indicator

---

[16] Levi also notes that an individual's self-interest may still allow for a range of behavior, from heavily altruistic to intensely self-regarding (1988: 3).

is separate from escalation and refers to a process by which actors devise previously unavailable collective and concerted solutions to extricate themselves from a given social dilemma. This does not mean that all actors will invent new operating procedures out of thin air. Here it refers to actors rethinking, refashioning, and revising existing procedures to fit new crises (Tilly 2000, 2007). I define an innovation in border administration as the adoption of a new operating procedure, norm, or policy that has been tailored to better respond to an existing problem or that has been developed in order to combat a new one. If existing routines persist in the face of new challenges to border control, then innovation has not occurred.[17]

The final indicator is corruption. A possible by-product of a boundary regime may be collusion among boundary officials. Border guards may extend protection to drug-smuggling networks; customs officials may solicit bribes in order to process goods faster or at reduced tariff rates. In each of the cases, I search for evidence that border authorities are engaging in corrupt activities. I specify the types of corrupt activities and gauge their extent. Detecting a specific instance of corruption is difficult as actors profiting from such activities are intent on hiding them. However, detecting the general types, presence, and extent of corruption is made possible by the presence of consular agencies of third-party states that monitor activities in border regions and international organizations and nongovernmental organizations that work in or near border regions and report on corrupt practices.

Corruption is a facet of all boundaries. It occurs in any situation where agents are entrusted with authority and have the opportunity to profit from an abuse of this authority (Kang 2002; also see Roebuck and Barker 1974; Sherman 1980; Rodden and Ackerman 1997). While I do not expect to find that boundary regimes are free of corruption, I am more concerned with demonstrating that the intent to profit from collusion and rent seeking are not the source of cross-border cooperation. To uncover some collusion in boundary regimes would be expected. To find that cross-border cooperation is motivated by a desire for personal profit would be damaging to the theory.

The next chapter investigates the emergence of a boundary regime along the nineteenth-century Ottoman-Greek land border. The border is an

---

[17] As Axelrod argues, actors are adaptive and will amend their behavior via trail-and-error processes if new situations call for it (1997: 47; see also 1983).

unlikely site for a boundary regime. It was established in an isolated region rife with banditry and rebellion. Despite local insecurity and fraught diplomatic relations between the Ottoman Empire and Greece, border guards jointly and cooperative administered the boundary. I fuse the claims already presented with a rich archival record to show how border guards organized to craft a boundary regime under the most adverse of conditions.

3

Border Guards, Bandits, and the Ottoman-Greek Boundary Regime in the Nineteenth Century

The Greek-Ottoman land boundary was the product of protracted ethnic and civil conflict that devastated the Ottoman Empire's southern Balkan provinces during the 1820s. The Great Powers saw the conflict as an unlimited war of extermination between Muslim and Christian populations, and they decided to create an independent Greek state with a boundary that would ensure tranquility through a complete partition of the area's ethnic and religious groups.[1] Although the delimitation commission set out to create a perfect barrier between the two states, the demarcation commission that walked the boundary in 1832 reported that the border had done little to seal off the two sovereign territories from one another.

The boundary cut across the migratory paths of nomads, and residents of certain villages suddenly found their crops and water sources on opposite sides of the boundary.[2] Moreover, as the boundary commission began to survey topography and to lay down stone pyramids, thousands of refugees, Christian and Muslim alike, abandoned the new Greek state for Ottoman

---

This chapter relies extensively on manuscripts from three archives. Manuscripts and documents used appear in footnotes with brief annotations. The following abbreviations are used in the footnotes to avoid repetition of archive names: BBA (Başbakanlık Arşivi, the Archives of the Prime Ministry, Istanbul, Turkey); AYE (Historiko Archeio tou Ypourgeiou Eksoterikon, the Historical Archives of the Greek Foreign Ministry, Athens, Greece); FO (Public Record Office, Foreign Office Files, London, UK). Dates are presented as they appear on documents. Dates based on the Ottoman *hicri* calendar are also converted into their Western equivalents (e.g., 1260/1844).

[1] BBA, HR.SYS, 1677/2, 1827–7–6, 19 February/2 March 1832; "Memorandum on the New Delimitation of Greece."

[2] BBA, Hatt-ı Hümayun, 47760-B, 1249/1833–34; Hüseyin's description of the delimitation procedure and the boundary zone; AYE, 1833, 4/4, 25 April 1833; petition of residents of Sourbe to the Greek government.

territories. Unhappy minorities were given eighteen months to request indemnity and immigrate (Georges 1996: 70). Terrified, the Muslims of a border town that was to remain on the Greek side directly petitioned the sultan to be transported out of Greece.[3] Other villages, rather than immigrate to the other side of the border, took measures to ensure that the neighboring state migrated to them. Villagers in the central district of Agrafa, whose unity was to be split in half by the boundary, conspired to provide the delimitation commission and engineers who were building guardhouses with false place names to throw off the demarcation proceedings and to ensure that they would end up in Greek territory.[4]

Foreign observers warned that the boundary was ill-conceived and left both states less secure. Instead of sending well-armed military regulars to defend the border, the Ottoman and Greek states commissioned and deployed a group of former bandits, mercenaries, and domestic police units to take up positions along the boundary (Strong 1842: 263). Despite predictions that the boundary was primed for more unrest, within several years it became a site of cooperation between Ottoman and Greek border guards, who innovated procedures to administer the boundary jointly with minimal escalation of incidents.

How were two ragtag border guard teams of former bandits and inexperienced irregulars transformed into innovative and professional managers of an international boundary? This chapter explains the emergence of a boundary regime along the Greek-Ottoman land border (from the 1830s to the 1860s) in two steps. In the first stage, I use archival documents concerning the boundary and its border guards to demonstrate that from the 1830s to the 1840s Ottoman and Greek guards moved from a state of administrative confusion and disarray to a system of cooperation and information exchange that facilitated the task of boundary administration (i.e., prevention of smuggling, irredentism, banditry, and border jumping). Three conditions were necessary and jointly sufficient for cooperation. In order to cooperate across the international boundary, border guards required (a) a common definition of the cooperative dilemma, (b) an arena in which to communicate and propose solutions for administering the boundary, and (c) the capacity to monitor implementation of proposed solutions.

---

[3] BBA, Hatt-ı Hümayun, 21694-C, 1248/1832; petition from the town of Patracık to the sultan. Also BBA, Hatt-ı Hümayun, 47762-H, 1250/1834.

[4] BBA, Hatt-ı Hümayun, 47730-B, 1254/1838; and AYE, 1853, 4/1a, 4 February 1844; report of mayor of Ktemenion.

In the second stage, the administration of the boundary moved from limited cooperation to a boundary regime. Border guards along the length of the boundary innovated to suppress banditry, cooperated diffusely, and solved disputes locally and jointly without triggering escalation and diplomatic crises. However, I discover that this institutional shift required a fourth condition: a third-party monitor located along both sides of the boundary. I argue that a local, external monitoring mechanism pushed the border guards to cooperate more broadly and to innovate long-term solutions for administering and protecting the boundary.

Although the events of this chapter are set along a boundary that no longer exists, they serve the purpose of theory building outlined in the previous chapter. Specifically, I use the literature on institutions and the evolution of cooperation to explain how and why local authorities will tend toward cross-border cooperation if given the opportunity to interact, irrespective of the state of diplomatic relations. Local authorities in this chapter include border guards, border captains, customs officials, and mayors located at or near the Greek-Ottoman border. Central state agencies encompass official institutions such as Ottoman and Greek diplomatic organs, offices of war, and foreign and interior ministries.

Evolution of a Boundary Regime

Agreement on the location of the border was difficult to achieve. Part of the difficulty lay in the maximalist demands of the Greek delegates at the talks that the Great Powers sponsored. The Greek delegates wanted a border that would incorporate a maximum of Ottoman territory in the southern Balkans, including large towns such as Larissa, Arta, and Volos. The Ottoman delegation resisted this demand, citing the substantial Muslim peasant and land-owning populations in these areas. The Great Powers consequently brokered an agreement giving the provisional Greek state approximately 30 percent less territory than it had desired (Chrestos 1999).

Affixing the border was more than a matter of coordinating how much the Ottomans were willing to lose with how much Greece was willing to gain. The Great Powers – and in particular the British delegation – wanted to carve a boundary between the two states that would use natural geographic barriers in the region to partition the area's ethnic groups. The planned border was to bisect an area that was wild, mountainous, and remote. This area began in the east along the Gulf of Volo and ran westward through rough and forested mountain chains until it reached the Gulf of Arta (see Map 3.1). Delegates in charge of delimiting the boundary attempted to make use of natural features as much as possible in order to make the location of the boundary clear and to provide a strategic buffer between the two sovereign territories.[5]

Geographic considerations trumped attempts to create a neat partition of the area's ethnic and religious groups. Like many of the Ottoman Empire's territories, the frontier areas were appreciably multiethnic. They contained Christian, Muslim, and Jewish populations who spoke a multiplicity of languages that included derivations and dialects of Greek, Turkish, Albanian, and Vlach. In 1828, ahead of the demarcation of the boundary, Greek delegates proposed that Turkish residents living on what would be the Greek side of the boundary immigrate to the Ottoman Empire (Georges 1996: 77). A substantial portion of Greece's Muslim population in other areas had already fled to escape the conflict.

The Treaty of Constantinople of 1832 determined the new border and attempted to ease ethnic and religious issues by giving those living in border areas eighteen months to immigrate to the other side.[6] Both Ottoman and Greek delegates warned that such legalities would be abused by the other side in order to push out unwanted minorities. Nonetheless, they accepted such provisions. Although the treaty and demarcation resolved the conflict between the Ottoman Empire and Greece, the placement of a border where none had existed created problems for both states. The boundary created a new set of legal realities that had to be enforced. It cut across the migratory paths of nomads, and many residents suddenly found their crops, forests, water sources, and relatives on the other side. Accessing them was now an

---

[5] The *Journal of the Royal Geographical Society* published a map, titled "The Northern Frontier of Greece, 1834," which enumerated the landmarks and showed the path of the boundary line over physical features. Much of the western half of the boundary followed the course of rivers and mountain streams. The eastern half of the boundary ran along the ridges of the Othrys mountain range in what appears to be a more or less horizontal manner. Although the map exaggerated the extent to which the mountains formed an unbroken and wall-like barrier, the attempt of the British to affix the line along such physical features underscores their desire to deter future conflict between the two states. It was not uncommon in the European cartographic tradition to exaggerate physical features in frontier areas. In discussing the case of early modern France, Sahlins (1990) shows how rulers' obsession with maintaining natural boundaries compelled cartographers to sketch physical barriers such as mountains and rivers even where none existed.

[6] The right to request an indemnity and immigrate appears to have gone into force in 1835 only after the Great Power representatives handed over the boundary map to Ottoman authorities. For more details, see Georges (1996: 70).

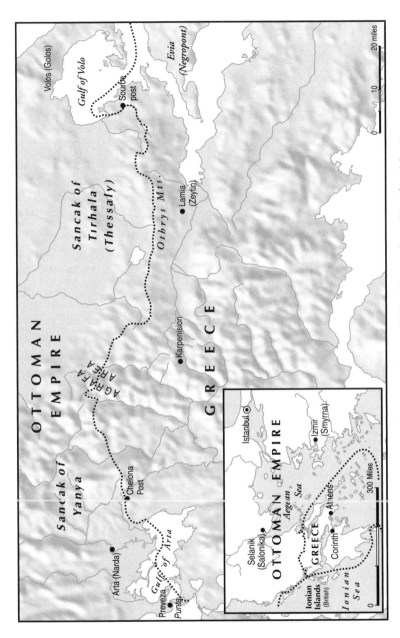

Map 3.1. The Ottoman-Greek boundary, 1832. *Source:* Phillip Schwartzberg, Meridian Mapping.

illegal and punishable act. At the same time, the boundary created tremendous opportunities for crime and violence. Bandits could commit crimes along one side of the border and flee to the other side confident that security forces giving chase would not be able to pursue them over the boundary.

The problem of banditry was one that had been endemic to the region in the decades prior to the Greek revolt. By the end of the eighteenth century, much of the interior of the southern Balkans had slipped out of the Porte's control due to a combination of economic decline, overtaxation, and administrative malaise.[7] This triggered the ascendance of three groups: local potentates (*ayan*) such as Ali Paşa, who ran virtually autonomous principalities within Ottoman territory and who amassed sizeable coercive and extractive power by consolidating the holdings of peasants and becoming their creditors; bandit chiefs who alternately pillaged and sold their services as mercenaries to Ali Paşa and other well-paying employers; and networks of pastoralists who organized themselves in cooperatives (*tselingato*) in order to provide collective security for their members and flocks (Koliopoulos 1987). Peasants, merchants, and urban populations found no security and miserable economic fortunes in such a system.

According to traditional explanations, the Greek War of Independence represented liberation from the oppression and poverty of the Ottoman Empire.[8] Yet alternative accounts suggest that the Greek revolt was based on a loose coalition of semibandit chiefs and Christian landlords whose primary goal was to achieve local autonomy as had occurred in other parts of the Ottoman Empire (Chirot and Barkey 1983). Tellingly, the proto-administrative structure of the Greek state appears to have consisted largely of landowners and tax farmers (primates of the Peloponnesus), bandit captains, and ship owners and merchants in the islands (Petropoulos 1968; Koliopoulos 1987: 3).

This background is crucial to understanding the nature of the boundary and its subsequent administration. For both the Ottoman Empire and Greece, the new border had to confront banditry as a continuing dilemma for state rule and territorial control. Suppressing banditry and crime meant using methods that had substantial precedent in Ottoman administration.

---

[7] At the time the term "Porte" was commonly used to refer to the Ottoman government in Istanbul. The term is a partial translation of the Turkish *Bab-ı Ali*, the exalted gate.

[8] This is part of an enduring nationalist narrative in Greece. For such accounts, see Paparregopoulos (1932). For criticism of these approaches, see Herzfeld (1986). The Ottoman word for the conflict was *ihtilal*, or rebellion.

In her work on the centralization of Ottoman authority, Barkey (1994, 2008) demonstrates how officials suppressed bandit activities by strategically offering brigands official positions in the extractive and coercive apparatus of the state. In the processes of co-opting select bandits as tax collectors and policemen, she argues, the Ottomans effectively converted bandits into bureaucrats. Köksal (2006) shows a similar process unfolding in the nineteenth century among tribes in the Anatolian interior of the empire. The state carefully and selectively incorporated tribal leaders into its lower-level administration in order to settle the tribes, reduce criminal activity, and enhance the ability of the state to extract resources.

Such practices were not limited to the Ottoman state. They were widely practiced from northern Europe to East Asia. In a study of banditry on the eighteenth-century Dutch frontier, Blok lucidly demonstrates how bandits helped state officials suppress the society from which they rose (2001: 16). In late nineteenth-century China, Cohen documents how state officials discriminated among criminal elements; they sanctioned a marginally licit group known as the Big Swords to suppress less fortunate bandits (Cohen 1997: 19). In her study of sovereignty in early modern Europe, Thomson (1994) shows how European rulers struggled to end the widespread use of commissioning mercenaries and privateers to fight on their behalf. Such well-organized, armed private groups allowed state authorities to rent fighting forces on a case-by-case basis, but often created rival sources of authority and prevented state rulers from controlling the use of international force.

Given such widespread practices in the Balkans and elsewhere, it is not surprising that bandits and brigands featured prominently in the administration of the Ottoman-Greek border. In the wake of the controversial demarcation, the Ottoman and Greek states amnestied and commissioned large numbers of former bandit captains and their entourages to serve on their respective borders. Former bandits were charged with the task of providing security against other bandits along the border in order to prevent crime and violence and to restore the region's shattered economy and infrastructure.

From Confusion to Cooperation

Ottoman and Greek authorities were in a state of confusion over how to administer the rugged boundary. Although the demarcation commission laid down 95 stone markers along the 150-mile border, Ottoman provincial authorities refused to recognize Greek territory pending an official decree from the center.[9] Local Ottoman *derbent* – officially appointed to protect bridges and roads and to guard strategic areas in the interior of the Ottoman *sancak* of Tırhala (Thessaly) – shifted their activities to the boundary zone.[10] They policed the area to suppress banditry and freely entered Greek territory in pursuit. Although Greek diplomats complained, local authorities in Greece – both confused about their duties and intimidated by the Ottoman *derbent* – did nothing to oppose their movements in the wake of the demarcation.[11]

In addition to the disagreement regarding the position of the boundary, local authorities were in a state of substantial administrative disarray. They did not agree on procedures for regulating passage, implementing quarantine, taxing goods, restricting access to grey zones, or coordinating patrols to prevent banditry and border jumping. Yet within a few years, Ottoman and Greek border guards developed a substantial capacity to cooperate in order to administer the boundary. Moreover, they adopted a common definition of what constituted criminal acts such as border jumping. Escalation was substantially reduced along the boundary, as were incidents of banditry and weapons smuggling.

What factors explain the ability of Greek and Ottoman border guards to adopt common procedures to police and administer the boundary? In order to avoid gathering and interpreting data only to verify my own hypotheses, I looked for evidence supporting two alternative views that offer plausible and parsimonious answers to the question. The first alternative is that cooperation came about because states handed down precise administrative directives on how to manage the boundary. This alternative deserves thorough investigation because a literature in comparative politics on historical and contemporary boundaries converges on the assumption that modernizing, centralizing states treat borders as vital institutions of state security and territorial control. In a marvelous study of the history of the French-Spanish boundary in the Pyrenees, Peter Sahlins (1991) demonstrates how the two capital cities increasingly tried to regulate and micromanage day-to-day operations along their border, even as locals resisted and evaded state

---

[9] AYE, 1833, 4/4, 1/13 May 1833; letter from a local boundary inspector to Rizos (Greece). Also see "The Northern Frontier of Greece, 1834," a map of the demarcation posts that was published in 1837 by John Murray for the *Journal of the Royal Geographical Society of London*.

[10] The only substantial work on the *derbent* institution is in Turkish (Orhonlu 1990).

[11] AYE, 1833, 4/4, 20 April/2 May 1833; report of a Greek official who was afraid to approach the boundary for this reason.

directives. In a study of Soviet borders, Andrea Chandler (1998) demonstrates that Moscow aggressively micromanaged security affairs on its borders in order to prevent the exit and entry of goods and people. Although these studies are set in different centuries and contexts, they suggest that states have interests in micromanaging and directly administering their borders (though they may lack the capacity to do so). Thus, I searched for evidence that the Ottoman and Greek states organized and administered their borders through unilateral, specific, and aggressive codes and directives. Specifically, I looked for evidence that they handed down precise instructions on policing, suppressing border jumping, reporting territorial violations, and the like.

An examination of both Greek and Ottoman documents in the period before border guards took their posts and in the several years following the recognition of the boundary do not indicate that the Ottoman and Greek states handed down specific instructions on how to administer the boundary. This chapter will show that when border guards along both sides petitioned their respective states to provide instructions and to help them solve specific disputes, both states simultaneously responded that solutions to managing the boundary ought to be locally determined.

The second plausible explanation is that border guards cooperated because of self-serving interest. Border guards received a regular salary, and, given the scarcity of resources and opportunities in the region, it was to their benefit to carry out administrative duties and police the boundary. Not carrying out duties could lead to sanctions and punishment, namely, loss of position and income. If this explanation is correct, it is likely that administrative order along the boundary is not a result of cooperation between border guards on both sides; rather, it is a function of guards carrying out their duties simultaneously but independently.

While the category of border guard seems uniform as a type, guards along the Ottoman-Greek land border were socially complex actors. As will be shown, the Ottoman border guards were composed of armed toll collectors, domestic police, mercenary captains, amnestied bandits, and, in some cases, local peasants. Along the Greek side, border guards were generally a mix of irregular captains, former bandits, settled peasants, and some military recruits (Koliopoulos 1987). Neither side was part of a regular military element, nor was either side specifically trained to guard an international boundary.

Specifying a set of preferences for an array of local actors is an unproductive task. The literature on cooperation and conflict has increasingly distanced itself from the necessity of specifying preferences at the onset of a given social or institutional dilemma (Axelrod 1997). Personality type will certainly affect an actor's preferences. Some individuals may be willing enforcers and quick to punish defectors. Others may be willing cooperators, while some are predisposed toward quick defection (Laitin 1998; Ostrom 2000). Above and beyond this difficulty, in the case of the border guards it is difficult to determine what social and personality characteristics are represented at particular border posts. Some guards may prefer to carry out some of their duties but smuggle when they can. Some may find it prudent to fall back on their bandit habits given the isolation of the boundary, while others may become efficient managerial border guards if they desire an upwardly mobile career in the boundary authority. Specifying preferences in situations involving myriad local actors across multiple sites of observation may be counterproductive and inaccurate (Gould 1995; Tilly 1998; Kalyvas 1999). Preferences change according to the backgrounds of particular border guards, according to particular border posts, according to issues of administrative duty, or according to a combination of many factors.[12]

Instead, I focus on the context of interactions and argue that cooperation between Ottoman and Greek border guards was the result of three local conditions: (1) a common definition of the institutional/cooperative dilemma, (2) the ability to interact to propose solutions to the problem; and (3) the ability to monitor compliance to determine if the other side was implementing joint solutions. All three were necessary in order for the boundary to switch from unilaterally (mis)managed to jointly managed. This section demonstrates the presence of all three prior to the advent of cooperation.

Condition 1: In order to jointly and cooperatively administer the boundary, it is necessary that border guards along both sides share a common definition of the cooperative dilemma they face. The Ottoman and Greek states provided this common definition rather unintentionally. In the period

---

[12] As stated in Chapter 2, I intend to avoid guesswork regarding the intentions of local actors. Instead, I focus on their interactions and the context of these interactions. Many scholars who study banditry and tribes do the same. Blok (2001) criticizes attempts to create an account of banditry based on types of bandits. Instead, he studies the ability of bandits to shift in and out of roles and professions. In a study of Montenegrin tribal feuding, Boehm (1984) focuses on the interactions and sanctioning mechanisms that have created specific and highly precise rules on feuding and escalation. Such rules overshadow the nuances of individual personalities.

immediately after the recognition of the boundary, border guards along both sides were quick to fire off petitions to their respective states to complain about the other side's guards and to request intervention. Along the eastern edge of the frontier near Sourbe, Greek local authorities wrote to the Ministry of Interior requesting clarification of locals' immigration rights and of general administrative procedures.[13] Along the western section in the Chelona (Chalones) area, boundary authorities complained that Ottoman units had overstepped the Greek boundary and demanded diplomatic action to ensure that the Ottoman guards responsible for the violation be punished.[14] In the same area, Ottoman authorities complained that Greek national guards had invaded Ottoman territory and carried off domesticated animals. While some issues, such as the smuggling of arms, seemed to arouse particular concern in the capital cities,[15] high-level ministries along both sides expressed displeasure that border authorities were requesting intervention without due cause. Complaints and requests for intervention exasperated the Greek secretary of state, who fired off an angry letter demanding that local authorities stop harassing the state and start cooperating with Ottoman border guards in light of the impossibility of unilaterally administering the boundary.[16] The Ottoman state made similar demands of its own border authorities.[17]

Throughout the early 1840s, the Ottoman and Greek states repeated these instructions.[18] While such instructions provided little information on how border guards were to administer the boundary, they did serve to clarify the general aims and principles of boundary management. First, the states demanded that border guards cooperate and avoid provoking incidents between the two governments. Second, the states highlighted banditry and border jumping as the primary administrative dilemma along the boundary.[19] Bandits posed a particular problem for both the Ottoman and Greek states in the border region. Bandits regularly pillaged villages

[13] AYE, 1836, 4/1b, 3 November 1836.
[14] AYE, 1836, 4/1b, 2 September 1836.
[15] AYE, 1836, 4/1, 13 March 1836; from the Ministry of the Interior to the Greek foreign minister.
[16] AYE, 1836, 4/1b, 30 July 1836.
[17] BBA, HR.SYS, 1677/2, 6 July 1837.
[18] BBA, Cevdet Hariciye, 8995, 2R1262/19 April 1846; AYE, 1840, 4/1, 3/15 March 1840; AYE, 1842, 4/1, n.d.; order of the Greek minister of war to the troops and gendarme in Lamia; and AYE, 1843, 4/1d; n.d.; letter of Tayyar Mehmet Paşa, *Kaymakam* of the *Sancak* of Tırhala to the Greek consul in Salonika.
[19] BBA, HR.MKT, 7/41, 1260L11/24 October 1844.

in the area and often kidnapped individuals in hopes of ransom payments. They traditionally alternated between stealing and bargaining with the state for amnesty and appointment to the security apparatus (Koliopoulos 1987, 1999; Barkey 1994). A fraction of the bandits managed to secure a regular salary as border guards. The majority of bandits, however, had to continue their traditional ways of survival and found the boundary a prime area in which to operate given the initial confusion among authorities. The outbreak of banditry both embarrassed and alarmed Ottoman and Greek officials, and they resolved to crush brigandage.[20] In 1842, the Ottoman and Greek states appointed many new border captains to ensure the security of the boundary. These captains marched to the boundary with yet another entourage of inexperienced soldier-clients.[21]

Although the Ottoman and Greek states dispatched large and untrained forces to face off across the boundary for the first time, the instability and clashes predicted by British foreign observers did not occur. The prevailing order was partly a consequence of the instructions of the Ottoman and Greek states, which presented boundary authorities simultaneously and uniformly with information that made clear the general goals of boundary administration. The central states expected their boundary authorities to cooperate with one another to administer the boundary, to prevent the escalation of disputes, and to focus on banditry and border jumping by third parties (rather than on the territorial violations border guards themselves committed). While such information provided no specific solutions or procedures to administer the boundary, it unambiguously defined boundary administration as a joint task.[22]

Condition 2: Cooperation across boundary authorities requires the presence of an arena in which actors can pose solutions to an institutional problem. This arena came in several forms along the boundary. First, guardhouses were placed along the boundary sufficiently close to those of the

---

[20] FO 196/19, 7 March 1842; cipher from Canning in Istanbul to the Foreign Office. In addition to security concerns, the issue of embarrassment was central to Ottoman and Greek officials. Great Power diplomats often condemned Greece as a barbaric sociopolitical order, completely estranged from its ancient civilized roots. Austrian Foreign Minister Metternich once referred to Greece as a "republic of bandits" (Seton-Watson 1955: 113).

[21] BBA, Cevdet Zaptiye, 554, 22R1257/13 June 1841; and BBA, HR.MKT, 8/8, 1260Za22/3 December 1844.

[22] The central states were precise in some respects ("Catch bandits!" and "Work together!") and extremely vague in others. They did not present border guards with lists of suspects or a definition of acts constituting banditry and border jumping.

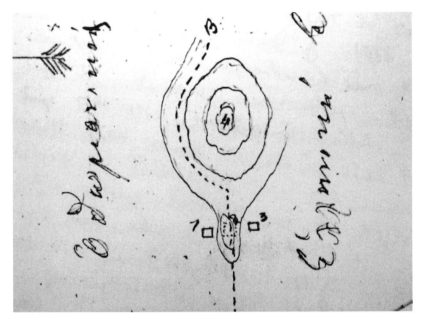

Map 3.2. Border post positions. *Note:* Sketched by Greek border captain to show the final positions of paired Ottoman (1) and Greek border stations (3) in Chelona. *Source:* AYE, 1866 4:2b; courtesy of the Historical Archives of the Foreign Ministry of Greece.

other side to permit both visual and communicative contact (see Map 3.2).[23] Such interfacing allowed border guards to walk over to posts on the other side to discuss procedure, coordinate patrols, and exchange information on suspects.[24] Second, the area's linguistic pluralism did not impede communication. Although a multiplicity of languages were spoken, including Albanian, Greek, Turkish, and Vlach, many border guards were multilingual or had an interpreter readily available. This ensured that language did not pose a communicative barrier.

Condition 3: Cooperation required the presence of a system to monitor compliance that included agreed-upon administrative solutions. This condition is based partly on the second condition. The physical proximity of guardhouses often allowed immediate and automatic monitoring of activity

---

[23] This observation is also derived from the documents, which describe the relative closeness of the other side's guard houses.

[24] AYE, 1856, 81/1, 22 November 1856; discusses the monitoring ability of two proximate border posts.

along border posts. For instance, if a paired border post had agreed to coordinate patrols and did not show up to begin patrol the following day, this would become obvious. If the two sides shared a list of suspects and one side allowed a suspect on the list to exit, this too would be difficult to mask from the other side. Even in cases where border posts were not within immediate visual range, monitoring was possible in various ways. An increase in border jumping from the other side did not necessarily mean that that side's border guard was negligent in policing the boundary, but it did warrant a joint meeting and an informal investigation.

Throughout the 1840s, these conditions allowed border guards to organize, coordinate, and monitor behavior. These cooperative outcomes are expressed in the data in the form of three shifts – two procedural and one normative. The first shift was the procedure that border guards set up in order to share information and discuss boundary administration. During the period immediately following demarcation, border guards tended to communicate indirectly with the other side by writing petitions or complaints to their own higher authorities. The high state organs would then lodge a diplomatic complaint with the other state, which would forward the complaint and begin an inquiry down its administrative hierarchy.[25]

By the 1840s, the shared arenas of communication allowed border guards to set up more direct information relay systems. Investigations were increasingly conducted in tandem before informing central state authorities; walkovers to collect information from opposing border posts became routine; local officials such as mayors were allowed to cross in order to collect information on security issues; and meetings along the border at predetermined posts became increasingly common to discuss procedure and conflict resolution.[26] Such meetings seem to have become expected and even routine. Border posts where local authorities did not meet were considered to be in violation of shared administrative procedure.[27]

---

[25] AYE, 1842, 4/1, 4 February 1842; in this document a list of the names of the bandit gang of Hajistergiou is forwarded by Ottoman guards to the Ottoman state. It is then forwarded to Athens, where the minister of the interior sends it to a governor, who forwards it to a Greek boundary captain stationed near the Ottoman guards that were the source of the list.

[26] AYE, 1841, 4/1b, 16/28 June 1841; on a joint investigation conducted in the presence of Veiz Ağa; and AYE, 1842, 4/1, 9 September 1842; on information gathered at the Mautsare blockhouse.

[27] AYE, 1840, 4/1. In these documents, the border post of Komboti is criticized for not meeting with its Ottoman counterpart to discuss procedures.

The second shift in procedure along the boundary concerns the suppression of border jumping and banditry. As discussed, early bandit pursuit was conducted unilaterally and often led to accusations of territorial violation when authorities chasing bandits overstepped the boundary. By the 1840s, certain positions along the boundary began to coordinate their efforts with the other side's authorities. For instance, as one side pursued bandits in the area, it would relay news of the pursuit to the other side's border authorities. The bandits would then be chased over the border toward an ambush set up by the other side.[28] This system of trapping bandits was an appreciable innovation and was far more efficient than the old system of unilateral pursuit.

The third transformation in the 1840s was normative. Initial complaints from border guards were rife with accusations about the corruption of the other side or its intent to harm.[29] During the 1840s, border authorities tended to replace accusations of corruption or mal-intent with insinuations of indifference. These accusations tended to downplay allegations of corruption and instead focused on the willingness of the other side to cooperate.[30] Border guard reports reveal that such cooperative behavior was valued irrespective of actual outcomes in suppressing banditry or the apprehension of fugitives. Escalated incidents demonstrate that border guards were willing to sanction the other side if it did not cooperate and coordinate activity even if the other side was observed to be successful in its unilateral administration of the boundary.

The Emergence of the Boundary Regime

The institutional evolution of the boundary went far beyond the information relay systems and chase-ups described in the previous section. By the 1850s, Ottoman and Greek border guards shared a growing repertoire of procedures and norms that included the following: (a) cross-territorial pursuit (or the reciprocal right to enter foreign territory while in hot pursuit of suspects and border jumpers), (b) joint pursuit of bandits, (c) local

---

[28] BBA, Cevdet Zaptiye, 2872, 1259/1842; and BBA, İrade Yunanistan, 147, 1264/1847.

[29] FO 195/153, 15/27 November 1840; Paicos describes a boundary meeting in which the Ottomans accused Greek border authorities of complicity with banditry. Also see AYE, 1842, 4/1, 24 November 1841; on Greek border authorities harboring the brigand Velentzas.

[30] AYE, 1842, 4/1, 26 February 1842; AYE, 1841, 4/1b, 16/28 June 1841; and AYE, 1843, 4/1d, 14 February 1843.

extradition of army deserters and fugitives on shared lists, and (d) a definition of border jumping that unofficially exempted local communities from quarantine and customs duties during certain boundary crossings.

These developments are puzzling given the increasingly bad relations between the Ottoman Empire and Greece. The Greek state had begun to intervene in internal Ottoman affairs on issues such as citizenship rights and protection of the Ottoman Empire's Christian subjects. Moreover, Athens had adopted irredentist rhetoric against the Ottoman Empire and had begun to lobby the Great Powers to revoke their guarantees of the empire's territorial integrity. Cooperation between Greek and Ottoman border guards not only became more durable and innovative during this period but also served as a deterrent to would-be Greek irredentists and weapons smugglers who aimed to infiltrate Ottoman territories.

What explains the innovation and increased cooperation among Ottoman and Greek border guards? Historians view these developments as the result of diplomacy and treaty brokering. They argue that the Great Powers were alarmed at the growing irredentist sentiment in Greece and at Greek willingness to promote rebellion in Ottoman border provinces following the Crimean War in 1854 (Dakin 1972; Davison 1978; Veremis 1990; Georges 1996). In 1856, they pressured Greece and the Ottoman Empire to sign the Convention on the Suppression of Brigandage, which bound both states to adopt more measures against bandits, smugglers, and irredentist border jumpers along the sensitive boundary zone. While the convention stipulated cross-territorial pursuit and extradition practices, border captain reports reveal that such practices had been in use along sections of the boundary at least since the late 1840s.[31]

In the 1850s, relations between Ottoman and Greek border guards moved decisively into the category of a boundary regime. The necessary condition leading to the creation of a boundary regime was the establishment of a local, external monitoring mechanism (condition four). The mechanism was present along both sides of the boundary and pushed border guards toward more innovative cooperation by threatening the possibility of external enforcement and intervention from above. This monitoring condition was satisfied in two forms along the boundary.

External monitoring mechanism 1: A highly specific pool of information independent of particular border posts became commonly available

---

[31] BBA, İrade Yunanistan 147, 1264N11/11 August 1848; and 1264S29/5 February 1848; reports of Hüseyin Paşa.

to authorities at the provincial level along both sides of the boundary. This information included publicly available as well as privately held information. Publicly available information included newspapers from border towns, which were read along both sides of the boundary. Both Greek speakers in Ottoman territories as well as local provincial authorities read newspapers from the Greek border city of Lamia. These newspapers reported incidents taking place along the boundary and were a rich source of information on the general state of the border. Private information was also regularly exchanged in the form of reports, which border captains sent across the boundary throughout the 1850s.[32]

The content of the information was broad. The Greek side, for instance, was able to obtain specific reports on appointments to the Ottoman border guard. As a case in point, Greek border authorities reported great concern when an Ottoman captain who was supposed to be outgoing managed to retain his post unexpectedly.[33] Border captains also held information on crime trends and suspect whereabouts.[34]

Border authorities used such public and private information to monitor the other side's administrative measures as well as to censor and threaten when the other side's measures were considered insufficient or improper. In one example, an Ottoman border captain was able to pinpoint the location of a wanted bandit right down to a specific family's house in a Greek border village.[35] The captain indicated the Greek border post that was nearest to the area and lectured on the danger of the post's inaction. Such letters were sent off to high-level agencies as a last resort in instances of cooperation breakdown. In another example, Ottoman border authorities, following a series of successful cross-territorial pursuits, complained that their Greek counterparts were underreporting the Ottoman side's contribution. To make their case they used evidence from Greek provincial newspapers that carried reports on the state of the boundary.[36] Neglecting to give proper credit for successful administration was the equivalent of spreading false information and a breach of trust.

Border captains used the general pool of information on the state of the boundary zone to reveal problems in administrative procedures and to

---

[32] See procedure in BBA, A.MKT.UM, 91/18, 1268Ra15/8 January 1852.
[33] AYE, 1853, 4/1st, 7 March 1853; relayed by the mayor of Sourbe to the nomarch in the provincial town of Lamia (Zeytin in Turkish).
[34] See BBA, HR.SYS, 1721/19, approximately 1852.
[35] AYE, 1856, 4/1g, 22 July/3 August 1856.
[36] AYE, 1864, 4/1b, 20 April/2May 1856.

sanction border posts that were not performing according to certain standards. When they met along the boundary at designated sites, they used this information to suggest improvements, devise new procedures, and sanction posts not operating optimally.[37] Details of these meetings suggest that border captains became increasingly willing to try new methods. Shortfalls in experimental procedure could be discussed and corrected at the next meeting.

External monitoring mechanism 2: Local actors settled close to the boundary acted as external and local monitors on the administrative efforts of border guards. While peasants had been present along the boundary since the demarcation, it was only in the late 1840s that border populations began to actively monitor the actions and administrative successes of border guards. This is a function of harsh criminal laws that the Ottoman and Greek states passed simultaneously in 1849. These laws declared local populations criminally liable for providing room and board to suspected bandits.[38] The drafting of the criminal laws was not intended to be simultaneous but seems to have coincided with a massive outbreak of banditry throughout the Balkans.

Settled populations along the boundary became subject to unprecedented scrutiny from border guards and police as their villages were perceived to be likely destinations for fleeing bandits, who tended to commit crimes on one side of the border and seek refuge on the other. These villages suddenly found they had a stake in a well-administered boundary, and they monitored nearby border posts to make sure guards were vigilant in keeping bandits out of their vicinity.[39] While some border posts maintained an aggressive stance toward nearby villages, going so far as to torture false confessions from villagers they suspected of harboring bandits, other posts maintained a more symbiotic relationship with local residents.[40]

One incident demonstrates how border guards found it difficult to act without being carefully monitored. In the winter of 1850, Ottoman and Greek border guards were jointly pursuing bandits near the Ottoman village of Vigles. The bandits had taken a hostage, who was fatally injured during a shootout. Psaroyannis, an Ottoman border guard, found the body of the hostage and brought it to the Ottoman village of Berbitso (Vorvitzis). Under

---

[37] See BBA, A.MKT.UM, 91/18, 1268Ra15/8 January 1852.

[38] FO 195/494, n.d.; in this document the governor of the *sancak* of Tırhala (Thessaly) threatens to banish such individuals (called *yatak*) along with their families to remote Anatolian provinces in the Ottoman Empire.

[39] BBA, A.MKT.NZD, 185/69, 1272N18/23 May 1856; and AYE, 1856, 24 January 1856.

[40] FO 32/198, January–March 1852; reports from Consul Wyse.

cover of night, the guard moved the body over to the Greek side of the boundary, fearing that villagers would be falsely accused of harboring and abetting bandits.[41] The mayors of Berbitso and the Greek towns of Idomene and Thyamos immediately met and collected depositions from locals, who provided minute details on the actions of the border guard. Locals from Idomene and Thyamos cobbled together a group of men to pursue and capture the fleeing guard.[42] While this incident demonstrates the potentially symbiotic and corrupt relationship that border guards might form with local residents, it also demonstrates that locals were keen monitors of border matters and willing participants in investigations.

The monitoring role of local populations had traceable effects on the cooperation of boundary authorities. Local populations were quick to complain to provincial governors when they believed border guards in their vicinity were not doing enough to keep bandits out of the boundary zone. Rather than face charges of aiding and abetting bandits, local peasants preferred to sanction their border guards by requesting the intervention of higher authorities. As a response to this, border posts in remote regions began to discuss ways to suppress cross-border crime and banditry more effectively. They devised a scheme whereby they could enter into each other's territories while in hot pursuit of bandits. This practice was an innovative solution to two problems. On the one hand, it suppressed banditry more efficiently. On the other, it preempted local complaints, which could lead to central state intervention and sanctions against border guards. Another innovation was that of joint pursuit. In this practice, guards would call on one another for assistance, organize ambushes in each other's territory, and fight bandits as a joint company.[43] These practices indicate that border guards increasingly managed the boundary as a common institutional zone with sets of precise norms and procedures governing conduct (see Table 3.1).[44]

In addition to cooperative management, a boundary regime should have the capacity to handle new events and crises without internal collapse. It should also demonstrate a substantial capacity to deter illegal activity and

---

[41] AYE 1850, 4/1, 24 January/5 February 1851.

[42] Psaroyanni was later caught in Greece and prosecuted. See FO 195/374, 1851.

[43] FO 195/494, 20 August 1855; FO 195/494, 3 October 1857 and 13 January 1857; FO 32/262, 13 August 1858; and as reported in the provincial Greek newspaper *Faros tes Othryos*, 8 December and 15 December 1856.

[44] BBA, A.MKT.UM, 91/18, 1268Ra15/8 January 1852; report from the post at Dervenkarya following an instance of joint pursuit and follow-up meetings at the boundary.

Table 3.1. *Evolution of the Ottoman-Greek boundary regime*

	Cooperation between Ottoman and Greek Guards	Policing Measures against Banditry
1830s	No cooperation: confusion over procedure and escalation over territorial violations	Unilateral and infrequent pursuit
1840s	Moderate cooperation: frequent meetings at border posts, joint investigations	Coordinated chase-ups and trapping; information of fleeing bandits relayed to the other side
1850s	Extensive cooperation and trust: unwillingness to escalate, durable expectations of cooperation, precise administrative repertoires	Reciprocal right to cross border in hot pursuit; formation of joint Ottoman-Greek pursuit units; local extradition of fugitives

conflict. Two events demonstrate that the Ottoman-Greek boundary fit the definition of a boundary regime and functioned as an autonomous and locally embedded institution. The first event demonstrates the boundary regime's ability to absorb new crises and resist collapse.

In 1853, the Ottoman state made a series of sudden high-ranking appointments to the boundary. This policy was unrelated to the performance of boundary officials but was part and parcel of the Ottoman state's institutional reforms, which required periodic rotation of mid- and high-level officials.[45] This intervention at the border was unprecedented in scope. The new border captains and a large number of their clients were expected to take positions along the boundary (Koliopoulos 1999).

Fearing a loss of salary, the current captains and their border guards incited disorder along the boundary and triggered a massive rebellion among the border populations, mainly on the Ottoman side (Koliopoulos 1987, 1999). Greek state officials used the rebellion as an excuse to send army units to the boundary, many of which proceeded to infiltrate Ottoman territory. This invasion came to an abrupt end. The Great Powers engaged in a rapid punitive expedition against Greece and occupied the main port city of Pireaus, while provincial authorities in the Ottoman Empire quickly moved to crush the rebels. The rotation of officials and the consequent rebellion, however, did not compromise the boundary regime. Within a few months, Greek and Ottoman border guards were suppressing banditry and weapons smuggling along the boundary using the same procedures

[45] These reforms are discussed in more detail in the following chapter.

as before the 1853 events. Moreover, the Greek border guards managed to absorb scores of Ottoman border guards who had lost their positions following the Ottoman state's rotation of officials.[46]

The second indicator of the boundary regime's effectiveness was its ability to deter irredentists and smugglers and shift illegal activities away from the boundary. British consular officials reveal a growing concern that smugglers and irredentists (often moonlighting as bandits) were shifting their activities from the land boundary to the sea. Unable to freely operate across the land border, irredentist activity shifted to the region's port cities.[47] Officials of the British protectorate of the Ionian Islands, located along the western coast of Greece and the Ottoman Empire, reported sharp increases in nationalist and bandit activity at the same time that boundary regions experienced a dramatic decline.[48]

Variation across the Border

The evidence presented so far represents an average trend from nascent cooperation in the 1830s to the boundary regime of the 1850s. However, not all border posts demonstrated a linear cooperative trajectory. Some posts along the boundary remained sites of unilateral management, conflict, and escalation. This section discusses the variation in cooperative outcomes across post pairs in order to test the proposed conditions. From the twelve principal paired posts set up along the boundary, I selected three on the basis of variation in the outcomes. They were located respectively along the western, central, and eastern segments of the boundary (see Map 3.1).

At the time of demarcation, all three paired posts demonstrated high levels of conflict and administrative disarray. There was no agreement on quarantine policy or regulation of passages; there were positional disputes regarding grey areas along the boundary and the placement of the border posts; and bandit activity in the area was substantial. All three pairs interfaced, allowing Greek and Ottoman border guards the potential for

---

[46] AYE, 1853, 4/1b, 15 April 1853; reports on Ottoman guards who negotiated employment with the ninth boundary regiment of Greece.

[47] See, FO 32/195, 19 October 1851; the British vice consul on the Ionian isle of Corfu writes that bandits and irredentists are using port cities as entry points to the British-controlled Ionian islands.

[48] British vice consuls in provincial towns report that the frontier guards have successfully deterred banditry along the boundary zone. See FO 32/198, 14 March 1852.

regularized contact. Despite initially similar conditions, only one of the three border posts demonstrates significant advances in joint management.

Post 1: The Chelona border post – located on the western edge of the Ottoman-Greek boundary near the Gulf of Arta (Narda) – is a case in which a boundary regime did not emerge. The post was unable to reach even the initial stage of cooperation. This would seem to cast the theory in doubt, since all three conditions necessary for cooperation are present. The posts were proximate, satisfying both the arena for interaction requirement and the monitoring requirement. The posts also received orders, as did other posts, to cooperate jointly to manage the boundary, satisfying the condition that guards share a definition of the problem. Yet archival data reveal that the third condition was not fulfilled; the Greek and Ottoman states sent information and agents to the boundary that established contradictory definitions of the cooperative dilemma.

In the wake of the demarcation of the boundary, Ottoman and Greek border guards stationed in Chelona were involved in a positional dispute regarding the location of the Ottoman guardhouse. The guardhouse was initially built directly on the boundary line. Following the obstruction and complaints of Greek border guards, the post was torn down and moved further inside Ottoman territory.[49] In their final positions, both guardhouses were equidistant from the line and proximate enough to have frequent physical and visual contact. Yet tremendous tensions persisted. Several years later, in 1840, it was reported that the border guards on the two sides were refusing to meet with one another to discuss coordination of patrols.[50] Throughout the 1840s, there was very little coordination and information exchange on bandits and illegal passage. Border guards on both sides tended to engage in disputes regarding quarantine and customs policy. While other sections of the boundary experimented with information exchanges and coordinated procedures to suppress banditry, border guards in this area were engaging in recriminations, accusing one another of illegally detaining people and unfairly taxing goods.[51]

The lack of cooperation along this section of the boundary is based on two factors. First, Chelona and its satellite posts guarded passes and roads

---

[49] AYE, 1836, 4/1a; Soutsos to the minister of foreign affairs; and AYE, 1842, 4/1; 23 July/14 August 1842.

[50] BBA, HR.SYS, 1680/3, 22 July 1858; a series of reports on unresolved problems and conflicts between border authorities.

[51] AYE, 1847, 4/1; letters exchanged between Greek and Ottoman provincial authorities.

linking relatively large provincial cities and ports located along both sides of the boundary. The British held a group of islands on the westernmost edge of the boundary, and they emphasized the need to effectively quarantine goods and people in order to prevent disease.[52] Second, and more importantly, the large volume of traffic in the area presented local Greek and Ottoman officials with an opportunity to collect customs duties to supplement their perpetually strained provincial budgets. Local officials deployed customs officials to the area's ports as well as to the border crossings just inland. While central government officials in Athens did not place a heavy emphasis on customs duties, local officials attempted to collect revenues even when such extraction was technically illegal. The attempts by local officials to collect duties and to prevent the spread of disease contradicted the high-level request that boundary authorities locally and jointly administer the boundary and focus on banditry and border jumping. At this post, relations remained conflict-prone because Ottoman and Greek guards were unable to arrive at a common view of the institutional dilemma.

The imperative to tax goods and quarantine arrivals meant that the boundary was not flexible enough to accommodate informal crossover to discuss policy, least of all cross-territorial pursuit of bandits. One particularly explosive incident demonstrates the administrative autism along this section of the boundary. A party of guards found the body of an Ottoman border captain just on the other side of the frontier. When the Ottoman guards followed the traces of the murderer into Greece, a Greek detachment ordered them to return, accusing them of violating sanitary regulations. The argument escalated into a shoot-out, and two Ottoman guards were killed before reinforcements arrived to restore order.[53]

Post 2: The Agrafa border post – located in the central sections of the boundary – demonstrates entirely different outcomes in cooperation. At this paired post, all four conditions were present, and the area demonstrated possibly the most rapid and substantial advances in administration along the boundary. The post was located in an isolated boundary area notorious for bandit activity and social unrest. Demarcation procedures in the rugged mountains and dense forests of the area had also been less than perfect, leaving behind numerous grey territorial areas. That Ottoman and Greek border guards in this area were able to solve such positional disputes and

---

[52] BBA, A.MKT.UM, 154/54; 1270C21/21 March 1854; reports on illegal collection of *iane* (customs tax) at Preveze.

[53] BBA, HR.SYS, 1680/3, 3/15 August 1858; and FO 32/262; 13 August 1858, from Wyse.

make the most progress in suppressing banditry suggests the robustness of the proposed mechanisms.

Cooperation between Ottoman and Greek border guards at the Agrafa post seems to have begun immediately around the time of the demarcation. Local villagers had attempted to fool the commission in order to ensure that they would wind up in Greek territory.[54] While they seem to have succeeded in convincing the commission to use the wrong reference point in marking the boundary, local authorities knew better. Ottoman guards built their post adjacent to the site in question, and the Greek guards did not object. Border authorities did not publicize the deception and allowed the villages to maintain their ambiguous national status. However, both sides built posts sufficiently close to the site to monitor the villages and to curb any future deception.[55]

The existence of natural resources that straddled the boundary promoted cooperation. Forest resources (used locally for construction and heating) as well as tracts of pasture were left in grey areas as the placement of the boundary had disrupted the continuity of paths in the region. Residents traveling within Ottoman Agrafa found their trip involved a necessary foray into Greek territory. Local border authorities realized that they faced a dilemma. Border guards could cooperate to guarantee residents of both sides access to paths and joint use of natural resources. If either side prevented access, the other was likely to reciprocate. Neither side would be able to use the paths and land.[56] Border guards chose to cooperate with one another, ensuring mutual access.

This initial management of the boundary and its resources led the posts of the area to expect issues to be jointly discussed. Furthermore, the proximity of locals to border posts and the social networks across the boundary ensured that most actions of border guards would be transparent and relayed to the other side. Given these factors, it is not surprising that border guards stationed in this area made the quickest advances in cooperation. Ottoman and Greek border guards quickly converged on an understanding of the boundary as a common institutional zone and were among the first to implement cross-territorial and joint pursuit as means to capture bandits.[57]

---

[54] AYE, 1853, 4/1, 2 March 1853.

[55] BBA, HR.SYS, 1680/3, n.d.; reports on *hudud vukuatı*/border incidents.

[56] AYE, 1858, 4/2b; border guards admit that both sides allow residents to cross over the boundary freely.

[57] *Faros tes Othryos*, 1 October 1860.

Border guards in the Agrafa region were the first to make an unofficial distinction between border "jumping" and "clipping." The former refers to activity, such as smuggling and banditry, that guards considered illegal, while the latter tacitly permitted local residents to make short-term trips across the boundary and to carry over a certain amount of tax-exempt goods.

Post 3: In the case of the Sourbe-Taratzes post, located on the eastern edge of the boundary, border guards developed partial capacity to cooperate in order to administer and secure the boundary. However, their border post never reached the cooperation levels that can be classified as innovative or as contributing to the boundary regime.

In this particular case, all three initial conditions were fulfilled. An arena for interaction was provided as the two posts were a mere 250 feet apart. This proximity also fulfilled the condition that border posts have monitoring capacity. The posts were in full visual range and were located next to a caravan road, allowing them to observe mutual regulation of border crossing and patrol styles. Condition three is also present as both posts were given unambiguous instructions on the principles of boundary management. In fact, the Greek post at Sourbe was the first to receive instructions from the minister of interior in Athens that border posts were expected to cooperate with their Ottoman counterparts.[58]

Relations at this post were at times cooperative and cordial but also prone to sudden breakdowns. For instance, investigations and information relay systems were set up, and the posts coordinated their activities in chase-ups (that is, the practice of chasing bandits up to the boundary toward the other side's security forces). However, this cooperation was limited. When an unprecedented incident or issue outside the immediate scope of usual relations occurred, border guards tended to escalate and accuse one another of corruption. Border guards at this post resisted implementing more advanced cooperative procedures such as cross-border pursuit, even after such procedures had been certified by the 1856 Convention on the Suppression of Brigandage.

In this case, however, local boundary residents did not act as external monitors of border guard activity. They instead turned into a manipulative force. Residents of the town of Sourbe on the Greek side of the boundary were furious that the demarcation had left both their fields and their irrigation system just beyond the Sourbiotico River on the Ottoman side. At the

[58] See AYE, 1836, 4/1b, 3 November 1836.

same time, many of these residents had acquired residency papers in both Greece and the Ottoman Empire, despite the illegality of dual status. This created a unique situation as these locals now had an incentive to switch residences according to the harvest seasons and according to the burdens of customs and tax duties. Whereas villages along other parts of the boundary were most concerned with banditry and monitored border guards to ensure that they vigilantly kept bandits out, peasants in Sourbe became invested in a boundary that was fluid, poorly secured, and that allowed them to slip over with goods and property unmolested.

Instead of acting as external monitors, locals in the Sourbe area learned to manipulate border guards and border policy. Although locals intended to evade customs policy and border checks, their manipulation also compromised the overall cooperation and trust between the two border posts. In extreme cases, locals recognized the mistrust between border posts and used it to their advantage.

In October 1855, the mayor of a nearby town reported that Greek guards had crossed the frontier, attacked Ottoman guards, and stolen food and sheep.[59] The Ottoman guards reportedly fought back, pushing the Greeks over the demarcation line. An investigation later revealed the true causes of the conflict. A Sourbe local had found he could not carry his sheep over to the Greek side without attracting the attention of the Ottoman guards stationed nearby.[60] He ran over to the Greek side under the cover of night and informed the Greek guards that bandits had stolen his property. Under the pretext of rescuing his property, Greek guards crossed the boundary and carried off the sheep. In the darkness of night, the Ottoman guards mistook the Greek guards for bandits and opened fire. A skirmish ensued and escalated into a diplomatic row. Such events prevented cooperation between Ottoman and Greek border guards at this post. Relations between authorities in the vicinity were so conflict-prone that in 1856 the Ottoman state made the site the location of several new strategic border towers.[61] The Sourbe post stands out as a pocket of conflict, escalation, and institutional disarray on an otherwise well-functioning border.

The comparison of the cooperative Agrafa post to the conflict-ridden Sourbe post allows for two observations. One concerns geography. Agrafa

---

[59] FO 195/494, 15 October 1855.

[60] FO 195/494, 16 October 1855.

[61] On the construction of blockhouses, see BBA, A.MKT.NZD, 180/60, 1272B24/31 March 1856; and 180/80, 1272B25/1 April 1856.

was a wildly remote and mountainous area in the center of the border, while Sourbe was a crossing in a coastal plain with relatively high traffic and located at a caravan road. It is notable that the isolated and remote geography of Agrafa was a site of cross-border cooperation and calm in contrast to the Sourbe crossing, which was geographically more accessible and near centers of provincial power. The remoteness of Agrafa was not an impediment to stable border control. Indeed, its geography may have contributed to its stability. A far distance from state agencies, Ottoman and Greek border authorities in Agrafa turned geographic remoteness to their advantage. They set up a system of crossing and policing to suit the isolated area, which ensured that populations on either side would have unfettered access across the frontier. This observation on geography is revisited in later chapters.

A second point concerns local populations and their support for border control. The divergent attitudes of local populations toward border authorities indicate that whether locals choose to reinforce or undermine border control is an empirical question. The role of local populations will be further examined in subsequent chapters. For the moment, it is possible to note one striking fact about the posts examined here. The dynamics of local relations with border guards did not involve conflict along ethnic lines. In the Agrafa area, villagers along both sides of the boundary cooperated with Ottoman and Greek guards to maintain an open and secure border. In Sourbe, locals manipulated Ottoman and Greek guards alike. These observations imply that the importance of a boundary lies less in whom it divides than in how it is managed.

Theoretical Implications

The examination of the dynamics of the Ottoman-Greek boundary goes beyond documenting an extinct and forgotten border. The boundary regime has implications for the study of collective action. The cooperative dilemmas of the border guards in this story are, in the abstract, a case of social networks and arenas of interaction that contribute to cooperation and the creation of micro-level institutions. From Gould's work on insurgent uprisings against central authority in nineteenth-century Paris, we know that collective action and cooperation in high-risk situations requires the presence and perception of common patterns of durable social ties and not convergent interests (1995: 19). Gould's work may shed light on how cooperation intensified along the boundary and how it diffused to other border posts. Many of the former bandits who subsequently became border captains were appointed to the boundary precisely because they exercised strict control over the men they commanded as outlaws. Their positions as captains were well defined and hereditary, and they were expected to function as strict disciplinarians (Koliopoulos 1987). Each captain controlled a tightly regulated band of individuals who would follow agreements brokered by the captain.[62] This network of ties effectively meant that cooperation by one post could elicit an equal contribution from the post on the other side. At the same time, the captains who had contact with other captains on their side could diffuse the cooperative practices to adjacent posts on their side. Over time, cooperation spread across and along the boundary.

Ostrom's work shows that common arenas for interaction are necessary if actors are to propose solutions to administrative and social dilemmas. In her study of irrigation systems in the parched agricultural plains around Valencia, she shows how farmers created common meeting sites to discuss the use of scarce water, devised complex procedures to share canals, and set up monitoring mechanisms to ensure compliance and punish those who took too much precious water. The farmers of Valencia may not be that much different from Ottoman and Greek border guards. Given the ability to interact with their counterparts, discuss administrative problems, devise potential solutions, and monitor one another's compliance, both the farmers of Valencia and the Ottoman-Greek border guards tended toward cooperation in their respective settings.

Cooperation, however, may have an illicit side. While I have established that the Ottoman and Greek guards generated a resilient policing regime along the border, there is the possibility that this cooperation hid a substantial amount of corruption and extortion. In other words, cooperation in matters of policing could be hiding collusion to fleece nomads, peasants, and merchants crossing the border.

There are several reasons why corruption along the border appears to have been ubiquitous yet restrained. First, the states paid border guards' salaries instead of having security officials live off transit fees as had been standard practice before the border was established. When salaries were in arrears, the border guards were likely to riot, flee their posts, and create

---

[62] Captains acted as brokers. Brokerage, defined as the linking of two previously unlinked sites, is used in studies of contentious politics to explain how practices spread from one venue to another (McAdam, Tarrow, and Tilly 2001; Tilly 2005b; Tilly and Tarrow 2005, 2007).

disorder. This suggests that salaries, rather than bribes and illegal tolls, were the primary sustaining force for the guards and their families. Second, individuals passing through the border had multiple outlets to report corruption by border guards: local consuls, mayors of border towns, as well as the other side's security forces. The fragmentary reports that appear on border guards' improprieties suggest that bribes were solicited often but in very small amounts. Third, because the border guard system was locally embedded and relatively autonomous, both sides had tremendous incentive to restrain themselves and the other side in order to avoid unnecessary scrutiny from above.

This chapter has also demonstrated that the macro and micro dynamics of border control have countervailing tendencies. The administration of the border took place in the absence of direct monitoring from above and despite the macro-level hostility and belligerence of Ottoman-Greek relations. Diplomatic relations between Greece and the Ottoman Empire were generally not perceptible at the boundary where the two sovereign territories came into contact with one another.

The case thus raises a compelling question: why do states let go of their boundaries when the stakes of border security are so high? This is the question that motivates the next chapter, which shifts the focus upward to the pinnacles of the Ottoman and Greek states. The aim is to explain why they allowed their border officials such a high measure of autonomy and why they eventually destroyed their well-functioning border.

4

The View from Above

The previous chapter limited the treatment of the Greek-Ottoman boundary to the interactions of its border guards. Despite the poor quality of diplomatic relations, the Ottoman and Greek states shared a well-managed boundary from the 1840s to the 1860s. The states were quick to devolve administration to local authorities and expected their border guards to manage the boundary jointly. Both Greece and the Ottoman Empire demonstrated an unwillingness to escalate border incidents, even those that involved disputes over the location of the boundary.

By the 1870s the situation was very different. Despite a growing alliance between Greece and the Ottoman Empire, the two states began to militarize their boundary, intervene in the day-to-day administrative tasks of border authorities, and restrict the activities of their own border guards in ways that made it difficult to effectively protect the boundary against bandits and smugglers.

Why did the Ottoman and Greek states replace successful joint management practices with a unilateral and inefficient border administration that lent itself to escalation and crisis? To answer this question, the chapter shifts the focus to the pinnacles of state administration. It traces the institutional history of the Ottoman-Greek land boundary from its inception in the 1830s to the 1880s. It examines border administration, territoriality, and dispute escalation from the perspectives of both the Ottoman and Greek central states to demonstrate that the states initially managed their borders as broad zones. They devolved authority to the local level, overstaffed their borders to create employment, and triggered locally embedded forms of cooperation in order to prevent escalation of incidents. In the process they gave up the chance to extract customs duties aggressively, and they incurred substantial costs in order to keep the boundary regime functioning. Yet by the 1870s the shared land border was a site of militarization, hostility, and constant escalation. Both states perceived it as the limit of their threatened sovereignty, and they vigilantly policed it.

This chapter explains the change from cross-border cooperation to conflict by investigating the simultaneous processes of Ottoman and Greek state formation. It argues that individual yet convergent state-building processes allowed the two states to devolve authority and cooperate over the policing of the border. The main concern in both capital cities was that the border serve as a tool of state coercion, especially in deterring banditry. Overriding concerns with coercion explain why the states did not use their borders as sources of customs revenues. Yet over time, state formation processes increased the degree to which the states (especially Greece) intervened along their borders. State agencies increasingly monitored events at their borders and restricted the administrative autonomy of their border guards. While such intervention was meant to modernize and streamline the administration of the boundary, it had the effect of hobbling the autonomous, efficient, and locally embedded boundary regime. Consequently, the pages that follow provide evidence for two of the claims elaborated in the second chapter: (a) strategies of state building determine how high-level authorities design their border administrations; and (b) the more directly states intervene to manage their borders, the greater the limits on cross-border cooperation.

This chapter also explores hypotheses that offer rival explanations about Ottoman-Greek conflict and cooperation over the boundary. These hypotheses are drawn both from existing historical analyses of Ottoman-Greek affairs and from general theories concerning interstate borders. The idea here is to frame the case against rival explanations in order to avoid sketching an account based solely on confirming evidence. This maximizes use of Ottoman, Greek, and British consular documents.

Rival Explanations

A dominant approach to Ottoman-Greek relations treats the border as a tool of ethnic and nationalist claims (Dakin 1972; Veremis 1990). Greece was a young, ethnically based, and nationalizing state. The Ottoman Empire remained multiethnic and multiconfessional. While the Greek state had purged many of its Turkish-speaking Muslims, the Ottoman Empire contained sizeable populations of Greek-speaking Christians to which Athens lay claim. One set of such claims implies that the Greek state used the border to siphon contraband and individuals into Ottoman territories in order to foment separatism among the remaining Ottoman Christian populations. The implication is that the Greek state, from its inception, saw its border as a tool of irredentism. If this is the case, documents should reveal a willingness among state makers to use the boundary for this purpose and an unwillingness to cooperate with the Ottoman state to police the border.

An alternative to this approach takes a broader view of the effects of the international system on Ottoman-Greek relations and border affairs. This approach highlights the Ottoman Empire's precarious geopolitical situation in the nineteenth century. The empire's expanse across three continents had become a liability rather than a sign of strength. European continental powers, particularly Russia, began a competitive aggrandizement of the empire's territories. The competition for Ottoman territories proved so fierce and destabilizing for inter-European relations that the British and French formally made the Ottoman Empire a member of the balance-of-power system and extended guarantees of its territorial integrity (Harari 1958; also see Schroeder 1986; Krasner 1999; Mitzen 2001a, 2001b). While such studies disagree on the mechanics of and explanations for Great Power motives, there is a general consensus that the stability of Ottoman borders depended almost entirely on the forbearance and protection of the Great Powers (Bailey 1970; Tatsios 1984; Veremis 1990; Davison 1992; Macfie 1996; Christos 1999).

Some studies in this tradition focus on the first half of the nineteenth century (Harari 1958; Davison 1978; Zegin 1978). In a study of the Treaty of Erzerum of 1847, which governed the Ottoman Empire's eastern boundary with Persia, Harari demonstrates how the British intervened in order to prod Istanbul to militarize its border (1958: 78).[1] Other studies are devoted to an examination of high-level diplomatic treaties and border changes affecting the Ottoman Empire in the 1870s and beyond (Türkgeldi 1957; Davison 1983; Üçyol 1988; Ioannidou-Bitsiadou 1993). Strategic and military considerations dominate these studies given the serious Austro-Hungarian and Russian duress visited upon the Ottoman Empire's territories during the late nineteenth century. The impression they create is that the Ottomans had no choice but to militarize their borders in order

---

[1] For alternative approaches to Ottoman frontiers that offer a mix of military and nonmilitary considerations, see Abu-El-Haj (1969), Kafadar (1994), Khoury (2001), and Blumi (2003). The first two focus on premodern and early modern frontiers. Khoury focuses on tribes in Ottoman Arab lands, Blumi on Ottoman Montenegro.

to prevent territorial aggrandizement by large powers and their assertive Balkan clients – among them Serbia and Greece (Yasamee 1996; Hatipoğlu 1998). All of these explanations prioritize the effects of the international system on Greek-Ottoman affairs and say little about the domestic sphere. This omission is potentially a serious one; after all, the Ottoman Empire was engaged in massive domestic reforms called the *Tanzimat* (1839–78), while the Greek state was attempting to create administrative institutions from scratch.

The Bird's-Eye View

The remainder of the chapter investigates the Ottoman-Greek boundary from its creation in 1832 to its erasure in 1882. The sources on which the case is based include Ottoman, Greek, and British archival documents as well as newspapers. The case study is broken up into time periods in order to capture changes over time. Documents are also used to reveal the state-building priorities of the Ottoman and Greek states and each side's interaction with local authorities at the border. The case study attempts to gauge the effect of international factors relative to domestic ones.

State Actions in the Wake of Demarcation

As Ottoman and Greek delegates sat down in London in 1832 to sign a peace treaty that would create an independent Greek kingdom, British officials brokering the conference expressed great anxiety about how to carve out a boundary between the two states. They awarded the island of Evia to Greece in order to secure the spine of the Greek mainland and the peninsula of Punta to the Ottoman Empire in order to secure shipping in the Gulf of Arta. A British diplomatic memorandum circulated prior to the delimitation of the boundary argued that the overriding aim ought to be the complete separation of the populations through a boundary that minimized contact between the two sides.[2] The British were hoping to pass on to the Greek and Ottoman states a view of the border as an instrument of sovereign power. The two states would enhance their sovereignty and lower the costs of territorial control by monitoring and restricting contact along the boundary, defending the boundary against military threats from

---

[2] BBA, HR.SYS, 1677/2, 6 July 1827.

the other side, and extracting a set of customs duties from goods and people passing through the boundary. In short, the two states were to take careful and deliberate measures to mark their territories as exclusive and to seal them off from challenges coming from the other side.

Yet Greece and the Ottoman Empire did precisely the opposite of what was expected. Instead of actively monitoring events at the boundary, they demanded that boundary authorities solve administrative and positional disputes locally without requesting assistance from high-level ministries. Flooded by a large number of complaints, claims, and requests from local boundary authorities, the Greek secretary of state made an exasperated (and apparently often-repeated) request that the minister of interior prevent local boundary authorities from harassing Athens with information on border events and disputes.[3] The Ottomans simultaneously made similar demands down their administrative hierarchies and demanded that their border guards cooperate with their Greek counterparts instead of asking for intervention.[4]

As border guards and engineers took positions along the boundary in 1836, a series of disputes occurred regarding the construction of block-houses and their proximity to the boundary. These disputes are fascinating, not because of their content, but because the Ottoman and Greek states treated them as nonevents. Border guard reports that reached the capitals were forwarded to diplomatic agencies with little or no urgency, despite the fact that some blockhouses violated territory and were intended to house large numbers of armed guards.[5]

In 1842, such a dispute took place between border authorities in the area of Molocha. Border authorities reported that the Ottomans had begun construction of a new blockhouse a quarter-hour within Greek territory at a source of potable water called Armatolobryse. The Ottomans had begun construction after a water source on their side dried up.[6] Instead of accusing the Ottoman state of provocation and territorial violations, Greek state officials noted that the construction of the blockhouse could potentially harm relations among border guards, violate quarantine laws, and affect

---

[3] AYE, 1836, 4/1b, 30 July 1836.

[4] AYE, 1840, 4/1, 3/15 March 1840; AYE, 1842, 4/1, n.d.; order of the Greek minister of war to the troops and gendarme in Lamia; and AYE, 1843, 4/1d; letter of Tayyar Mehmet Paşa, *Kaymakam* of the *Sancak* of Tırhala to the Greek consul in Salonika. Also see BBA, Cevdet Hariciye, 8995, 22R1262/19 April 1846.

[5] AYE, 1836, 4/1b, 2 September 1836; Greek interior minister to minister of foreign affairs.

[6] AYE, 1843, 4/1b, 3 March 1843 and 1 March 1843.

public health. The Ottoman foreign minister's response was to order an end to the construction, without confirming whether the territory in question actually belonged to Greece.[7]

It is telling to note that the language of exclusive territoriality in disputes such as this one originates with local authorities. Border guards, captains, and municipal authorities along the border initially accused the other side of territorial violations and comfortably spoke in the name of defending national territory.[8] Central state agencies, on the other hand, did not act according to such a territorial imperative and either ignored or downplayed local reports on violations of the boundary. If the Ottoman-Greek boundary was to mark the end of one sovereign territory and the beginning of another, Istanbul and Athens were acting with an alternate understanding.

Although the boundary separating the Ottoman Empire and Greece was new, both states implemented existing institutional practices to administer the boundary. The *derbent* institution of the Ottoman Empire traditionally served as the primary provincial police force. *Derbents* were armed guards who were chosen from the local populations – both Muslim and Christian – and stationed at strategic points such as caravan roads, bridges, and important passes linking towns and provinces (Orhonlu 1990: 61). The *derbents* were the best candidates for the new border guard positions, since their former duties had included the protection of roads and strategic passes from criminals, restriction of access to bridges and caravan roads, and the collection of tolls. Consequently, they would require little training for the tasks required. Greek state officials discussed sending regular armed forces to guard the border, but by the time the boundary was diplomatically recognized in 1837, local chieftains and their clients had already taken their posts. Although an 1838 decree incorporated the border guards into the army with higher pay, in actuality the *derbents* were in full control of boundary administration (Strong 1842: 263).

Two observations are crucial with respect to the *derbent* institution. First, it was contained to the provincial level. In other words, *derbents* were tied to local mayors and their clients. As long as they received their pay, the system carried out its functions with little need for the central states to intervene. Second, *derbent* posts were geographically fluid. Villages and *derbents* could switch duties among themselves as well as their positions (Orhonlu 1990:

[7] AYE, 1843, 4/1b, 23 November/5 December 1843.
[8] On a similar process along the nineteenth-century Spanish-French border, see Sahlins (1991).

61–64). The mobility and revolving nature of the *derbent* gave the system a zonal quality. Although many *derbent* zones were well defined, and guards did not interfere in each other's affairs, they were expected to cooperate when necessary. They also held legal and financial responsibility for crimes committed in their areas, which meant that they monitored locals and other *derbents* alike to ensure that criminal and bandit activity did not spill over into their zones of jurisdiction.[9]

The Ottoman *derbent* institution and its replication on the Greek side allowed both states to satisfy their need for border security and to pursue more pressing domestic institutional reforms. The Greek state, in particular, faced a problem inherent in its independence: how to construct state institutions from scratch. The Ottoman state faced an internal economic crisis, a revolution from within on the part of Mohammed Ali (the renegade leader of an autonomous Ottoman Egypt), and was on the verge of promulgating the *Tanzimat*, its most ambitious and extensive reform policies.

It is not surprising, therefore, that both states resisted advice to militarize their borders and did not adopt a view of their boundary as a hard line of sovereign defense. Indeed, Ottoman and Greek state officials were surprised that the institutions that they had charged to secure their boundaries were not acting autonomously. Devolution remained the order of the day.

State Formation Under Way

By the 1840s the Greek state was attempting to extend its newly designed institutions into the Greek countryside and into matters of the economy, while the Ottoman Empire was investing huge efforts in the ambitious *Tanzimat* reforms. Although the Greek state borrowed from certain Ottoman institutional holdovers (such as the *derbent* or *armatolik*), it generally found itself creating institutions from scratch. While coercive and extractive organizations of the state were nonexistent in the Greek countryside, it should be noted that the capital itself displayed only symbolic elements of statehood. Foreign architects were called in to redesign the streets of minuscule Athens and to build grandiose government buildings in neoclassical Greek style.

While Greece built ministries and state structures where none had existed, the Ottoman state found itself aggressively reorganizing many of its institutions from 1839 onward during a period known as the *Tanzimat*.

---

[9] See BBA, Hatt-ı Hümayun, 1256M5/9 March 1840.

Early work on the *Tanzimat* argued that Ottoman officials embarked on these reforms in order to centralize, modernize, and streamline administration throughout the empire (Davison 1963; İnalcık 1973; Shaw and Shaw 1977; Heper 1980; Issawi 1980; Ortaylı 1985; Çadırcı 1988, 1997; Yıldız 1992).

While early studies argued that the reforms were borrowed wholesale, unimaginatively, and ineffectively from European models, recent work by historians and sociologists has been kinder to the *Tanzimat* (Rogan 1999; Köksal 2002, 2006; Quataert 2003; Barkey 2008). In a study of state centralization across Ottoman provinces, Köksal finds that in some regions the state became more adept at coercing recalcitrant populations and more efficient at raising revenues (2002: 43–107). In light of the newness of the Greek state and the reorganization of Ottoman coercive and extractive practices, this section examines the effects of these state-building trajectories on the management of the border.

Coercion: In the early years of the boundary, the Greek state attempted to implement draconian measures to settle nomads along the boundary, destroy the huts of mountaineers, and relocate villages that were suspected of causing frontier unrest (Koliopoulos 1987: 107). These coercive policies represented basic attempts to expand state control in outlying regions. The policies are comparable to those described in much of the state-building literature on the projection of state power (see, e.g., Weber 1976; Tilly 1992, 1999; Scott 1998; Migdal 2001). By settling populations and expanding the realm of state control, the Greek state was attempting to stabilize residence as grounds for obligation and service to the state. The state was well aware that such measures would meet fierce resistance but implemented them anyway.

Tight border controls can enhance the coercive capacities of states by removing the exit option for those who refuse to submit to the obligations and extractive policies demanded (Hirschman 1978; Sahlins 1991). However, the Greek state did not have to monitor its border directly or vigilantly, since it was aware that its Ottoman neighbor was taking similar measures to settle nomadic populations, eradicate banditry, and expand control over the countryside via substantial structural and fiscal reorganization of its provincial administrative apparatus.

An example from archival documents is instructive. A relatively large number of Greek mercenary captains found themselves in the Ottoman city of Tırhala (Trikkala) near the boundary. The number of captains and their entourage totaled 168, and most had committed crimes of banditry throughout Greek and Ottoman territories. Local authorities had housed and fed the captains and wrote to the Porte asking whether salaried posts could be given to the captains along the boundary. The Porte responded with an interesting decision. The captains were to be transported and settled in the Anatolian city of İzmir on the other side of the Aegean. They were not to be settled anywhere near the land boundary as this would upset the security of the area and give the Greek side license to make similar appointments in the future. The captains and their followers, despite having committed crimes in Greece, were to be returned to Greece only in the event that settlement in the İzmir area failed.[10]

This decision represents an emerging obligation on the part of the two states to cooperate diffusely to secure the boundary zone. In the same year that this event took place, Hacı Hüseyin Paşa, head of the Ottoman *derbents* in Tırhala, reported to İstanbul that domestic security in Greece was in shambles and unlikely to recover anytime soon. "Bandits are everywhere and there is no security to speak of. The Greek people don't know what to do and are too scared to even stick their heads out of their houses."[11] The Ottoman state monitored the insecurity in Greece. In settling the captains in its own internal territory, it was helping maintain the overall security of the border zone at the expense of its other provinces.

Extraction: Borders are potentially important sites of extraction for states. Governments have traditionally found it convenient to set up customs posts at borders to collect duties, excise, and value added taxes.[12] These modes of extraction contribute to the fiscal solvency of governments, especially those that have weak internal surveillance capacities and that are not in ideal positions to monitor income and prevent tax evasion. Yet high extraction rates at borders can trigger interstate disputes on customs policy. High extraction rates on the part of one state can strangle trade and

---

[10] BBA, İrade Yunanistan, 129, 1264M6/14 December 1847.

[11] BBA, Cevdet Zaptiye 2372, 1264S29/5 February 1848; Hacı Hüseyin was also the Ottoman representative to the delimitation commission (translation mine).

[12] Customs taxes are duties, tolls, or imposts imposed by law on imports or exports; excise taxes are internal taxes that are levied on the manufacture, sale, or consumption of a particular commodity; a value-added tax (VAT) is an incremental excise that is levied on the value added at each stage of the processing of a raw material or the production and distribution of a commodity. On the relationship between taxation and rule, see Ardant (1972), Levi (1988), and Tilly (1992).

hurt the import economy. They can also provoke evasion, smuggling, and crime.

The Ottoman and Greek states had weak extractive capacities relative to their European counterparts (Kasaba 1988). Yet the border did not become a site of competitive customs extraction.[13] Disputes over customs policy seem to have been localized. A cursory examination of the border zone's remoteness and sparse population might explain the lack of emphasis on customs collection.[14] Simply put, too many costs would be required to collect too few duties from too few cross-border traders. Few passports were issued to travelers heading out of boundary zones in Greece in comparison to the number of passports issued for port arrivals.[15] Indeed, relative to duties and customs levied at port cities in various parts of the empire and the Kingdom, both states seem to have paid little attention to the implementation of customs functions along the boundary.[16] The heavy volume of goods carried in and out of port cities gave the states more concentrated and easier sites for levying duties and generating revenue.[17] The Ottoman port of Volos, a day's ride from the border, was one of the more active ports in the area owing to the substantial production of wheat, iron, and copper in the province. Golos, as the port was called in Ottoman documents, at times rivaled the volume of the much larger Ottoman city of Selanik (Salonica) to the north (Farley 1862: 142). The large volume of trade coming to and from such ports made the job of customs assessment

---

[13] Indeed, the range of control that the Greek state exhibited over its economy was meager. The state perpetually teetered on the brink of bankruptcy. In the first two decades of its independence there was no perceptible increase in revenues. The Greek state tried as much as possible to collect taxes in kind and had to pay to warehouse goods. Moreover, state officials made careless choices. Officials in the treasury forgot to estimate the value of silver before minting one particular coin. The public began to melt the coin down and sell the more valuable silver, and the coin was pulled from circulation. The economy was undermonetized, and diplomats in the 1850s report that Turkish coins continued to circulate widely in Athens (About 1855: 208).

[14] Cities near the border like Lamia, Volos, and Tırhala each had well under 10,000 inhabitants. For details, see accounts in Leake (1835) and Stamatake (1846). Also see FO 32/124, 24 March 1843. For details on Ioannina (Yanya) and Preveza, see Ortaylı (1994).

[15] AYE, 1841, 54/1; on sanitary and quarantine regulations involving major points of entry. Also see Georges (1996: 116).

[16] Chapter 3 demonstrated that the impetus to collect customs duties at the boundary came from local or provincial officials who were not related to the border guard.

[17] Kasaba's outstanding study of the political economy of the nineteenth-century Ottoman Empire gives an excellent indication of the overall dynamism of Ottoman port trade and revenues (Kasaba 1988). Although it does not discuss revenues at border crossings, it gives us an indication of the emphasis on sea rather than overland trade.

Table 4.1. *Greek government revenue and expenditures (in Greek drachmas)*

	1834	1836	1838	1840
Indirect tax revenue	2,922,424	2,996,000	4,057,000	4,287,311
% of total tax revenue	26.2	21.9	28.2	24.5
Revenue collection expense (for both indirect and direct tax)	1,310,903	1,242,810	1,325,000	1,609,721
% of total govt. expenditures	6.1	7.6	8.1	9.6
Army expenditures (includes border guard and gendarme)	9,029,921	4,870,000	5,500,000	5,073,580
% of total govt. expenditures	41.8	29.6	33.6	30.3

Source: Strong 1842: 250, 251.

and collections infinitely easier for state officials.[18] The Greek state likewise attempted to collect customs taxes from its ports rather than at the land boundary.[19] Of the ten primary treasury divisions, seven were located at ports. None were at border crossings. Indeed, the jurisdictions of the customs zones were drawn to maximize coverage of the coast and islands; only 10 percent of the primary and secondary class treasuries of the state were located in interior towns (Strong 1842: 207). The expenditures of the Ottoman and Greek states along the boundary outstripped any customs duties they collected from the passage of goods and people (see Table 4.1).

Both the Ottoman and Greek states commissioned a larger-than-necessary force of military captains and their clients to watch over the boundary and the border zones.[20] Those appointed to the boundary were part of the region's traditional security forces. However, the guards of both sides included a large number of former bandits. In extending amnesty to many of the bandits and offering employment along the boundary, the states were attempting to pacify the area. The policy was a rather smart one, tried and proven before in Ottoman state building. It pacified bandit elements, amnestying and employing some while suppressing and punishing the rest via coercive practices (Koliopoulos 1987; Barkey 1994). It also maximized

---

[18] According to an 1852 assessment, customs revenues made up nearly 12 percent of the Porte's budget. Government expenditures on the army accounted for 41 percent of government revenues (Horton 1854: 98).

[19] One economic assessment shows that import duties were levied at 10 percent and export duties at 6 percent. Those caught in the act of smuggling were by law to pay eight times the legal duty.

[20] FO 169/19, 7 March 1842; in this dispatch the British also express concern about the large number of security forces dispatched by Greece to the border.

border security relative to state input. Hiring bandits effectively removed a substantial number of individuals from the pursuit of criminal acts (levying unofficial taxes, establishing protection rackets, etc.) by giving them a stable and decent salary in an otherwise impoverished region. Moreover, these former bandits knew the tricks of the bandit trade and were adept at taking measures that effectively suppressed and captured those that remained on the margins of state authority.[21]

Two observations can be made at this point. First, the state-building measures just discussed demonstrate that the two states saw the security of their boundary zone as a mutual undertaking. In their exchanges regarding the boundary, the Ottoman and Greek states demonstrated (a) an understanding of the boundary as an interdependent security zone, (b) an obligation to absorb certain costs domestically in order to help maintain the security of the other side, and (c) a forecast that such interaction would continue. As a result, the boundary was insulated from the frequent ups and downs that characterized Ottoman-Greek relations. While the Ottoman Empire and Greece repeatedly came to the brink of war over trade, the treatment of diplomats, and the sponsorship of irredentism in Ottoman territories, the boundary remained a well and locally managed institution.

The second observation concerns the role state coercive policies played along the boundary. While the new Greek state adopted some rather restrictive legislation and high-handed tactics in order to pacify populations in the provinces, such policies operated separately from the administration of the boundary. These policies were meant to help maintain security in border zones without interfering or prescribing specific procedures in the actual administrative practices of the border guards. The coercive policies of the Ottoman state were likewise interesting. The overall centralization reforms seemingly bypassed the border guards. Indeed, reforms of police forces did not take place until the second half of the nineteenth century in the Ottoman Empire.[22]

The International System, State Capacity, and the 1854 Rebellion

By 1853 the Ottoman Empire was engaged in open conflict with imperial Russia. Sentiment in Athens was highly pro-Russian, and the Greek

---

[21] This policy represents an interesting deployment of local knowledge as a means of gradually expanding state authority. On the general topic, see Scott (1998).

[22] I owe this point to Yonca Köksal.

government began to make public claims on Ottoman territories where Greek-speaking Christians constituted a large part of the population. In 1854, a large rebellion swept through the Ottoman provinces of Epirus and Thessaly (the *sancaks* of Yanya and Tırhala). Greek forces took part in this rebellion, besieging Ottoman border cities such as Narda (Arta) and Tırhala (Trikkala). The rebellion resulted in the severing of diplomatic relations between the empire and Greece. Ottoman forces later swept through the area to suppress disorder. Meanwhile, the British and French launched a punitive expedition against Greece and occupied its main port city Pireaus (Driault and Lheritier 1925: 393).

On the surface, these events seem to be a turning point. The Greek state demonstrated an increased capacity to threaten the Ottoman Empire and a willingness to use the boundary as a front for irredentism. Although historiographers and observers at the time argued that Greece was using its boundary as an offensive line, much of the historical record suggests that the disturbances were both unintended and not under any form of state control. The revolt seems to have begun when captains in the Ottoman border guard feared unemployment. The Ottoman state had appointed yet another series of border captains who were coming to take positions with their clients at the expense of the existing guards (Koliopoulos 1999). The salaries of the existing guards had been in arrears. The guards left their posts and began a violent spree, hoping to force their reinstatement. Military circles, political parties, and the press in Greece wrongly perceived the cross-border violence as evidence of ethnic discontent and began to speak of seizing the moment to grab Ottoman territories.

Greek army captains and regulars stationed in provincial cities defected en masse and headed for the boundary zone (Domna-Visvizi 1972). A large and uncoordinated push into Ottoman territory began, with bandits, army deserters, and former border guards burning and pillaging indiscriminately. Although Greek irredentist circles celebrated when the Ottoman city of Narda (Arta) was besieged, it became clear that much of the attack was less nationalist and patriotic than had been previously thought. Insurgents robbed and burned Muslim and Christian villages alike and even created disturbances in Greek provincial cities. Lamia (Zeytin), the eastern head-quarters of Greece's border guard, was attacked, its prisons opened, and its residents robbed.

Despite the massive disorder and violence, the Ottoman and Greek states initially did not attempt to implement a more direct form of control over boundary matters. Under British diplomatic pressure, the two states restored diplomatic ties and signed into force the Convention on the Suppression of Brigandage in 1856. In the previous chapter it was argued that the convention essentially codified practices that already existed at the local level. These included cross-territorial pursuit, information exchange, and direct extradition of suspects. Following the signing of the convention, the two states fell back upon their previous views of the boundary as a local zone of employment and mutual security. Border guards again cooperated with one another as if the events of 1854 had not occurred.

However, the convention of 1856 represented a turning point. It certified the existing boundary regime at the same time that the border was coming to the forefront of Greek political discussions. Moreover, the codification of the boundary regime contained a clause stipulating that only regulars could be stationed along the border. This clause would become a point of contention, despite the continued practice of amnestying bandits and commissioning them as frontier guards.

Centralization and Contradictions, 1856–1865

Following the signing of the convention, both the Ottoman and Greek states began to invest increasingly larger pieces of the budget in the boundary. The Ottoman state, in particular, announced its intent to renovate radically its border infrastructure. More and bigger blockhouses were to be built along the length of the boundary.[23] This would enable the guards to carry on their duties properly and would also address the issue of housing.[24] Traditionally much of the border force was either housed in crude wooden shacks or burdened local villagers for room and board. The new construction, however, required better maps and topographical surveys. Engineers were sent to the boundary to survey territory and to select positions for the stone blockhouses. The new blockhouses were built just behind the boundary line, allowing border guards to continue interfacing. This promoted the ability of border guards to cooperate, communicate, and monitor one another.

In order to build the blockhouses, engineers descended on the boundary with newer and more precise maps in hand. These maps presented the

---

[23] BBA, İrade Dahiliye, 26785, 1274S24/14 October 1857; and 28670, 1275/approximately 1858. See also FO 195/494, 22 October 1855; description of new plan as reported to British consular agents.

[24] On general styles of architecture and methods of construction in the region, see Mega (1946).

boundary line in more specific detail and revealed mistakes in the demarcation of the boundary. Border guards had managed such disputed spaces quietly without involving higher authorities.

Detailed maps and topographical surveys were the result of advances in cartography in European capitals (Black 1997; Biggs 1999). Greece, for instance, had contracted French military officials to carry out a huge geographical survey. The survey was published in 1850 in the form of a massive book itemizing villages and other man-made features. It also included a huge multifoil map that showed Greece and the boundary zone in unprecedented detail.[25] At the same time, the Porte was busy at work with the French in setting up courses on map making at the military academy. By 1860, as more blockhouses were being put up, the academy was turning out map officers (*Harita Subayı*) and sending state officials to France for advanced studies in cartography (Ülkekul 1998).

Scholarship on mapping and cartography argues that maps promote national identity. When maps of a national territory are published and disseminated in print or in the classroom, subjects become able to imagine that they are part of a broader territory (Anderson 1997; Black 1997). In studies of nation building and mapping in the nineteenth-century Ottoman Empire and Greece, Fortna (2005) and Peckham (2001) argue that putting maps in the classroom educates students about the reach of their state, their membership in it, and the value of protecting its sovereignty.[26] Goemans (2006) demonstrates that maps function as crucial focal points that define the precise extent of a national homeland. They define a homeland with clear boundaries and signal to those inside the borders that they have the obligation to fight for the security of that territory (also see Carter and Goemans 2007).

Here, I make a more limited argument concerning the effects of maps on state builders. In the case of the Ottoman-Greek boundary, the availability of more precise maps enabled state makers to picture the microgeography of the land border. As a consequence, they began to rethink their existing approach to border control. This had been unthinkable in prior decades

---

[25] This commissioned project is described in AYE, 3/1, 11 May 1850; "Peri katartiseos geografikou chartou tou basileiou tes Hellados."

[26] It is interesting to note, however, that in his study of Greece, Peckham explains that the use of maps heightened national identity and support for the irredentist project. Fortna, on the other hand, shows that school maps in the Ottoman Empire were a boon for national identity but at the same time forced students to confront the humiliating aggrandizement of the empire by surrounding states.

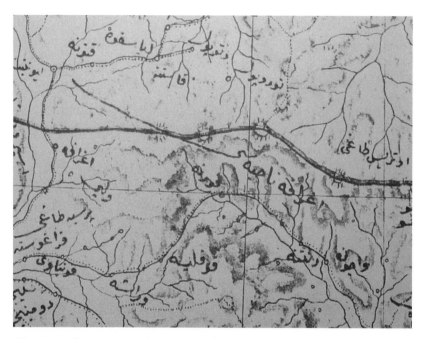

Map 4.1. Ottoman map showing Agrafa (Agrafe Nahiyesi). *Source:* BBA, Harita Kataloğu; courtesy of the Archives of the Prime Ministry, Istanbul, Turkey.

given the crudeness and imprecision of maps. Years after Greece became an independent state, authorities in Istanbul continued to use a map predating independence. Cartographers had brought the map up to date simply by hacking a rough, thick line across it to represent the boundary (see Map 4.1). Such maps and mistakes in demarcation had left behind numerous grey areas, omitted many villages, and even located some on the wrong side of the border (see Map 4.2). In the previous chapter it was shown that Ottoman and Greek border guards managed such indeterminate areas jointly, making the issue of sovereignty moot. However, guards had done so tacitly, usually without the knowledge of central government officials.

New surveys and maps gradually revealed such grey areas, making it difficult to ignore the issue of precision and sovereign ownership. New maps exclusively and precisely split up territory into Ottoman and Greek ownership. They revealed neutral zones and grey areas and presented a more detailed inventory of resources along the boundary. Where older maps omitted many villages and even located some on the wrong side of the border, newer and larger maps made the nationality of border villages entirely

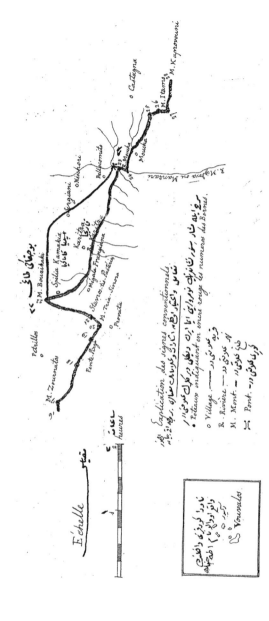

Map 4.2: Sketch revealing grey/disputed areas on the Ottoman-Greek border. *Source:* BBA, HR.SYS 1680/3; courtesy of the Archives of the Prime Ministry, Istanbul, Turkey.

clear. This precision did not create territorial claims or positional disputes. It also did not generate a more precise awareness of national geography; newspapers in Athens regularly misplaced Ottoman towns in Greece when reporting events.[27] However, these new maps gradually began to contradict state officials' zonal image of the boundary.

A second factor that affected state views on the boundary was a series of political claims originating at the local level. Residents living near the land boundary began to demand a share of state investment in the form of either salaried positions along the boundary or building contracts. Such claims began in 1856 and persisted throughout the 1860s. Boundary residents in the Ottoman Empire were particularly ingenious in manipulating petitions in an attempt to secure jobs, subsidies, and contracts pertaining to boundary administration. One village requested that it be declared regional headquarters for border security and that surrounding villages be tied to its jurisdiction.[28] It noted that the sizable budget required for this task would be well worth the increase in security given the threat across the boundary. Elsewhere residents asked for tax relief in light of the frequent bandit disasters visited upon their villages given their proximity to Greece.[29]

Such petitions from Muslim and Christian villages alike consistently share two themes. The petitioners underscore their strategic value given their proximity to the Greek boundary, and they demand a slice of the budget in order to implement territorial defense against a perceived Greek threat. Villages along the boundary treated one another as competition for limited funds. They outdid each other in describing their strategic value and in casting the specter of invasion over the boundary. So tight was the competition for funds that one cluster of villages sent a plan to the Porte underbidding surrounding settlements. They described in detail their plan to protect a stretch of the boundary and informed the state that their perman cost was the lowest on offer regionally.[30]

Although a new provincial law forbidding towns from directly petitioning Istanbul had come into effect in 1864, many local political claims had

---

[27] See the complaint about poor geographical knowledge in *Faros tes Othryos*, letter to the editor, 12 May 1856.

[28] BBA, A.MKT.NZD, 1272N18/23 May 1856.

[29] İrade Dahiliye, 30255, 1276S15/13 August 1859.

[30] FO 195/801, 18 May 1864; as reported by the British vice consul stationed in the Ottoman provincial city of Yanya (Ioannina).

already made their way to the Ottoman state.[31] They alleged corruption and violent behavior by the other side's boundary authorities, and they contradicted the state view of the boundary as a zone to be locally managed. Provincial governors, whose powers and budgets were increased, now found themselves having to address such petitions. Although they did not forward all petitions to the Porte, they themselves were clearly influenced by their content.[32]

The political debates on citizenship were the third factor that pushed the central states to regulate the work of border guards. In the late 1850s and 1860s, the Greek state was confronted with two facts that were in direct contradiction with its citizenship policy. First, a substantial number of its border guards were Ottoman citizens. Certain members of the ninth regiment, which had been stationed along the more remote stretches of the border and had demonstrated excellent ability to cooperate with Ottoman guards, did not meet the criteria for Greek citizenship in light of their Muslim background (Koliopoulos 1987: 156). Second, in the 1856 convention (and its renewed version in 1865), the Greek state legalized the extradition of Ottoman army deserters. While this had been a long-standing local practice, the Greek state found itself in the awkward position of extraditing Christians who otherwise would have qualified for protection and a Greek passport.[33]

By the late 1860s a major contradiction had come into existence concerning the Ottoman-Greek boundary. While boundary authorities continued to cooperate with one another to administer the border as a common institutional zone, the Greek and Ottoman states shifted to an understanding of their boundary as a line of territorial defense that deserved active monitoring and intervention. Detailed maps and surveys made it easier for the

---

[31] On the implementation of the provincial law, see Çadırcı (1989), Rogan (1999), and Köksal (2002).

[32] FO 195/801, 18 May 1864; reports on revised plan.

[33] AYE, 1866, 4/2a, 14/26 December 1865; on discussion of extradition and composition, of the army. A few words on the citizenship dynamics of the time: Since its inception, the Greek state had made a habit of extending passports to Greek-speaking Ottoman Christians upon completion of a brief residency requirement. Through this process the Greek state was able to extend nationality and protection to Ottoman Christians outside its territory. The Ottoman Empire tried to end such extraterritorial claims on its citizens in a variety of ways. One was by withdrawing diplomatic recognition to pressure Greek authorities to give up the policy (Georges 1996). Another initiative came in 1856, when the Ottoman state declared the formal equality of all its subjects, irrespective of religion (Karpat 1982). Ottoman nationality became a juridical fact, and non-Muslims were to serve in the army. Before this, military service was reserved for Muslims and converts to Islam. The formal equality of all subjects made the holding of foreign passports unnecessary and illegal.

central states to view their boundary as an exclusive line and to follow developments with specific reference to place and territory. Local political claims had likewise territorialized the boundary and contradicted local reports that enumerated cross-border cooperation. The citizenship debates also revealed the divergence between theory and practice. For the first time, the Greek state was confronted with the fact that its border guard looked little like the nation it purported to defend.

The Ottoman and the Greek states began to monitor the boundary more vigilantly, and they increasingly restricted the administrative autonomy of the local level. It became increasingly difficult for border guards to cooperate. This shift becomes clear when considering events that took place in 1867 along the central region of the boundary. The Greek prime minister reported that he had received a report of a serious violation of Greek territory on the part of Ottoman troops. The report claimed that Ottoman guards had penetrated one hour into Greek territory, entered villages around Karitza, killed a woman, carried off seventy oxen, and threatened to come back and punish the district more severely.[34] A captain in the Greek border guard answered the inquiry by stating that the reports had been greatly exaggerated and that, facing a similar situation, he would have acted no differently than the Ottoman guards.[35] The exchange demonstrates that the content of interactions between the state and its border authorities had changed. State officials in the capital had become suspicious of local cooperation and uncomfortable with the territorially loose boundary administration. At the same time, the border guards resented having to defend long-standing administrative practices.[36]

In addition to the increased willingness of states to interfere in the administrative micromanagement issues of the border, the 1856 and 1865 conventions created a convenient template for Greek diplomats and political leaders to criticize the Ottoman state. This period witnessed a peak of diplomatic complaints registered with the Ottoman state and with other major European powers by the Greek foreign ministry. These complaints focused on Ottoman noncompliance with the articles of the convention. Greece accused the Ottoman Empire of failing to staff the border posts adequately,

---

[34] FO 195/868, from Greece 1866–67; 14 February 1867.

[35] FO 195/868, from Greece 1866–67; 23 February 1867.

[36] In a similar incident, an ad hoc commission of Greek high state representatives "naturally" rejected an Ottoman offer to declare the zone neutral and open to mutual use. See BBA, HR.SYS, 1530/1, 29 August 1866.

and Greek diplomats alleged that the Ottoman state was continuing to use irregulars disguised in army uniforms. These complaints had some basis in fact, but the motives of the Greek state were to convince British diplomats that the Ottomans were uncivilized and barbaric and, hence, undeserving of Great Power protection.

While the Ottoman Empire was continuing to treat its boundary zone as an institution that would strike an optimal balance between job creation and the need for security, the Greek state was shifting to a view of the border as a line of control requiring unilateral management. It may seem counterintuitive for a nationalizing state with irredentist designs to prod its neighbor to replace a lightly armed group of irregulars with a professionally trained and well-armed military. Yet this proved to be the only means by which the Greek state could foreclose cooperation with its neighbor and assume more direct control over the actions of its border guards.

Many Greek provincial governors applauded this projection of central authority. These governors were centrally appointed figures and often the very source of complaints regarding the Ottoman use of irregulars. Newspapers of Greek border towns found themselves on the losing side in a battle against their own provincial and central authorities. These provincial newspapers issued severe criticisms of high-level policies. They accused Athens of exaggerating the Ottomans' lack of professionalism and fabricating provincial crime statistics in order to assert direct control over security matters.[37]

The increasingly divergent state-building practices along the border would prove debilitating to the functioning of the regime. While the Ottoman state maintained devolution of authority along the boundary, Greece aggressively centralized its control of the border. It set up direct channels of communication from the boundary to the capital and intervened in the day-to-day affairs of the border guards. The growing scale of direct intervention from the Greek side increasingly prevented border guards from cooperating with their Ottoman colleagues to administer the boundary.

The Demise of the Boundary Regime and an Irredentist Epilogue

Historians describe the 1870s as a period of rapprochement in Greek-Ottoman relations. Diplomatic relations had been restored, public and joint

---

[37] See issues of the provincial newspaper *Faros tes Othryos* for this sustained theme.

efforts to stamp out brigandage in the border zones had been declared, and the two states jointly campaigned against Russian interference in Ottoman affairs (Sergeant 1897; Dakin 1972; Tatsios 1984). Russia's influence over the Ottoman Empire was in ascendance. Russia made public its sweeping plans for the autonomy and independence of Ottoman territories with Slavic populations. Many of these territories were populated by Greek speakers and Christians tied to the Patriarchate, and this created panic among Greek leaders and diplomats who wanted these territories under their influence and eventual sovereignty (Kofos 1975).

At the same time, both states announced their intent to cooperate and decisively stamp out banditry following high-profile bandit kidnappings of British officials (Koliopoulos 1987: 179–190). The Dilessi Incident, as it came to be known, attracted unfavorable foreign attention to the domestic situation in Greece and the Ottoman Empire. A series of high-level meetings took place along the border to discuss security and administration, and governors along both sides of the boundary offered joint rewards for the capture of border jumpers, deserters, and fugitives.[38] State officials also implemented mixed regiments of Ottoman and Greek border guards along the boundary.[39]

Despite the rapprochement and seemingly cooperative nature of boundary administration, the locally embedded boundary regime was gone. The states had adopted an understanding of the frontier that was more territorial and linear than zonal. Substantive meetings along the boundary, which had once taken place between local border officials, were now replaced by superficial spectacles of pomp and circumstance. High-level officials were given twenty-one-gun salutes as they crossed the border.[40] The fanfare served as an indication that crossing the boundary had now become a formal and tightly regulated act.

The states restricted the access of the other sides' guards even as they recertified the practice of cross-territorial pursuit. In May of 1871, military

[38] British consular officials reported that the Greek and Ottoman states offered a joint reward for the capture of the elusive bandit Takos. The Greek side offered 20,000 drachmas and the Ottoman government 1,000 lira, a huge sum by the standards of the day. See FO 195/952, 6 July 1870. In another instance, the governor of Tırhala telegraphed the nomarch of Lamia to announce that he was offering a reward of 300 Turkish lira for the capture of border bandits. A local newspaper created a stir when it published one such offer, sending a huge wave of volunteers to the boundary in search of bandits. See *Faros tes Othryos*, 16 November 1874.

[39] AYE, 1840, 4/2b, 19 May 1870.

[40] See "He eleusis tou Mechmet Ali Pasa eis Lamia," *Faros tes Othryos*, 18 May 1874.

and government officials discussed the implementation of mixed companies along the frontier. Ottoman and Greek border guards were to fight bandits using a coordinated strategy under a single captain.[41] While the right of cross-territorial pursuit was affirmed, a set of restrictions was placed on the companies. The companies could meet, communicate, and cross over only at two select points along the entire border.[42] Diplomats agreed that the companies should act at nightfall to surprise border jumpers and bandits, but they also demanded that the companies first request permission from governors in whose territorial jurisdiction the ambush was to take place.[43]

The mixed regiments were a failure. The companies could not operate under the conditions the states attached to the execution of their duties. Border jumpers and bandits seem to have been aware of the procedural limitations placed on the companies, and they eluded the regiments by cropping the frontier along points where passage was not certified.[44] The mixed companies found their activities frustrated in other ways. The quarantine houses and officials, which multiplied along the boundary,[45] routinely detained mixed regiments in hot pursuit as they entered Greece, citing sanitary regulations.[46] The regiments looked on helplessly as the bandits escaped.

The advances in boundary administration made during the 1850s and 1860s unraveled. Reports and exchanges between Ottoman border guards demonstrate a swift return to primitive methods of tit-for-tat cooperation that were reminiscent of the first years of the boundary. Basic issues of coordinating information exchange and patrolling dominated border guard communiqués. Each side began to manage the boundary exclusively and unilaterally, with little coordination of activity or shared procedures.[47]

As a result, border guards found themselves working unilaterally and more furiously to combat banditry and crime along the boundary.[48] The

---

[41] See the discussion on the boundary between government officials in AYE, 1871, 4/1e, 19 April 1871.

[42] AYE, 1871, 4/1e, 25 June 1871; minister of foreign affairs reports to consulates in London, St. Petersburg, Paris, etc.

[43] AYE, 1871, 4/1e, 4/16 February and 17 February/1 March 1871.

[44] FO 195/980, 16 December 1871.

[45] On *lazarettos* (quarantine houses) established on the border at Derven Fourka, Sourbe, Stamos, and Nea Myzele, see FO 195/980, 10 December 1871.

[46] FO 195/980, 26 December 1871.

[47] FO 72/2294, 1873; on domestic measures and rewards to troops.

[48] FO 195/952, 5 January 1871. This document describes an incident in which Ottoman *hududiye* (border guards) were ambushed, resulting in the death of two officers, twelve soldiers, and four villagers.

decline in administrative capacity meant that problems that otherwise would have been solved jointly and locally were now escalated. Boundary authorities also became more willing to attribute disorder and crime on their side to the negligence of their foreign counterparts. Before the major crises of irredentism (1896 and 1912), the Russo-Turkish War (1877), and any obvious decline in their relations, the Greek and Ottoman states centralized their border and declared martial law in most of their frontier provinces.

In 1881, the Ottoman *sancak* of Tırhala (Thessaly) and the region of Arta (Narda) were incorporated into the Greek state. The Great Powers granted the region to the Greek state at the Congress of Berlin, which followed the stunning defeat of the Ottoman Empire in the Russo-Turkish War of 1877 (Halavart 1973). The Congress aimed to roll back Russia's de facto territorial gains. Although Greece had not taken part in the war, the Congress hoped to satiate Greek irredentism permanently with a slice of Ottoman territory (Anderson 1966; Davison 1983, 1999; Macfie 1996; Yasamee 1996). The British brokered the terms of the handover (Commission Europèene 1883). Ottoman forces were to evacuate Tırhala piecemeal and cede control to Greek authorities town by town, garrison by garrison (Paganele 1882; Sfeka-Theodosiou 1989). Meanwhile, the Great Powers prepared a detailed map of the new frontier for distribution to Ottoman and Greek authorities.[49] By the spring of 1882 the Ottomans had evacuated Thessaly, and Greek armed forces had taken up positions along the new boundary.

Several positions along the new boundary came under immediate dispute. Greek captains and Ottoman officers refused to relinquish their positions, and numerous skirmishes took place along both sides of the border. Soutsos, commander of the Greek frontier troops, attempted to meet with his Turkish counterpart to broker an agreement, but he was quickly replaced by high-level ministerial order. Grivas, the captain taking his place, was ordered to take a status quo position and not to relinquish any territory until the situation could be diplomatically resolved. Negotiations regarding the final positions of the border guards continued into the summer of 1882, while skirmishes erupted along multiple posts.[50] Grivas and the Greek prime minister rejected an offer to declare the disputed areas neutral. Athens also refused to renew the convention of 1865, arguing that

---

[49] FO 32/537, 11 August 1881, Greece; on Greek frontier rectification.
[50] Namely, at the points of Zorba, Platania, Stephani, Kedri, Trochali, Kapnos, and Prophetes Elias. See FO 32/541, 31 August 1882.

cross-border pursuit was anachronistic, unnecessary, and bound to be abused by Ottoman authorities.[51]

Although many of the border posts were paired and in full view of one another, contact appears to have been minimal. Relations between the two border authorities in the mid-1880s remained adversarial and hostile. Alleged customs infractions, border banditry, and smuggling incidents were escalated rapidly to respective capitals. In 1886, skirmishes erupted along multiple sections of the border, resulting in dozens of border guard deaths, substantial territorial incursions by both sides, and destruction of border posts.[52] The Ottoman response was militarization. The eastern edge of the border alone was fortified with eighteen battalions and ten field artillery units (War Office 1890). This militarization did not prevent an increase in banditry, which plagued the boundary for the rest of the century.[53]

Conclusions

What conclusions can be drawn from the Ottoman-Greek case study? First, it is evident that cooperation relating to the administration of the boundary did not vary with the ups and downs of diplomatic relations. Cooperation occurred during both hostile and cooperative diplomatic periods. More-over, cooperation collapsed during a period of rapprochement as both states fortified and militarized the border. These actions triggered escalation and border disputes that quickly destroyed the diplomatic calm. This finding shows that states do not necessarily manipulate their borders for reasons of brinkmanship. The border was a locally contingent operation, and the interests and preferences of local boundary administrators did not match those of central states.

Second, the case uncovered a trade-off between coercion and extrac-tion. During the boundary's life span, both states emphasized the impor-tance of coercion and deterring banditry rather than the boundary's capac-ity to regulate the movement of goods and to generate valuable customs duties. Coercive state-building practices took precedence over extraction.

---

[51] FO 32/550, Greece, January–July 1883, May 16, 1883. Eventually the Ottoman charge d'affaires in Athens, Tevfik Pasha, made the same accusation against Greek soldiers. He alleged that Greek soldiers had stolen, incited populations, and spread propaganda when given the right of entry into Ottoman territory.

[52] See FO 32/573, Greece, March and April 1886.

[53] On events leading up to the Greco-Turkish War of 1896, see Bigham (1897) and Kodaman (1993). Following the Balkan Wars of 1912, the boundary ceased to exist altogether.

Subsequent case studies will attempt to further investigate the trade-off between coercion and extraction as it affects border control strategies.

Third, the case demonstrates that top-down intervention may prove both unproductive and destabilizing. Destabilization occurred as officials in Athens stripped their border guards of autonomy and vested themselves with the task of micromanaging the administration of the border. Consequently, they guaranteed that local incidents would not remain local. Incidents, conflicts, and violations were necessarily shifted upward, preventing border guards from engaging in cross-border cooperation.

However, the case did not identify a single intervention mechanism as the source of escalation. The institutional history of the border indicates different patterns and sources of top-down micromanagement. Cabinet ministers, members of parliament, and even media organs made political claims and intervened in the administration of the boundary. For instance, members of parliament debated border control and passed laws centralizing border control. Such oversight was not as direct as that of the executive, ministers of defense, and ministers of the interior, who in later years monitored events at the border and prescribed specific policies for policing. Especially on the Greek side of the border, captains found themselves trying to avoid the scrutiny of both Greek governors and members of parliament while also having to justify their cooperation with Ottoman border captains to their superiors in the ministries in Athens. While the case demonstrates the deleterious effects of centralization and top-down intervention, the case does not allow us to distinguish their relative weights.

Some of the dynamics of intervention were prone to unintended consequences. For instance, in the process of modernizing its border guard and making infrastructural improvements to the frontier zone, Ottoman officials became susceptible to lobbying from local populations, who skillfully manipulated and exaggerated security threats along the frontier in order to benefit from state investment. Better maps inadvertently revealed grey zones that Ottoman and Greek guards were managing jointly and quietly. Such by-products of state formation created momentum for further intervention in matters of border control. This was especially so on the Greek side, where centralization and top-down intervention disengaged Greek border guards from the boundary regime. Greece gradually administered the border with growing numbers of heavily armed combat units. The Ottomans would belatedly and reluctantly follow suit.

While the Ottoman-Greek case study provided for tremendous depth of analysis, it is not prudent to generalize excessively on the basis of a single case study. In order to better understand the connections between state building, centralization dynamics, and border control, the next chapter studies interstate borders in post-Soviet Central Asia. Central Asia's troubled boundaries provide an ideal setting to expand and refine the argument. Upon their independence from the Soviet Union, state builders had to expand their authority across inherited territory and police new boundaries. The creation of several new states allows us both to vary state-building policies and to select cases from over a dozen paired borders. The next chapter further examines the link between state building and border control in this varied contemporary context.

5

State Formation and Central Asian Peripheries in the Twentieth and Twenty-first Centuries

On the heels of the Soviet Union's collapse, the leaders of Central Asia's newly independent states made bold declarations promising regional cooperation and mutual economic prosperity. In 1992, Uzbek President Islam Karimov and Kyrgyz President Askar Akayev, whose states shared adjoining borders, pledged broad cooperation over mutual security problems such as border demarcation and Islamic extremism.[1] Yet by the close of the decade, many Central Asian borders were sites of conflict, escalation, and near wars. Islamic militants infiltrated and staged attacks near border areas, while the amounts of contraband slipping across borders reached staggering proportions.[2] The usual approach of authorities was to close many crossings permanently or to impose high bureaucratic hurdles for those crossing the border. The United Nations Development Program (2005) condemned such indiscriminate closures for suppressing trade and estimated that lifting such barriers would cause average incomes in the region to increase 50 to 100 percent over ten years. The region's states received little in exchange for the lost trade opportunities; indeed, the unilateral and often aggressive methods of border control themselves became the object of dispute and escalation.

Here there is an interesting and counterintuitive empirical puzzle to solve: how a seemingly straightforward coordination problem over border security turned into conflict and violent escalation between certain Central

---

[1] A speech made in the wake of independence by Uzbek President Islam Karimov highlights the region's two main security issues: border inviolability and militancy. See Official Kremlin News Broadcast, 15 May 1992, "Speaking of Borders Means Breaking Up Central Asia." Also see statements by Kyrgyz President Akayev in ITAR-TASS, 30 November 1992, "Kyrgyzstan Not to Choose Fundamentalism."

[2] BBC Uzbek, 12 May 2006, "Tojik-Qirg'iz chegarasida navbatdagi hujumlar."

Asian states. Many Central Asian borders should have been easy cases for cooperation. Uzbekistan and Kyrgyzstan both had a stake in preventing the flow of militants across their borders. International organizations such as the Commonwealth of Independent States (CIS) and the Shanghai Cooperation Organization (SCO) advocated regional cooperation and created specific opportunities for states to design and implement common security policies and visa regimes. Studies of cooperation in international relations would lead us to expect that such a dense network of international organizations would have fostered at least a minimal degree of coordination across borders (see Keohane 1984; Katzenstein 1996; Keohane, Moravcik, and Slaughter 2000).

Yet borders are not crafted with the sole aim of meeting external challenges. The previous chapter argued that understanding the sources of border security requires a theory of state-building practices. Much of the evidence for this dynamic was induced from a detailed case study covering the life of the Ottoman-Greek boundary during the nineteenth century. The case study linked state building to border control and demonstrated that coercive practices took precedence over extractive functions. Although both the Ottoman and Greek states favored the adoption of coercive practices in order to suppress banditry along the border, they allowed local authorities to design and implement such strategies autonomously. Cross-border cooperation was robust until the Greek state centralized the administration of its border guard. The sudden increase in high-level intervention and monitoring impeded the border guards' ability to cooperate and debilitated the boundary regime.

The chapter at hand moves forward in a number of ways in order to refine and extend the theory. The Central Asian case studies generate additional empirical support for the book's theory in a modern context. Uzbekistan, Kyrgyzstan, Tajikistan, and Turkmenistan – the states examined here – became independent simultaneously in 1991 following the dissolution of the Soviet Union in a climate that one could describe as part euphoria, part tremendous uncertainty (see Map 5.1).

Beissinger's (2002) outstanding comparative study of Soviet dissolution underscores how reluctantly Central Asia's republics embraced independence. Unlike other Soviet republics, which saw frequent and intense pro-independence protests, Central Asian elites and society were relatively mute. With independence, Central Asia's leaders faced the daunting tasks of extending authority over vast multiethnic territories and securing

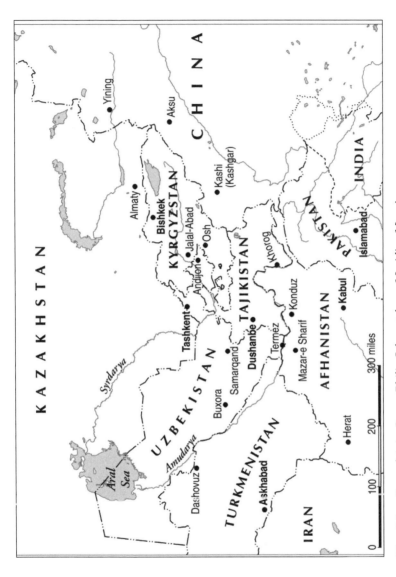

Map 5.1. Central Asia. *Source:* Philip Schwartzberg, Meridian Mapping.

95

international borders that had previously been unguarded administrative lines.

I do not argue that nineteenth-century historical borders function exactly as do twenty-first-century borders. I do, however, argue that the similarities between late-imperial borders and the contemporary borders of developing states are often striking and worthy of comparison. New borders divide territory and regulate access where the crossing of goods and people was previously unregulated.[3] The Ottoman-Greek boundary, for example, split the Agrafa, a highly cohesive district. The borders of Uzbekistan, Kyrgyzstan, and Tajikistan trisected the Ferghana Valley in Central Asia. Residents had been accustomed to unfettered access to jobs, markets, and relatives throughout the valley. States that today attempt to impose regulations such as visa requirements, duties, and passport controls across such networks necessarily encounter resistance as they have in the past (Sahlins 1991).

Another daunting problem is the nature of the threats that states encounter along and across their boundaries from nonstate groups. Along the Ottoman-Greek boundary, organized bandit groups challenged state authorities, robbed and pillaged local populations for sustenance and political influence, and evaded capture by fleeing to the other side of the border. The borders of the late-twentieth and early twenty-first centuries pose similar problems for overextended states and give opportunities to groups that use isolated borders to rival state authority (Fearon and Laitin 2003). The Islamic Movement of Uzbekistan (IMU) used the region's new borders to its advantage. Its members escaped across thinly protected territory to escape repression in Uzbekistan, trained and practiced along the rugged borderlands of neighboring Tajikistan, organized smuggling networks to ferry drugs and weapons across borders to sustain their activities, and engineered multiple and sustained attacks on border posts throughout the region and inside Uzbek territory.

While security problems endure, state responses to these problems vary. In a given group of newly independent states that must quickly extend authority across inherited territory with limited resources, it is likely that a variety of state-building strategies may be observed that involve various forms of extraction, coercion, and intervention. Given the simultaneous

---

[3] However, Carter and Goemans (2007) argue that the probability of conflict may be lower if new borders are based on prior administrative lines.

independence of five states in the Central Asian region, I expect to detect enough variation in state-building strategies to refine my earlier claim that new states tailor border control to suit their priorities in state building.

Moreover, the cases include within-country variation. Each state shares borders with several other states, allowing for the theory to be examined along different bilateral borders. Uzbekistan, for example, shares borders with Kazakhstan, Kyrgyzstan, Tajikistan, Afghanistan, and Turkmenistan. If the theory that general state-building dynamics condition how states perceive and defend their borders is correct, then we should see a state deploying a unitary policy along its entire border. We might refer to this crudely as "cookie-cutting" borders. If this is not the case, and we observe states deploying different policies at different points, then we might conclude that rival explanations are correct. It may be, for instance, that states tailor security strategies to meet specific threats at particular segments of their borders.

The argument in this chapter encapsulates the first two claims of the project: (a) state-building dynamics shape state preferences regarding border security, and (b) divergent state-building dynamics along two sides of a shared border will prevent coordination of border security strategies and trigger conflict. The first part of the argument relies on theories that see state preferences as prior to interactions with other states. Moravcsik's (1997) work on the subject rejects systemic and structural approaches in international relations, which argue that state interests derive externally from the international system. He argues that state preferences are domestically determined. I expand on this theme and show how unique trajectories of state formation constitute state orientations toward their boundaries.

There is precedent for this in the Central Asian context. Menon and Spruyt (1999) made a very astute observation, arguing that conflict and security in post-Soviet Central Asia would depend, not on the threats the new states posed to one another, but rather on the difficult processes that state builders would undertake to build effective political institutions and cope with economic development. Darden (2008) similarly shows that the participation of Central Asian states in regional and international organizations and trade relations is highly constrained by each state's unique post-independence trajectory. He locates the source of this diversity in leaders' beliefs about the relationship between economics and the state. By looking inside states it is possible to investigate how domestic political dynamics affect interactions with neighboring states, how perceptions of threat condition states' security strategies, and how boundary functions are organized to assist state formation.[4]

In this chapter, I deploy three categories that capture the gamut of functions that interstate borders serve: informational, extractive, and coercive. Delimitation and demarcation procedures signal information about the particular location of the border on maps and along physical features (Jones 1945; Prescott 1987; Rushworth 1997; Blake 1998; Wood 2000). Extractive functions along the boundary take place when customs officials assess duties and limit goods that may be brought into or out of a state. Coercive functions take place when immigration officials check documents and when border guards patrol the "green border" – the part of the boundary that falls between official crossing points. At a moment of independence or creation of a new boundary, none of these functions may be fulfilled, and states may face choices about which functions to implement and the types of organizations that they will deploy at the border. To simplify the measurement of preferences on border security, I measure the type of policy each state prioritizes and the timing and type of organization deployed to the border.

The second part of the argument posits that coordination of border security strategies became exceedingly difficult because Central Asian states adopted divergent state-building policies on their respective sides of a given boundary. Coordination problems are solved when two or more actors have matching preferences and convergent interests about a given outcome (Stein 1982; Snidal 1985; Kreps 1990; Goemans 2006). The statements of Central Asian leaders after independence portray the organization of border security as a straightforward coordination issue. Leaders agreed that it was in the best interests of all states to avoid disputing the location of borders and to focus instead on security against extremist groups. However, the actual practices of state formation in each state revealed highly distinct and inflexible means of attaining border security. Coordination is extremely difficult when actors declare that they prefer the same outcome yet make distinctly different choices about how to pursue that outcome (Stein 1982: 314; Schelling 1980: 87).

The chapter proceeds in the following order. First, it outlines the Soviet imperial legacy and the strategic context in which the Central Asian

---

[4] This domestic interest approach differs from other domestic approaches. For example, Bueno de Mesquita (2006) studies domestic politics and how domestic institutions create international outcomes. However, Bueno de Mesquita's unit of analysis is the leader and the institutions that keep that leader in power (selectorate theory).

states found themselves immediately after their independence. This context should have prodded the states to coordinate their policies in order to achieve secure and open borders. The second section explains why such cooperation did not result. The different state-building approaches adopted by each capital following independence triggered highly divergent preferences on border policy. This section measures state-building indicators such as coercion and extraction in Kyrgyzstan, Uzbekistan, and Tajikistan. It finds that extractive practices – defined as state strategies for generating revenue over national territory – had the greater weight on border policy. The third section argues that the implementation of these policies at the border prevented coordination over security policy and, in some cases, triggered conflict and escalation. In the process of pursuing policies tailored to its economic objectives, each state was effectively preventing the other side from implementing its own policy. A final section concludes the chapter by explaining why seemingly more obvious explanations are wrong. While alternative theories may see border security as determined by localized or external threats, the argument in this chapter is that border policy is determined primarily by domestic processes. These domestic processes are often inflexible in the face of particular circumstances that affect border security.

Imperial Legacies

Although Russian imperial expansion left its mark on Central Asia in the nineteenth century, it is the Soviet Union that most affected the economy, politics, religion, and demography of the region (Bunce 1999; Beissinger 2002; Beissinger and Young 2002; Cooley 2005). The following section discusses Soviet-era border delimitations, the suppression and revival of Islam, and the economic portfolios and infrastructures of the republics. These serve as background but also highlight the puzzling failure of cross-border cooperation.

Internal borders: Upon independence in 1991, Central Asian states inherited the territory and borders that they had held as Soviet republics.[5] These internal republican borders were institutionalized following numerous internal delimitations and changes between 1918 and 1936 (Tishkov

---

[5] The idea that internal political borders should become international borders without changes is a principle known as *uti possidetis*. This norm – for better or worse – has been a guiding principle in managing the transition toward independence of many states (Ratner 1996).

1997: 34). In 1918, officials in Moscow set up the Turkestan Autonomous Republic. In 1920, a further change was proposed aiming to separate Turkestan into Uzbekiya, Kyrgyziya, and Turkmeniya. By 1924, yet another change went into effect creating five administrative units: Uzbek SSR, Turkmen SSR, Tajik Autonomous SSR, and Kyrgyz and Kara-Kalpak ASSRs (Koichiev 2003). By 1936, the five essential predecessors of today's republics emerged (Jones Luong 2002: 65).

Soviet strategies of rule motivated these delimitations. One motive was to empower republics with titular nationalities and integrate them into the Soviet Union; another was to prevent ethnically based mobilization against Soviet rule (Cornell 1999). Cities such as Samarkand and Bukhara – part and parcel of ethnic Tajik history – went to Uzbekistan. Many Uzbek speakers found themselves part of the Tajik ASSR. The Ferghana Valley was split up among three republics, and internal borders were delimited to ensure that sizeable numbers of each ethnic group became a minority in a neighboring republic.

Commentary on the delimitations sees them as Stalinist *diktat* (Cornell 1999; Menon and Spruyt 1999). However, some of the delimitations were susceptible to bottom-up lobbying. The Ferghana Valley is a good case in point. Populated by Sarts, Tajiks, Uzbeks, Kyrgyz, Kipchaks, Turks, Kara-Kalpaks, Kurama, and Russians, the valley was to be delimited in 1924 between the Kyrgyz and Uzbek republics. Neither Uzbek nor Kyrgyz delegates were satisfied with the delimitation commission's proposals, and each side argued that the proposed boundary would prevent its ethnic unity. Additionally, the Uzbeks lay claim to Osh and Jalal-Abad, cities with large Uzbek populations. These cities were given to Kyrgyziya. The Kyrgyz objected to the incorporation of the city of Andijon into Uzbekiya, explaining that they intended to make it the capital of their republic (Koichiev 2003: 50). Such protests persisted even after Moscow declared a ban on lobbying.

The final delimitation left 109,000 Uzbeks on the Kyrgyz side and nearly as many Kyrgyz on the Uzbek side. Additionally, the lobbying created a series of enclaves that were not contiguous to the territory of the republics that owned them. The Uzbek enclave of Sokh, for instance, was surrounded by Kyrgyz territory. The lack of enforcement of the delimitation directives complicated the situation. Uzbek authorities seized control of Shakhimardan inside Kyrgyziya, creating another enclave that had not been authorized by the commission (Koichiev 2003: 56).

When these internal republics became independent in 1991, they did so with borders that were not coterminous with the locations of ethnic groups.

Uzbekistan's border provinces had substantial populations of ethnic Tajiks, while Kyrgyzstan's second largest city, Osh, had an Uzbek population of over 40 percent. Many scholars of ethnic conflict suggest that the proximity to international boundaries of dense minority populations is dangerous as it fosters incentives for secession on the part of the minority or attempts to seize the territory by a proximate motherland state (e.g., see Posen 1993; Van Evera 1994; Brubaker 1996; Gavrilis 1996; Toft 2003). On the eve of Soviet collapse, it was Central Asia's multiethnic republics – not those of Yugoslavia – that were often the focus of predictions of ethnic conflict. In 1990, violent riots in Kyrgyzstan's Osh *oblast* involving ethnic Uzbeks initially seemed to bode ill for the stability of Central Asian borders. As Soviet officials warned of a "medieval nationalism" spreading through the region, media reported the 15,000 Uzbeks had crossed into Kyrgyzia to aid threatened relatives in Osh (Parks 1990). Yet as Valerie Tishkov (1997) documents in his work, it was competition over scarce land and water resources that generated such violent conflict, not ethnic hatreds or secessionist goals.

Despite the hyper-ethnicity of Central Asian border regions, elites did not make revisionist or irredentist claims on neighboring ethnic populations. While Uzbek President Karimov did use a covert alliance with ethnic Uzbek warlords in Tajikistan to topple Tajik government officials who did not meet with his approval (Rashid 1994: 237), he refrained from making any claims on Uzbek co-ethnics in neighboring states that could be interpreted in irredentist terms.

Ethnic demography, however, did create two sets of problems concerning boundary management. First, during the Soviet period members of border populations had been accustomed to visiting relatives, holding jobs, and buying and selling goods in neighboring republics. This meant that any attempt to manage and restrict border crossings would meet local resistance. Second, although the borders of the Soviet republics had been officially delimited on maps in 1936, settlements and their infrastructures had grown right across the administrative borders of the republics (Megoran 2006: 631). Late Soviet military and topographical maps indicate that many towns and industrial sites located near the border of one republic expanded and spilled over onto the other side. Consequently, all of the boundaries of Central Asia's newly independent states required re-delimitation and on-the-ground demarcation.

Islam: During the Soviet period, elites employed strategies of repressing religious mobilization alongside the co-optation of religious elites to the service of the state. In the final decade of the Soviet Union, a period of revivalism was clearly detectable (Rashid 1994; Hiro 1995), particularly in areas such as the Ferghana Valley. By the late 1980s, there were numerous reports of Islamic mobilization throughout Central Asia, and in the wake of independence, "it appeared that the Ferghana was developing its own self-government independent of the state, and it was clear that religious leaders often enjoyed greater authority than their state counterparts" (Anderson 1997: 158).

The idea of revivalism and religious extremism worried Central Asia's leaders and elites. One Uzbek Interior Ministry official warned in 1993 that the Ferghana Valley was on the verge of exploding (Rashid 1994). The Karimov government clamped down on the Uzbek side of Ferghana, arresting some clerics, forcibly retiring others, and attempted to supplant religious intensity with nationalist fervor with slogans such as "The Homeland: As Sacred as a Place of Prayer" (Karimov 1995; Megoran 2005).[6] At the same time, Karimov and his counterparts pledged cooperation against religious extremism. Interestingly enough, such worries pervaded much of the elite hierarchy in Central Asia. In her extensive interviews with elites in Kyrgyzstan and Uzbekistan, Jones Luong found that concerns with the spread of religious fundamentalism were an overriding and nearly unanimous fear (2002: 194).[7]

Although an increase in public religiosity was neither surprising nor unusual following the Soviet collapse, fears of Islamic revivalism were heightened when Tajikistan collapsed into civil war in 1992. Major fighting broke out when the short-lived coalition government of the Islamic Renaissance Party (IRP) and the Socialists was ousted by the militia of the former government with Uzbek and Russian assistance. The region's elites saw the IRP government as tantamount to a fundamentalist takeover and urged broad cooperation to preserve the region's secular order (Rashid 1994: 43).

In Uzbekistan, repression fostered radicalization and led exiles and ethnic Uzbeks in Tajikistan to form the Islamic Movement of Uzbekistan (IMU), whose goal was to overthrow the secular republic and unify much of Central Asia into a larger Islamic state (International Crisis Group 2006a). In response, a host of multilateral initiatives were designed to combat extremism. Russian troops were deployed to the Tajik-Afghan border and the

---

[6] In Uzbek the expression is *Vatan, sajdagoh kabi muqaddasdir*.
[7] In Uzbekistan she found that 95 percent of central leaders and 97 percent of regional elites expressed the idea that Islamic fundamentalism was a great concern. The numbers were very similar on the Kyrgyz side.

Kyrgyz-Chinese border to prevent infiltration and weapons smuggling.[8] China – which borders Russia, Kazakhstan, Kyrgyzstan, and Tajikistan – also took the initiative to foster a series of meetings and accords on cross-border issues of terrorism, extremism, and separatism. By 1996, these meetings had solidified into the Shanghai Five association (Lukin 2004; Ong 2005).

Soon after independence, Central Asia's leaders converged on a mutual perception: the region faced an Islamist threat, and borders provided an opportunity to cross-border extremists to evade state authority. This agreement and the increasing number of bilateral and multilateral meetings provided arenas and opportunities for cooperation.[9]

Economy: The economic portfolios of the republics were subordinate to the needs of the Soviet command economy. Republics had economies that ranged from slightly diversified (e.g., Uzbekistan) to undiversified (e.g., Turkmenistan). Uzbekistan was a massive cotton producer but also had some light and medium industry. Kyrgyzstan produced agricultural goods, meat products, and vast amounts of water from glacial runoff and seasonal snowmelt, which it used to generate electricity and then sent downstream to irrigate Uzbek cotton crops. Turkmenistan's small population and massive gas deposits made energy extraction its main benefit to the Soviet economy, while Tajikistan was primarily a producer of agricultural products and aluminum. Tajikistan generated cheap hydroelectric energy and diverted much of it to the power-hungry aluminum plant in Turshunzade. That the plant made up 40 percent of Tajik GDP (Gleason 2003: 24) is a good indicator of the lack of diversification.

A glance at any Soviet-era map demonstrates that the republics' infrastructures were generally not self-contained. Infrastructure was built to channel production to the Soviet command economy rather than to give each republic exclusive roads, rail lines, and electric grids. Thus the only road connecting the Kyrgyz capital, Bishkek, with the second-largest city of Osh passed through Uzbek territory. Rail lines connecting Tashkent, the Uzbek capital, with Khiva in the Uzbek west passed through the Turkmen

---

[8] Publication of Kyrgyz Border Law, no. 530/17, 30 October 1992. The publication of the law bears the headline, "Borders of the Kyrgyz Republic: Sacred and Inviolable" (in Russian).

[9] Some scholars initially described the region's states as "Muslim Central Asia" (e.g., see Fuller 1992). Such terms emphasized Islamic unity rather than nationalism exclusive to each new republic. These terms become more common after the publication of Huntington's (1993) article "The Clash of Civilizations?" but eventually fell out of use. Also see Haghayeghi (1995) and Olcott (1993).

SSR (Badykova 2006). Independence left Central Asian states with undiversified economies, and in some cases leaders in the capitals could not reach their own cities over sovereign roads.

The combined effects of undelimited borders, fear of Islamic revival, and the interdependent economies of the states indicate that mutual cooperation would have been the preferred outcome. All of the states had interests in delimiting their borders and cooperating across those borders to prevent third parties from challenging state rule. They found themselves in a dilemma of common aversions where each should have coordinated border policy to ensure security against third-party threats.

Yet well into the first decade of independence, many of Central Asia's borders remained undelimited, and coordination of border security against groups such as the IMU was practically nonexistent. Most states not only failed to coordinate their activities against the IMU, but also adopted wildly variable policies on border security. Kyrgyzstan left its borders wide open even at the height of infiltration attempts, while Uzbekistan militarized all of its boundaries – including those where no threat was evident or probable. The security policies adopted and implemented along Central Asian borders were fraught with tension as states nearly went to war over one another's border policies.

From the perspective of international relations, these policies make little sense. The states should have been able to coordinate diplomatically to avert common threats. But this would miss the point. Border control policies were not designed as a reaction to specific threats at those borders; rather, states developed border control strategies to suit their individual state-building objectives. The new states did not see their borders as defensive sites against outside threats as much as they saw them as institutions that could be tailored to assist their domestic economic and coercive policies.

A Tale of Three Stans

This section investigates the link between state building and border control. It specifies two indicators used to measure state building: coercion and extraction. States use coercion and extraction to expand rule. Coercion was defined earlier as leaders' ability and willingness to limit challenges to their authority. Willingness is gauged via both the statements of Central Asian leaders and their deployment of the coercive arms of the state. Ability can be measured using a variety of indicators, including the size of a state's police forces. Extraction refers to the dominant mode of generating revenue for rule and the degree of economic intervention this mode requires.

Both mechanisms of state formation have consequences for how states define threat and how they organize their borders to filter out that threat. State authorities with strong coercive capacities may use police forces to suppress groups that make rival political claims within their territory, and they may use such forces to patrol their borders aggressively to prevent the exit and entry of these groups (Chandler 1998). Extractive practices also affect the claims states make at their borders (Ardant 1975; Levi 1988; Chaudry 1989; Barnett 1992). For example, if a state relies on a command economy to extract revenues, then it has a doubly vital interest in controlling its boundary. Work in comparative politics demonstrates that governments that rely on import substitution or foreign exchange controls necessarily have huge incentives to control the flow of goods across their borders (Bates 1981).

Second, by separating state building into different indicators, we are able to assess their relative weights. In the Ottoman-Greek case, we determined that revenue extraction was less important to the administration of the border than coercive measures. By examining three Central Asian states, I specify the relative weights of coercive versus extractive strategies on the organization and policing of interstate borders. The goal here is not to deduce how all possible trajectories of state formation affect border security. This is likely to be an empirical issue given the substantial variation in state formation across time and place. Rather, my objective is to specify separable and accurate indicators of the main processes of state building and to use the Central Asian case studies to induce a series of relationships between state formation and border security.[10]

I will proceed to examine three contiguous Central Asian states: Kyrgyzstan, Uzbekistan, and Tajikistan.[11] I measure extractive and coercive modes of state building pursued by the core leadership structures in each state.

---

[10] It is important to note that the relationship between coercion and border control may not necessarily be so direct. States that have the ability to police their entire territory may not need to patrol borders aggressively; individuals violating state policies may be subject to arrest deep inside territory. According to Wendt, very strong states may opt for fuzzy boundaries (1999), and even totalitarian states may choose to forgo aggressive border controls (Chandler 1998).

[11] Given space limitations I focus on the state-building strategies of these three states. Turkmenistan and Kazakhstan, while not discussed in this section, are addressed in other sections of this and the next chapter.

These measurements are taken in the initial five years of independence. To code state-building policy for each state I use the existing literature on state building and regime transition in Central Asia as well as international organizations' and nongovernmental organizations' assessments of Central Asia's economies and reform politics. These indicators allow me to create a state-building typology for each of the three states. Next, I specify the priority that such a typology implies for how states should administer their borders. A point of clarification is in order about who, if anyone, was guarding Central Asian borders at the moment of independence. Most of the "new" borders discussed here are ones that were shared between internal Soviet republics. In 1991 they were unguarded. However, other borders served as the outer limits of the Soviet Union (e.g., Uzbek-Afghan border and the Kyrgyz-Chinese border). After 1992, these borders became the external boundaries of the Commonwealth of Independent States (CIS), whose member states agreed initially to host Russian forces. The cases must thus explain not only the type of organization that Central Asian states deployed to new borders and the timing, but also the replacement or retention rates of Russian forces.

Uzbekistan the Autarch

Uzbekistan emerged as Central Asia's most populous state and largest economy. It is the only state to border on all of the region's other states, and it is centrally located in the area's transportation network and energy infrastructure. Delimitation issues concerning the location of the boundary arose with all of Uzbekistan's neighbors by the mid-1990s (Polat 2002). There is broad consensus among Central Asian scholars that the Uzbek state has the highest overall coercive capacity in the region (Olcott 1995, 2005; Jones Luong 2000; Ishiyama 2002; Weinthal 2002). From the moment of independence, the state asserted control over political activity and placed strict controls over the national economy.

Coercion: Early on, the Uzbek state systematically began to eliminate opposition, strip provincial leaders of powers, and tighten control over the media. Erk and Birlik, two oppositional caucuses that emerged during the move to independence, were banned in the early 1990s, and many of their members fled abroad. The main target of Uzbek state suppression was the political opposition, Islamic or otherwise. The Islamic Renaissance Party

(IRP) was banned. President Karimov took aggressive steps to arrest those perceived of Islamic political activism (International Crisis Group 2003b, 2003c). The crackdown intensified in 1997, when the government expanded a pilot program of repression from the Namangan area in the Ferghana Valley to the rest of the country (International Crisis Group 2002b; Kazemi 2003).

The Uzbek state developed the largest policing forces in Central Asia. Internal security forces are estimated at 200,000, and there is one police officer per 130 civilians (Cooley 2005).[12] These police forces began to operate aggressively soon after independence. There is evidence that their activities were not limited to Uzbek sovereign territory. In December 1992, Uzbek secret service agents kidnapped three Uzbek human rights activists suspected of having ties to the Islamic opposition from a conference in the Kyrgyz capital (Rashid 1994: 43).[13]

Extraction: In the five years following independence, the Uzbek state's policies of economic extraction were heavy in coercive tactics. Uzbek economic policy prescribes autarchy, a form of welfare authoritarianism that includes strict controls on foreign currency, banking, and trade (Rosenberg and De Zeeuw 2001; Gleason 2001a, 2003; Byrd and Raiser 2006).[14] One particularly instructive example involves Uzbek cotton farmers. State regulations require Uzbek farmers to sell their cotton exclusively to the Uzbek state at rates well below world market prices. The Uzbek state sells the cotton abroad at a profit and keeps the proceeds.[15] The state then uses this revenue to perpetuate its rule (Hanks 2000; Rummer 2005). It subsidizes the importation of consumer goods; it provides subsidies to domestic industry; and it pays the salaries of government bureaucrats and the growing ranks of police and military (Economist Intelligence Unit 2001).

---

[12] Compare with 1 per 258 for Kyrgyzstan.

[13] Further proof of the central state's coercive authority is the high dismissal rates of regional administrators. These *hokim*s were dismissed after failing to meet agricultural quotas. Still, some scholars doubt that the Uzbek state's coercive authority is truly deep (Noori 2005).

[14] In the decade following independence, the state's attempt to control its currency resulted in three exchange rates, two legal and one illegal. These are the official rate available at banks, the more favorable commercial rate available to approved businesses and importers, and the unofficial black market rate. *The Economist* reported a 245 percent spread between the official exchange rate and the one available on the black market (2001). In recent years currency controls have been eased.

[15] Cotton made up 41.5 percent of exports in 1998.

Uzbek Border Outcomes: It would not be surprising to find that Uzbek border policy plays a central role in Uzbekistan, where the state is highly centralized and the population tightly policed. Indeed, border control has been turned into a centerpiece of Uzbekistan's domestic security policy (Megoran 2005; Megoran, Raballand, and Bouyjou 2005).[16] The Uzbek state was the first in the region to deploy military units along all its borders and has passed border legislation that tightly centralizes and proscribes the behavior of the border guard. However, the imperative to protect state revenues and extractive policies dominates border security.

Upon independence, the Soviet border guards who were serving along the Uzbek-Afghanistan border were transferred to the authority of the Uzbek National Security Services.[17] Within a year, limited numbers of these guards were shifted northward to posts along the Tajik border to prevent refugees from the civil war from seeping into Uzbekistan. At the same time, Uzbekistan entered into delimitation talks with all of its neighbors. It was not until 1999, the year that coincided with the first major IMU attacks, that Uzbekistan passed a comprehensive law to standardize the border guard.

On the surface, these events indicate that border security policies have little to do with domestic state-building imperatives and more to do with the actual threat emanating from the other side of a border. After all, in the wake of Uzbekistan's independence Afghanistan and Tajikistan were in a state of failure.

Yet threat-based explanations cannot explain Uzbekistan's general border security strategies. By 1999 Uzbekistan had militarized all of its borders, including those with Kazakhstan and Turkmenistan, where there had been no security threats or potential for cross-border extremism. The border bill that was passed in October 1999 standardized, militarized, and centralized the administration of the border. Subsequent to this, the state adopted aggressive policies along many stretches of its border. While mines were placed along sections of the Kyrgyz and Tajik border, much of the Uzbek border was lined with barbed wire and policed by military units. Populations

---

[16] Uzbekistan's border legislation effectively links the border guard to the army and places the border at the forefront of state security. The law on border security charges combat units with the defense of the border, prescribes tight centralization of security procedures, and forbids cooperation with the border authorities of neighboring states. See Uzbek Law on the Border, no. 8820–1, 20 August 1999.

[17] Interview, with an anonymous official formerly in the Uzbek border guard, Tashkent, Uzbekistan, 4 September 2006.

that lived along sections of the border deemed sensitive were forcibly relocated. Affected populations included ethnic Tajiks living in frontier zones where incursions had taken place, but also populations near the Turkmen border and a retirement community along the border with Kazakhstan.[18] Moreover, the drafting of policies to fortify the border did not coincide with security threats. A former Uzbek border security official speaking on condition of anonymity explained that the militarization of the border service and drafting of the border bill took place well before the first alleged IMU attacks in February of 1999.[19]

Uzbek economic and extractive policies provide an unexpected explanation. A closer look at the first years of Uzbek independence indicates that the first border guards deployed to the border were customs officials. During the period immediately after independence, large numbers of consumers from neighboring countries entered Uzbekistan to buy subsidized consumer goods. Foreigners crossing the borders to buy goods came in such large numbers that consumer stocks were depleted. By 1994 and 1995, customs officials were put on all roads into and out of Uzbekistan. By the mid to late 1990s a booming trade had begun, not only in loaves of bread and vegetables, but also in cotton and gas, which were being smuggled en masse over the border to be sold at much higher market prices. While work on Uzbekistan normally makes much of the Islamic militant threat, it discounts the scale and importance of smuggling and economic theft. Megoran reminds us that "the border was portrayed as the site where the prosperity of Uzbekistan leaked out. *Halq So'zi* [an official Uzbek daily] reported many instances of customs officers apprehending people trying to secrete over the state borders items such as money, an electric transformer, honey, and meat" (2004: 745).[20]

Currency controls and the state monopsony of gas and cotton largely sustained the Uzbek government. Herbst argues that states that set up currency controls and autarchic economic policies end up weakening the state over time, in part because they cannot retain control of their borders over the long run to protect the closed economy (2000). However, in the decade following independence, Uzbek officials managed to extract substantial

---

[18] See International Crisis Group (2002a: 12) and BBC Monitoring International Reports, 1 March 2002, "Uzbekistan to Resettle Border People to Ease Tension with Turkmenistan," Asia Africa Intelligence Wire.

[19] Interview with an anonymous official.

[20] Note that this crisis worsened as customs duties plummeted from 1.5 percent of GDP in 1993 to 0.7 percent in 1998 (International Monetary Fund 2000).

revenues from the autarchic economy.[21] This suggests that border controls were moderately successful.

In sum, within five years of Uzbek independence border policing strategies were tailored to support the autarchic economy and protect state intervention and monopsony. High customs rates, the deployment of customs officers along the border, and the expectation that border guards would support the administrative duties of customs officials all demonstrate the economic imperatives behind Uzbek border policy. By contrast, the Uzbek state's approach to delimitation was one of inaction. The most favored strategies of border security targeted extractive practices and the protection of the autarchic economy. This does not mean that securing the border against militants was unimportant. However, the argument here is that extractive policies are the most reliable predictor of security policies along all Uzbek borders.

Kyrgyzstan the Trader

The Kyrgyz Republic borders on both Uzbekistan and Tajikistan. Uzbek and Tajik minorities reside in its densely populated southern border regions. The Kyrgyz state was the site of the first ethnic riots in Central Asia during the transition to independence. The state inherited a noncontinuous border (Uzbek sovereign enclaves within its territory) as well as two territorial disputes (one with China and another with Tajikistan along its southwest border in the Isfara Valley region) (Polat 2003: 43). Faced with a difficult geography and a shattered economy, the Kyrgyz state attempted to survive by pursuing strategies of liberalization that would bring in revenues from trade flows while attracting foreign aid, investment, and technical assistance.

Coercion: Scholarship on Central Asia indicates that the ability of the Kyrgyz state to coerce and implement central authority is very anemic in at least two different spheres. In the first years following independence, Kyrgyzstan was characterized as a decisively democratizing state. The term "laissez-faire" is certainly more accurate. For example, the state technically outlawed Islamic parties and passed certain restrictions on political mobilization, but in principle it initially chose a hands-off approach

---

[21] A survey by the Economist Intelligence Unit (2001) estimated that unrecorded imports likely total anywhere from 10 to 40 percent of official import expenditure.

(International Crisis Group 2003b, 2003c, 2006a; also see Alymkulov and Kulatov 2001). The state was the only one in Central Asia to elect a president rather than extend his term via referendum (Olcott 2005). It was reluctant to clamp down on religious activity for much of the 1990s, even after legislation introduced in 1996 required religious groups to register with the authorities (International Crisis Group 2003c). The number of Kyrgyz internal police forces – estimated at 19,000 – means that Kyrgyzstan has the lowest police-to-population ratio in Central Asia (Cooley 2005).[22]

Extraction: In extracting most revenues, the Kyrgyz state performed miserably. Income tax made up approximately 1 percent of the GDP. In the initial years following independence, government revenues seem to have been drawn largely from grants, interest on bank lending, and the sale of water and electricity to neighboring states (Kaser and Mehrota 1996; Abazov 1999).[23] Hampered by a lack of effective revenue collection and weak auditing institutions, the Kyrgyz state instead focused its efforts on collecting revenues that involved a minimum of state effort. Customs taxes, for instance, are easier to collect as they can be obtained at designated ports of entry and border posts. Yet the Kyrgyz state did not pursue an aggressive customs collection policy in order to meet requirements for membership in the World Trade Organization or the International Monetary Fund. By July 1997, it passed a new customs code that allowed raw material to be imported duty-free, and it created Free Economic Zones from which goods could be exported duty-free. It also adopted a uniform customs rate for remaining taxable goods at 10 percent. The initial objective of the Kyrgyz state in matters of extraction seems to have been to facilitate a liberalization of the economy that would increase trade volume while attracting donor assistance and investment.[24]

---

[22] While some argue that Kyrgyz police forces are ineffective and corrupt (International Crisis Group 2002b), there is another observation worth making. The Kyrgyz state initially took a very different approach to maintaining internal security. Following the Osh events in 1990, officials made an effort to use the courts to dole out appropriate punishments in order to perpetuate the rule of law, deter future violence, and redress grievances. On this, see Tishkov's work (1995).

[23] In 1994, Kyrgyzstan received development assistance totaling $172 million (5.5 percent of GDP). By contrast, foreign direct investment in that year totaled a meager $25 million. For a snapshot of the general economic context in Central Asia at the time, see Pomfret (1995).

[24] This crash course in liberalization created tremendous dislocation and financial crisis (Gleason 2003).

Faced with the task of extending authority over a fractured territory, the Kyrgyz state chose a mode of state building that I label the "trader path." Unwilling to forcibly centralize its political authority over outlying regions and expand the domestic security apparatus to all sections of the country, the Kyrgyz state instead pursued economic liberalization in order to secure trade revenues, economic aid, and investment.

Kyrgyz Border Outcomes: Which of these state-building indicators best explains the Kyrgyz Republic's approach to border security? On the one hand, given low coercive capacity and strong regions with centrifugal tendencies, the state ought to be more concerned with break-up than with the de facto control of people and goods moving across its borders. Bordering states that are weak and do not effectively control their outlying regions prefer to recognize one another's territorial authority as a low-cost way of protecting and preserving their borders (Jackson and Rosberg 1986; Herbst 2000). Delimitation and legitimation of the new borders, rather than the actual use of force and coercion at the border, is likely to be the most-favored strategy. Delimitation would result in the de jure recognition of Kyrgyz territory and thus promote the integrity of Kyrgyz territory. Outlying regions with the ability to secede or evade central state controls would have little incentive to break away and would be hard-pressed to find an external state sponsor.

A look at the empirical record in the decade following independence corroborates the centrality of delimitation as a goal of securing the border. Kyrgyz authorities were the most outspoken advocates in Central Asia for border delimitation and dispute resolution. They moved very quickly soon after independence to begin talks with China on the delimitation of their common border and resolution of the territorial dispute (Fravel 2005). Authorities requested delimitation talks with neighboring Kazakhstan, Uzbekistan, and Tajikistan. Although delimitation talks with Tajikistan failed – in part because of a dispute over which Soviet-era maps to use in redrawing the border – the Kyrgyz made dozens of requests for delimitation and attended ten failed delimitation talks.[25]

However, it would not be correct to state that the actions of Kyrgyz authorities can be directly attributed to the weakness of Kyrgyz coercive institutions. The Kyrgyz state, despite the weakness of its police forces,

---

[25] I owe this information to Amanda Wooden, who was working at the Osh field office of the Organization for Security and Cooperation in Europe (OSCE).

inherited a Russian contingent of border guard troops on its border with China. Even after the Kyrgyz state nationalized the remnants of the Soviet army, it failed to deploy it to its borders. Kyrgyzstan's borders remained without border guards throughout the 1990s (Cherikov 2005).[26] This is surprising given the early incidents of conflict among Kyrgyz and Uzbeks in Ozgen and Osh near the Uzbek border and the collapse of Tajikistan, which sent floods of refugees into Kyrgyzstan.

This puzzle has two related explanations. First, Kyrgyz officials believed that the border must be delimited before border authorities could be deployed. Numerous high-level officials expressed this belief.[27] Second, the unwillingness to deploy border guards had much to do with the idea that borders should be sites to promote trade and state revenues rather than sites of restricting movement.

The state chose to tailor a border policy to promote its "trader" path of state building. In 1994 it took down customs posts that had been hastily erected along some of its borders, and in 1996 it considered getting rid of customs duties altogether (International Monetary Fund 1996b).[28] Here the Kyrgyz state faced a dilemma. Customs duties assessed at the border would potentially depress and discourage trade but would allow the state to collect revenues. However, lifting customs or lightening customs duties would encourage trade but force the state to look for revenue to other forms of taxation, such as income, foreign direct investment, and corporate profits taxes. While the Kyrgyz state repeatedly vacillated between these policies, both were consistent with its goal of state building via a trade economy.

However, the placement of customs officers created another dilemma for state officials. State agencies would not place customs officers along a border that was not yet delimited for fear of making a political statement about the location and legitimacy of the border line and thus complicating delimitation talks. Along the Chinese border, the Kyrgyz state resolved the

---

[26] An exception to this is the Kyrgyz-Chinese border. A Russian contingent remained there until the late 1990s, although the activities of the guards seem to have been limited and confined to the border guard bases rather than involving patrol of the boundary line.

[27] Interviews with Baktibek Ajibekovich Usupov, representative of the Ministry of Foreign Affairs to the South, Osh, Kyrgyzstan, 23 August 2006; and Japarov Sadir Nurgojoevich, member of parliament, Bishkek, Kyrgyzstan, 27 August 2006.

[28] Also see Kaser and Mehrota (1996), Abazov (1999), and BBC Summary of World Broadcasts, 11 February 1994, "Prices Drop in Kyrgyzstan after Closure of Customs Post on Uzbek Border," ITAR-TASS News Agency, Moscow (2 February 1994). Customs duties were to be imposed on goods in transit from non-CIS countries.

dilemma by collecting revenues from a customs post that was located miles inside Kyrgyz territory.[29]

Even in the late 1990s, as militants crossed into and out of Kyrgyz territory, the Kyrgyz state persisted on calling for delimitation talks.[30] Border guards were the last authorities to be deployed to Kyrgyz borders and even then were placed reluctantly or in reaction to infiltration. The primacy of early economic liberalization means that the Kyrgyz state preferred an open economic border – one without impediments to the movement of goods. Dead last on the Kyrgyz state's list of priorities was the stationing of border guards and military units.

Tajikistan the Smuggler

Tajikistan collapsed into a civil war soon after declaring independence. The former Communists won the first elections in November 1991. A coalition including social democrats and Islamists protested the results of the elections, subsequently ousted the president, and assumed control of the government. By late 1992 politically motivated violence was spiraling, and Kulyabi and Khujand (Khojent) militias stepped in to restore the former Communists to power with the assistance of Russian military forces (Horsman 1999). The civil war lasted from 1992 to 1997. It destroyed the economy, displaced populations, and delayed crucial reforms (Rubin 1993; Fletcher and Sergeyev 2002).

Coercion: During the civil war competing armed groups set up posts and patrols and requisitioned soldiers and supplies (Nourzhanov 2005). And while fighting was often fierce, insurgents and government elites struck alliances of convenience in order to preserve spheres of influence. When the Rahmonov government tried to deploy police and military forces in Khujand, a local warlord threatened to blow up the only bridge connecting the capital, Dushanbe, with the north of the country and to secede to Uzbekistan (Nourzhanov 2005). Post–civil war reconstruction has been extremely difficult in Tajikistan, largely because of the persistence throughout the territory of militias and warlord groups who prefer maintaining their spheres

---

[29] Both the Torugart and Irkeshtam checkpoints along the Kyrgyz-Chinese border are substantially set back from the boundary.

[30] BBC Worldwide Monitoring, 11 October 1999, "Uzbekistan to Draw Border with Kyrgyzstan following Militant Crisis," Uzbek Television first channel, Tashkent.

of influence and the tributary role they play in the central government to a full integration into the state and its security forces (Nourzhanov 2005).

Extraction: Shattered by the war and confronted with ruling a remote territory, the main policy orientation of the postwar Tajik state has been to extract revenues in order to perpetuate the state. Although foreign aid and the sale of cotton and minerals make up a large part of government revenues, during the civil war drug-smuggling networks presented a lucrative source of revenue to the state and warring factions alike.[31] Warring parties financed their participation either by directly engaging in the smuggling of contraband or by extending protection to existing smuggling networks. Smuggling networks originating in Afghanistan, which traversed Tajikistan to points north in the CIS, hardened during this period and persisted after the civil war ended (International Crisis Group 2001b; Jackson 2005).

Tajik Border Outcomes: The Tajik state survives precisely because it collects protection fees from these smuggling networks. By one estimate, Tajik authorities seize only 3–6 percent of the opiates that enter their territory from Afghanistan en route to Russia.[32] Research by some scholars suggests that high-level orders have been handed down to local authorities instructing them to extend protection to these networks (Lubin 2003). The Tajik border thus contributes to the perpetuation of the Tajik state by remaining open to contraband. Delimitation and the control of other flows – including cross-border militants – are not actively pursued. The Tajik state has participated only reluctantly in delimitation talks with its neighbors, including China, which has approached Tajikistan with a very lucrative offer in their mutual territorial dispute (Fravel 2005, 2008).

There is substantial evidence of the state's incentive to keep the border open to smuggling at the expense of other policies. Russian border guards who were in charge of the Tajik-Afghan border have been implicated in the drug trade in numerous ways. There have been instances of the border guard directly airlifting contraband from the border to airports in Moscow as well as evidence that the units (which were recently replaced by Tajik

---

[31] Official statistics on the Tajik economy collected during the civil war years are misleading. Consider the following example: Tax revenues in 1994 made up a massive 43 percent of Tajikistan's GDP. This was not due to the ability of the state to collect taxes. Rather, taxpayers paid their debts to the state in worthless noncash rubbles (International Monetary Fund 1996a).

[32] Jones Luong (2003) estimates that government revenues from contraband constitute approximately 50 percent of the total budget.

border guards) have collaborated with officials to keep smuggling networks in operation.[33] High-ranking Tajik officials have been caught with large sums of money and quantities of drugs in Kazakhstan and Russia.[34] Officials working with security agencies in Central Asia explain that a vast and well-protected trade crosses Tajikistan from the Afghan border to Kyrgyzstan.

Kyrgyzstan and Tajikistan entered into talks over delimitation of their common boundary later than any other pair of states in the region. Talks on delimiting the boundary seem to have begun only in 2004. Tajik officials have avoided participating in delimitation talks. There are two considerations that may explain why the Tajik state obstructed delimitation of its border. One explanation focuses on ethnic migration, another on profits from contraband. During and after the Tajik civil war, large numbers of ethnic Tajiks migrated northward across the Kyrgyz border. Many settled, bought land, and own businesses.[35] By stalling delimitation, it is possible that the Tajik government is attempting to buy time and eventually hopes to annex these territories. While such an analysis sounds plausible, it is unlikely that territorial considerations motivate Tajik leaders. Tajikistan has shown little interest in delimiting its border with China and dragged its feet on resolving a territorial dispute, even though China has effectively offered the Tajiks the lion's share of the disputed land.

Another explanation focuses on the consequences of delimitation on border deployments. Following delimitation, borders become the focus of commissions, reports, and on-site inspections that publicize problems involving the movement of goods and people as well as the incidence of trafficking in illegal substances. A delimitation and demarcation agreement with Kyrgyzstan would mean the permanent stationing of newly trained border guards and customs officials along the border. Such a stationing could disrupt the smuggling networks in which existing Tajik border guards seem to be involved.[36] The Tajik state's aversion to creating formal and lasting administrative structures along the Kyrgyz boundary is such that officials have turned a blind eye to Tajik locals near the border area who

---

[33] BBC Monitoring International report, 1 February 2005, "Two Tajik Border Guards Reportedly Taken into Afghanistan by Force," Interfax-AVN; and interview with Jerome Bouyjou, director of OSCE Osh field office, Bishkek, Kyrgyzstan, 27 August 2006.

[34] Interview with an anonymous international organization official, Bishkek, Kyrgyzstan.

[35] This migration and its effects on the micro level of border control will be taken up in the next chapter.

[36] Agence France Presse, 12 August 2002, "Tajik Border Guard Chief Detained in Kyrgyzstan after Heroin Seizure," International News, Bishkek.

periodically attack and destroy Kyrgyz customs and border posts.[37] While Tajik authorities regularly condemn illicit trade and drug trafficking, in reality their interest lies in preventing the delimitation and consequent deployment of officials and border guards to the boundary.[38]

The Central Asian cases demonstrate the variable relationship between state building and borders. They show that new states tailor their borders to suit domestic state-building strategies rather than security threats or flows at particular sections of border (see Table 5.1). Moreover, in assessing the relative impact of coercive and extractive policies of state building, I have determined that economic-extractive strategies of state building take precedence over coercive policies. In the case of Uzbekistan, this has meant tailoring border control to preserve the autarchic economy. The Tajik state, following the conclusion of the civil war, developed a clear preference for creating a border that would be wide open to smuggling networks. The Kyrgyz Republic adopted delimitation as its most-favored strategy, seeing it as the key to legitimating the border and opening it to the flow of goods and trade.

These strategies reveal a very selective repertoire of border control. Kyrgyzstan did nothing to prevent large numbers of refugees from entering its territory during the Tajik civil war and left its border wide open following an invasion by IMU extremists from Tajikistan. Uzbekistan, on the other hard, overmilitarized its borders and sent troops to protect the state from economic threats at the border.

These policies make sense when understood from the perspective of state formation. Each state's border policy was tailor-made to assist in the pursuit of desired economic and extractive policies. States may have pledged to cooperate across their borders in order to demarcate them and to control militant activities, but in actuality each developed and pursued border policies in isolation and in contradiction to its neighbors.'

---

[37] See BBC Monitoring Central Asia Unit, 4 January 2003, "Tajik Border Area Residents Destroy Customs Checkpoints, Kyrgyz follow suit," ITAR-TASS, Moscow; and 4 January 2003, "Southern Kyrgyz, Tajik Police 'Agree to Remove Unlawful Customs Posts'," Kyrgyz Television first channel, Bishkek.

[38] Note the statement of the head of the General Staff of the Tajik border troops: "Both sides have the right to set up border and customs posts on their territories, but since the territory is disputed, there should not be posts in any sides." See BBC Monitoring Central Asia Unit, 8 January 2003, "Tajik, Kyrgyz Border Heads to Meet 12 January to Tackle Dispute," Asia-Plus News Agency, Dushanbe (7 January 2003); and BBC Monitoring International Reports, 28 July 2004, "Kyrgyz, Tajik, Uzbek Border Issue Still Unresolved," Kyrgyz Radio, Bishkek.

Table 5.1. *State formation and border policy in Central Asia*

State	State-Building Path (1991–96)	Border Policy Preference	Actual Policy
Uzbekistan	Autarch: high-coercion; government revenues via strict currency and price controls	Control flows threatening to autarchic economy and security	Unilateral: first in region to regulate borders; deployed customs officials before military; border policing centralized and monitored by NSS and executive
Kyrgyzstan	Trader: low-coercion, liberalizing economy; government revenues via trade volume	Delimit border; open it to trade flows	Cooperative: first to propose delimitation and cooperative policing; deployed customs agents at official crossings; resisted deploying border guards to "green border" until delimitation could start
Tajikistan	Smuggler: civil war prevents state building; state functions dispersed to local warlords; state survived through drug revenues	Allow smuggling networks access into and out of Tajik territory	Ad hoc: resisted delimitation talks; few customs officials and border guards; large gap between de jure border laws and de facto unwillingness to police the border

A Coordination Problem Turns to Conflict

In this section I examine the interaction effects of security polices implemented along both sides of a boundary. This is an important part of the argument because it explains how a coordination problem over mutual issues of border security turned into open conflict. What does this mean? Central Asia's leaders initially identified delimitation and extremism as mutual security threats and pledged to coordinate policies. However, within the first decade of independence their unilateral state-building processes generated varying approaches to border security. These approaches were not always mutually exclusive; for example, the Uzbek and Kyrgyz governments could have coordinated the activities of their border guards in order to police against cross-border extremism while working toward bilateral delimitation of the border. Instead, each side attempted to implement its most-favored policy in a way that prevented policy coordination.

The following are a number of case studies of paired boundaries in Central Asia. The first case study takes place along the Uzbek-Kyrgyz border. In all the cases, state authorities confront two mutual problems – militancy and delimitation. However, the state-building trajectories vary (autarchy, trader, smuggler). The cases have been chosen because the mutual concerns with delimitation and militancy should have resulted in at least minimal coordination over border security issues. The lack of coordination requires explanation.

The lack of coordination and linkage along many Central Asian borders is particularly surprising given the presence of two powerful international organizations: the Commonwealth of Independent States (CIS) and the Shanghai Cooperation Organization (SCO). The CIS sponsored a visa regime and uniform customs tariffs and was a forum for many meetings dealing with issues of security.[39] At the same time, the SCO grew stronger and became a forum to discuss issues of extremism, secessionism, and terrorism as well as trade. Even Uzbekistan, which tended to shirk participation in many international organizations, was an active member of the SCO.[40]

The Uzbek-Kyrgyz case study is followed by two others (the Uzbek-Turkmen border and the Kyrgyz-Chinese boundary). These cases clarify the argument. By examining these paired borders, I am able to determine whether state-building policies resulted in uniform implementation along a state border. That is, if inside-out state-building dynamics generate border policy, we should observe Uzbekistan implementing the same policies along both its border with Turkmenistan and its border with Kyrgyzstan, irrespective of threats and conditions particular to segments of the border. While these cases hold constant state-building policy in Uzbekistan and Kyrgyzstan, they allow for variation on a number of factors: along the Uzbek-Turkmen boundary, concerns for militancy are muted and the

---

[39] By 1997 border guard commanders of CIS member states had met twenty-six times and signed thirty-three documents on visa regimes, economic zones, and border protection. See ITAR-TASS News Agency, 6 September 1997, "CIS Border Guard Commanders Sign Over 30 Documents," Bishkek.

[40] Uzbekistan quit the CIS in 1999 but joined the SCO in 2001.

border is well-defined; along the Chinese boundary, concerns for militancy are high and there is a territorial dispute. In other words, these two cases examine border pairs where the potential for conflict is very different at the moment of the creation of the border.

The Uzbek-Kyrgyz Boundary

By the mid-1990s, growing numbers of IMU militants had taken advantage of the collapse of the Tajik state to set up camp in Tajikistan's remote northern provinces. Militants used Tajik territory as a base to kidnap officials and foreigners and to launch attacks on Uzbek and Kyrgyz territory alike (Rashid 2002). Despite the militant activity along their shared border and their common interest in coordinating security strategy, the Uzbek and Kyrgyz states refused to cooperate and pool their resources. This boundary should have been an easy case for cooperation, especially as the Kyrgyz and Uzbeks did not have overlapping territorial claims. But instead of cooperating to deal with militancy, the two states allowed the boundary to become a site of violence, escalation, and frequent closure.

The conflict over border policy began in the mid to late 1990s as the two states attempted to implement modes of border security in line with their state-building preferences. The Kyrgyz insisted on delimiting the border and keeping it open to the flow of goods. The Uzbek state, however, quickly moved to prevent the flow of unauthorized crossings. This unilateral enforcement resulted in tremendous obstruction of the movement of people and goods. Between 1997 and 1998, Kyrgyz exports to Uzbekistan plummeted from $101.5 million to $38.6 million (Gleason 2003). It was these restrictive controls on travel and trade, rather than security problems, that triggered the first appreciable dispute on record.[41]

Throughout 1999 cross-border militant activity and violence spiked in Uzbekistan and Kyrgyzstan, and it became clear that extremists were operating across the border. The Uzbek state sent troops and border guards on expeditions into Kyrgyz territory to suppress extremist operatives. Kyrgyz authorities condemned the violation of their sovereignty, but, instead of reinforcing the border, they called for immediate delimitation proceedings and insisted that the border stay open. The Kyrgyz insistence on recognizing the location of the border led them to dismiss remaining Russian border

---

[41] BBC Monitoring Central Asia, 19 April 1998, "Kyrgyz MPs Appeal against Uzbek Customs 'Impudence'," *Vecherniy Bishkek*, Bishkek (10 April 1998).

guard forces on Kyrgyz soil, even as Uzbekistan increased the volume of threats, began to violate Kyrgyz territory, and quit the CIS.[42]

Rather than coordinate strategy to deal with the militant threat, the two governments allowed the management of the boundary itself to become the subject of conflict. The Uzbek state began to mine the border and construct barriers, watchtowers, and dead zones along the Kyrgyz border.[43] This strategy of unilaterally securing the border foreclosed cooperation, restricted the movement of goods, and denied the Kyrgyz state its most desired goal – the delimitation and demarcation of the boundary.[44] Kyrgyz state and border security officials were so determined to pursue demarcation that the head of Kyrgyz border security insisted that a bilateral commission physically walk and demarcate the boundary before it would be demined.[45] Indeed, many of these unilateral fortifications were constructed deep within Kyrgyz territory. The incompatibility of preferences in securing the border not only increased the level of conflict along the boundary, but also created a territorial dispute where none had existed.[46] Uzbek forces entrenched themselves on Kyrgyz territory and refused to leave.

The Kyrgyz-Chinese Boundary

The conflict along the Uzbek-Kyrgyz boundary is in stark contrast to the cooperation and security achieved along the Chinese-Kyrgyz boundary. This is surprising for several reasons. First, China and Kyrgyzstan inherited

[42] BBC Monitoring Central Asia, 11 April 1999, "Uzbek border guards try to build 'fortified position' on Kyrgyz territory," *Delo No*, Bishkek (3 November 1999); and *Defense and Security*, 26 July 1999, "Russian Border Guards Leaving Kyrgyzstan," *Nezavisimaya Gazeta* (22 July 1999).

[43] BBC Monitoring Central Asia, 11 April 1999, "Uzbek Border Guards Try to Build 'Fortified Position' on Kyrgyz Territory," *Delo No*, Bishkek (3 November 1999).

[44] BBC Monitoring International Reports, 26 December 2003, "Kyrgyzstan Has Fewer Border Guards than Neighbors," *Vecherniy Bishkek* (23 December 2003).

[45] BBC Monitoring International Reports, 28 June 2003, "Kyrgyz-Uzbek Border Can't Be Demined unless Demarcated, " *Slovo Kyrgyzstana*, Bishkek (27 June 2003).

[46] For example, see Viktoria Panfilova, "Territorial Disputes between Uzbekistan and Kyrgyzstan Lead to Bloodshed," *Nevasimaya Gazeta* (18 January 2002); BBC Monitoring International Reports, 21 January 2002, "Kyrgyzstan to Claim Uzbek Enclave in Ferghana Valley," Kyrgyz Infocentre, Bishkek; BBC Monitoring, 28 June 2003, "Kyrgyz-Uzbek border Can't be Demined unless Demarcated – Border Service Chief," *Slovo Kyrgyzstana*, Bishkek (27 June 2003); BBC Monitoring, 26 January 2004, "Uzbek Villagers Wish to Join Kyrgyzstan," AKI Press News Agency, Bishkek; and BBC Monitoring, 6 November 2004, "Kyrgyz-Uzbek Border Disputes Might Cause Ethnic Clashes," *Respublika*, Almaty (15 October 2004).

a long-standing territorial dispute following the Soviet collapse that could be expected to tip the two states toward conflict. Much of the literature on territorial disputes argues that such overlapping claims tend to increase the incidence or severity of conflict between states (Vasquez 1993; Huth 1996; Hassner 2006). Second, China was disproportionately threatened by Uighur separatists who had set up camp on the Kyrgyz side (Walsh 1993; Munro 1994; Raczka 1998). Third, the Chinese were capable – like the Uzbeks – of unilaterally and aggressively policing the border.

Yet the critical factor distinguishing the Kyrgyz-Chinese boundary from the Uzbek-Kyrgyz border appears to have been the compatibility of Kyrgyz and Chinese preferences on border functions. Both Kyrgyz and Chinese officials wanted a border that was open to trade. At the same time, both sides valued delimitation as a security strategy (Fravel 2005). By the mid-1990s delimitation along these boundaries had progressed speedily, and the two states had proposed and implemented troop reductions and demilitarization. Domestic opposition in the Kyrgyz Republic blasted the territorial settlement with China, arguing that it had been negotiated in secrecy and that it treacherously gave up national territory.[47] Regime elites and officials in the Foreign Ministry responded that the loss of some land was well worth the opportunity to delimit and demilitarize the frontier zone.[48] It would permit trade, allow cooperation in preventing separatism and terror, and ultimately shore up Kyrgyz sovereignty. While escalation, conflict, and infiltration are regular features along the Kyrgyz-Uzbek border, there is diplomatic cooperation between Chinese and Kyrgyz officials on border issues. Moreover, Kyrgyz border authorities have received assistance from their Chinese counterparts in the form of patrol vehicles and training in the martial arts.[49]

---

[47] The Chinese-Kyrgyz territorial agreement was ratified in 2002. Cooperation substantially predates the ratification. Chinese and Kyrgyz state officials demilitarized the boundary and negotiated a territorial settlement as early as the mid-1990s. Ratification was delayed twice by nationalist parties in the Kyrgyz parliament who demanded that Kyrgyzstan receive the entirety of the disputed territory.

[48] Dmitry Glumskov, 13 May 2002, "Though Small, Kyrgyzstan Can Still Afford to Give up Territory," *The Current Digest of the Post-Soviet Press* (5 June 2002); and BBC Monitoring Central Asia Unit, 27 November 2002, "Kyrgyzstan Did Not Sell Uzengi-Kuush to China for 3 Billion Dollars, Says Official," *Slovo Kyrgyzstana*, Bishkek (19 November 2002).

[49] For example, see BBC Monitoring International Reports, 8 December 2004, "China Grants 20 Cars to Kyrgyz Border Service," Kyrgyz Television first channel, Bishkek; BBC Monitoring, 22 September 2004, "Chinese PM, Kyrgyz President Emphasize Long-Term Cooperation," Xinhua News Agency, Beijing; BBC Monitoring, 3 August 2004, "Chinese Experts

It would not be accurate to ascribe the cooperation in security to the SCO. The SCO has certainly facilitated multilateral summits and bilateral talks on issues of border security, but it is not the cause of such cooperation. Initial talks and agreements between Kyrgyzstan and China predate the SCO as well as its predecessor, the Shanghai Five. The Chinese government spearheaded the SCO in order to promote its agenda for suppressing terrorism and secessionism near Chinese borderlands and designed it to guarantee future cooperation from Central Asian states (Fravel 2008).

The Uzbek-Turkmen Boundary

The case of the Uzbek-Turkmen border presents a variation of the argument. If divergent state-building paths generate incompatible border control strategies, then the similar trajectories of Uzbek and Turkmen state building should generate compatible types of border control. Turkmenistan is a coercive-intensive state with highly centralized institutions that police the population and intervene in the economy. The massive oil and gas deposits in Turkmenistan are state property and are used to subsidize most consumer and staple goods (Badykova 2005). Likewise, most governmental decisions on political and economic matters have required the scrutiny and direct approval of President Saparmurat Niyazov.[50] If Uzbekistan could be labeled an autarch, then Turkmenistan is certainly a "hyper-autarch."

As in Uzbekistan, border security would be expected to play a central role in preserving the hyper-autarchic economy. Turkmenistan's price controls and subsidies make Turkmen gas even cheaper than that produced on the Uzbek side, creating an incentive for petrol smuggling. Like Uzbekistan, Turkmenistan first deployed customs agencies to its borders to assess duties and prevent smuggling. Both states had a roughly compatible interest in preserving their internal markets. As a result, the customs agencies along the two sides of the Turkmen-Uzbek border have reportedly evolved to become the best staffed and provisioned of any administrators along Central Asian borders.[51]

Train Kyrgyz Border Guards in Martial Arts, Mountain Training," Kyrgyz Television First Channel, Bishkek (2 August 2004).

[50] Niyazov died in December 2006.

[51] Interview with Pierre-Paul Antheunissens, project manager for Turkmenistan and Uzbekistan, Border Management Program in Central Asia (BOMCA), Tashkent, Uzbekistan, 4 September 2006.

Given the ability of each state to attain its most-favored policy of economic control, diplomats were able to move quickly to address the issue of border delimitation. On September 21, 2000, the Turkmen and Uzbek presidents signed a treaty in the Turkmen capital, Ashgabat, defining their shared 1,867-kilometer border (International Crisis Group 2002a). This agreement was the first of its kind among Central Asia's post-independence states. It was all the more notable given the existing disputes between the two states over the Uzbek leasing of oil and gas facilities in Turkmenistan and over the use of an oil and gas field straddling an eastern section of the border.[52]

Yet soon after the delimitation, violence and escalation along the border began. With the delimitation complete, both sides began expanding the number of border posts. The Turkmen president toyed with the idea of creating a fence along the entire length of the border (International Crisis Group 2002a); instead, an estimated 50,000 recruits were called up in November 2001 to serve in detachments along the borders, including those with Uzbekistan and Kazakhstan.[53] As the security situation and relations with Uzbekistan and Kazakhstan had been relatively calm and static, there was no clear outside threat requiring such as massive deployment.[54] However, the deployment makes more sense in light of the Turkmen state's extractive practices and concern with smuggling. In the year prior to the deployment, President Niyazov had enacted a six-dollar charge for Turkmen citizens crossing the border. The fee was an astronomical sum in a region where monthly salaries are under thirty dollars. Both sides of the border contained mixed populations of Uzbeks and Turkmen reliant on a brisk shuttle trade. The attempt to manage the movement of populations and trade backfired. There was a spike in reported smuggling and an increase in violence along the border involving locals and border authorities (International Crisis Group 2002a).

---

[52] See International Crisis Group (2002a) and BBC Monitoring International Reports, 14 January 2003, "Uzbekistan, Turkmenistan Settle 'Dispute' over Oil and Gas Fields on Border," Interfax News Agency, Moscow.

[53] BBC Monitoring International Reports, 24 January 2002, "Turkmenistan Beefs Up Borders," Kyrgyz Infocentre News, Bishkek. It is interesting that many of the border guards were deployed to Turkmenistan's northern borders rather than to its border with Afghanistan, despite the instability and spillover effects of the United States operations there.

[54] Relations worsened the following year when the Turkmen president accused the Uzbek ambassador in Ashgabat of plotting an assassination attempt against him.

The case of the Turkmen-Uzbek border highlights the link between economic state-building policies and border control strategies. Turkmen authorities militarized the border with Uzbekistan in order to enforce the visa fees and prevent smuggling. More interestingly, they did so by deploying forces away from the Iranian and Afghan borders, where the security situation and potential threats to the state from cross-border militants were graver.[55]

The case further demonstrates that the hyper-centralization of border control places limits on cross-border cooperation. The centralization of border control on the Uzbek side and its hyper-centralization on the Turkmen side meant that cooperation could not extend to the local level. Given the tight oversight, the two states prevented their border guards from having an arena of interaction in which to discuss disputes and crises that arose. While Turkmen border guards have a satellite uplink to communicate with headquarters in Ashgabat, their only means of communicating with their Uzbek counterparts is to raise a white flag in hopes of convening a quick exchange in neutral territory.[56] Border guards choose to report events upward rather than make time-consuming and crude attempts to resolve disputes with their counterparts several kilometers in the distance. Consequently, isolated incidents in 2000 spiraled into frequent shootings and large-scale violations. In December 2001, several hundred Uzbeks broke through border guard fortifications and entered Turkmenistan in order to make a visit to a cemetery on the other side. They overwhelmed Uzbek and Turkmen guards and returned only when Turkmen military reinforcements threatened the use of force (International Crisis Group 2002a).

This brief case study indicates a crucial variation of the argument. Among the series of claims outlined in Chapter 2, I posited that the greater the degree of direct state intervention, the lower the ability of border authorities to cooperate across a border (even if their state-building strategies converge). The high degree of monitoring and oversight that the Uzbek and Turkmen states have over matters of border control has resulted in two highly centralized border control agencies on either side of the border that operate distinctly and unilaterally. Despite the compatibility of their state-building policies and initial agreement that delimitation is critical,

---

[55] Afghanistan exported refugees and militants, and Iranian-Turkmen relations were occasionally marked by tension.

[56] Interview, Tamas Kiss, project manager for Kyrgyzstan and Kazakhstan, BOMCA, Bishkek, Kyrgyzstan, 21 August 2006.

both states foreclosed cross-border cooperation and created monitoring channels that ensure that all incidents along the border – no matter how minor – escalate to agencies in capital cities.

Conclusions

The findings in this chapter cast doubt on a number of plausible explanations regarding the sources of border control. One claim is that external threats condition state preferences on border security. Such threats may include ethnic separatism among border populations. Riots in and around the Kyrgyz city of Osh involving Uzbeks in 1990 were seen as a sign of future ethnic conflict. The collapse of Tajikistan into civil war may also have caused specific measures to be taken along adjoining Kyrgyz and Uzbek borders, especially given the role of Islamic insurgents in opposition to government forces. In order for this proposition to hold, it is necessary to observe states responding to an increase in threat or potential threat with a requisite increase in policing. The greater the threat, the more intensive the policing and the more likely the border is to be militarized. Conversely, a section of a border where there is no perceived or apparent threat should not be policed as aggressively.

On the surface, the issue of threat seems to explain Uzbek state policy in guarding its border. The state was quick to set up border controls along the Tajik border to prevent the civil war from spilling over into its territory. But these border posts were inadequate and understaffed. In the late 1990s and onward, the threat of cross-border militancy seems to explain the increasing militarization of the Uzbek border with Tajikistan and Kyrgyzstan. Yet the Uzbeks fortified their border and passed aggressive border legislation before the IMU attacks and without any indication that such attacks were possible down the road. Moreover, the scale of threat does not explain Kyrgyz behavior. At the height of IMU attacks, the Kyrgyz resisted militarizing their border and insisted on the importance of delimiting the border first. This is a curious reaction given the threat that IMU incursions from Tajikistan posed both for both Uzbekistan and Kyrgyzstan. The level of threat is not consistent with outcomes along Central Asian borders.

Another plausible explanation concerns institutional legacy and its effects on how states manage their borders. In other words, states may deploy to their borders whatever institutions are available for the task, irrespective of the level of threat at the boundary. For instance, we may expect Uzbekistan to militarize its border given that it inherited the Turkestan Military

District. Simply put, Uzbekistan possessed an army that it could readily throw to the border. This explanation seems to explain all three states: the Uzbeks, which turned out to be the most aggressive militarizers, inherited the most powerful Soviet military district in the region, while Tajikistan had to use its institutions to fight a civil war rather than to guard its border.

A closer look at the empirical evidence demonstrates that this proposition does not hold. First, Central Asia's states seem to have deployed guards only in the late 1990s. By leaving their borders unguarded for the first years of their independence, they demonstrated that there was no single institution that any of them inherited that could readily be assigned to the task of border control. Second, the Turkestan Military District did not pass into Tashkent's control intact. In his work on organizations and transitions in the former Soviet Union, Cooley explains, "without Moscow's central coordination, command, and resources, the Soviet army in the post-Soviet republics degenerated into a set of isolated pockets of bases, installations, and deployments. The collapse of the Soviet military also brought its ethnic imbalances into the nation-building spotlight as new national units had very few senior officers or high-ranking officials who were indigenous nationals" (2005: 111). Even if we take this institutional degeneration as temporary and assume that the Uzbek government regrouped, reformed, and deployed the army, this does not explain why Kyrgyz officials did not employ the armed forces that they had inherited.

A related claim would suggest that military capacity may explain why some states chose to manage their borders unilaterally rather than pool their resources with their neighbors. Uzbekistan is the most populous Central Asian state and has inherited the largest military. Uzbekistan's lack of cooperation may be a logical outcome given the military preponderance it developed soon after independence (see Table 5.2).

One possibility may be that Uzbekistan has deliberately retained a degree of ambiguity on border delimitation in order to signal its dissatisfaction with existing boundaries (Polat 2002: 49). The Uzbek state has no incentive to delimit its borders if delimitation will cause it to loose territory or strategic border outposts. Yet empirical evidence dispels the assertion that the Uzbek state was concerned with gaining territory.[57] In a border dispute with

---

[57] Indeed, military preponderance has not made Uzbekistan immune to threats from neighboring states. In May 2006, the governor of Kyrgyzstan's Batken region threatened to unilaterally close the border and prevent Uzbekistan access to its enclaves in Batken. In June of the same year, Tajikistan's much weaker and ill-equipped border guards attacked

Table 5.2. *Military expenditures and armed forces in the Central Asian region*

	Military Expenditures (in Millions of Dollars)			Armed Forces (1,000s)			Armed Forces (per 1,000 Persons)		
	1992	1995	1999	1992	1995	1999	1992	1995	1999
Kazakhstan	2,490	1,260	671	15[a]	20	33	0.9[a]	1.2	2.0
Kyrgyzstan	85[a]	135	285	12	13	12	2.6	2.9	2.6
Tajikistan	28	60	80	3	8	7	0.5	1.4	1.1
Uzbekistan	1,230	503	933	40	21[b]	60	1.9	0.9	2.5
Turkmenistan	NA	337	542	28	21	15	7.3	5.1	3.4
China	50,100	58,700	88,900	3,160	2,930	2,400	2.7	2.4	1.9

Source: U.S. State Department, *World Military Expenditures and Arms Transfers.*
[a] For year 1993.
[b] Between 1995 and 1997, Uzbek armed forces tripled in size (from 21,000 to 65,000).

Kazakhstan in 2002, the Uzbek state moved quickly to reach a settlement and handed over to its weaker northern neighbor territory that included a large reservoir, mineral resources, a hydroelectric dam, and villages populated in part by ethnic Uzbeks.[58] The Kyrgyz and Chinese cooperated in the context of a territorial dispute. These two examples recall an earlier point on territoriality: the function of a boundary may matter more than its location.

I now return to the argument established in this chapter. Through a series of case studies involving the borders of Central Asia's recently independent states, two broad claims were defended: (1) border security strategies are tailored to the needs of state building, and (2) cross-border cooperation is unlikely if neighboring states pursue divergent state-building policies (even in the context of mutual threats). Specifically, the cases demonstrated that strategies to extract revenues from national territory had a weighty effect on border policy. Economics trumped security.

Central Asian borders are unable to meet the challenges of new security threats. Yet seeing borders as inefficient would miss a more nuanced point. While lagging in their reaction to external threats, the borders make absolute sense when viewed through the lens of state building. Each new state has tailored its borders to serve economic functions and holds fast to these

Uzbek border posts. This information was obtained during the author's visit to the Osh *oblast* in the summer of 2006.

[58] BBC Monitoring, 9 September 2002, "Kazakh, Uzbek Presidents Sign Accord Resolving Border Issues," Interfax-Kazakhstan News Agency, Almaty.

policies despite the resistance of neighboring states. In light of this finding, Chapter 7 will conclude the project by explaining what international organizations can and cannot do to change border security practices and promote cooperation. But first, Chapter 6 returns to the micro level and explains a series of dynamics that affect the functioning of border organizations in Central Asia.

6

The View from Below

The previous chapter presented a bird's-eye view of how central states see their boundaries. Geographically and administratively distant from their borders, governments in capital cities formulate policies that reflect the central states' distinct preferences on what their borders ought to do for security, economy, and authority. But as Migdal (2001) demonstrates in his work, the pinnacles of the state rarely accomplish what they set out to do. The implementation of a given state policy reveals resistance at the societal level, manipulation by local agents, and the inherent limitations of the policy (Scott 1998). This chapter makes a necessary downshift to the local level to examine a crucial set of relations that affect the implementation of policy and the functioning of interstate borders. The sets of relations are those of local border authorities with (a) other boundary authorities, (b) their superiors, (c) local populations, and (d) traffickers of contraband.

These relations are examined here for a number of reasons. First, this chapter advances the theory on boundary regimes. Previously I argued that border guards who have the ability to interact with their counterparts on the other side of a shared boundary will tend to cooperate to jointly administer that border. Along the nineteenth-century Ottoman-Greek boundary (Chapter 3), Ottoman and Greek border guards used the proximity of their posts and neutral meeting grounds to discuss border administration. Over time, they devised and tested new and more complex policing procedures. By examining the presence, absence, and use of such spaces of interaction along present-day Central Asian borders, I broaden the regional and temporal focus of the project. This chapter finds a positive relationship between arenas of communication and the scale of cooperation across border authorities. When border guards are given the chance to interact with their counterparts, they pool their resources and develop cooperative procedures to police the boundary. Because of the relative newness of

Central Asian borders, it is important to note that we are unlikely to find highly evolved forms of local cooperation across boundary authorities. Thus we search for proto-boundary regimes where cross-border cooperation is in the early stages.

Second, I examine cross-border cooperation against evidence of corruption. If border guards can use arenas of communication to devise joint administrative strategies across a shared border, then it would be logical to expect such arenas to promote collusion as well. Local authorities may agree upon bribery rates for crossing the border or devise methods to assist smugglers who contravene official restrictions.

The argument here is not that boundary regimes fully resist corruption. Corruption exists along all international borders. Instead, this chapter examines two potential explanations for how jointly managed borders may limit corruption more than unilaterally managed boundaries. One plausible explanation is that boundary regimes value their administrative autonomy and thus avoid excessive corruption in order to prevent high-level intervention. Another plausible explanation is that the price of a bribe decreases along borders where guard stations are paired and policing is coordinated. Along such borders, bribe revenues must be shared among larger numbers of guards along both sides. Guards will solicit smaller bribes and attempt to make up for the shortfall through an increased volume of traffic. This drives down the price of a bribe. By contrast, along unilaterally managed borders the guards on one side are able to set the price monopolistically and the scale of individual bribes may be unrestrained.

Finally, this chapter argues that the pairing of guard posts alters the relationship of local communities to the functioning of the border. I examine a series of official and unofficial crossings to show that when border guards communicate and interact with their counterparts, they compel border populations to monitor and assist in the functioning of the border. A balance of power results between local interests in an open border and the interests of the two sides' authorities in policing that boundary. Conversely, when border guards of one side find themselves policing remotely and without contact from the other side's posts, locals have an incentive to impose their own regime for crossing the border.

The Border Authorities

Border guards who have the ability to interact with and monitor their counterparts along the other side of the border will tend toward cooperation.

Earlier chapters outlined three conditions that are necessary and jointly sufficient to trigger such cooperation: shared parameters, an arena of communication, and monitoring capacity. Along the Ottoman-Greek boundary, the two central states handed down similar objectives and goals on border management to their local administrators. The guards on the two sides benefited from the proximity of their border posts and neutral zones along the boundary. They regularly communicated with one another to pose solutions to security issues and to coordinate joint policing efforts.

But do these conditions have similar effects across time and place? The following discussion examines the conditions along three paired borders in Central Asia: the Kyrgyz-Kazakh border, the Kyrgyz-Chinese border, and the Kyrgyz-Uzbek border. These cases lack the depth and span of the Ottoman-Greek case. The investigation of that border from its inception (1830s) to its disappearance (1880s) allowed a deep study of the evolution of cooperation. As Central Asia's states have been independent only since 1991 (and some of its border guards formed only in the late 1990s), the cooperation that we attribute to the proximity mechanism is likely to be very formative.

Since all three of the cases include the border authorities of Kyrgyzstan, we are able to hold one security organization constant while examining the effects of variation with its neighbors' authorities. Each case describes the geography of the border, issues of security and policing affecting the zone, placement of the border guards, and the extent to which guards cooperate with the other side or unilaterally patrol the border. The aim of these cases is to explain why border authorities on the two sides cooperate or not and what result this choice has for the escalation of incidents and the provision of security along the border. The data in these cases is almost entirely composed of primary source material – a combination of interviews, on-site observation, legal documents, and news reports from border zones.

Before proceeding to the three cases, I provide information on local border authorities in Central Asia concerning organizational make-up, ethnic composition, and salary. While the reader will find this background useful, the information is intended to establish that such factors are not variable but constant across Central Asian states. In light of such similar starting points, the different cooperative outcomes are doubly interesting.

Along Central Asian borders, authorities belong to one of two state agencies: paramilitary and customs. Customs agents are tasked with the job of assessing duties on goods and preventing the flow of illegal items across border points. Border guards are usually conscripts with military training whose job it is to check documents and passports and police the border against the illegal flow of persons.

Border guards may be placed at official crossings or on the "green border."[1] The term "green border" refers to the parts of the boundary that fall between official crossings. As crossing is generally restricted, though not entirely prohibited, along the green border, guards stationed there must patrol in order to prevent illegal activities.[2] The green border is particularly important as most attempts to cross illegally or infiltrate another state's territory do not take place on or near official crossings.[3] Customs officials in most states, including those in Central Asia, are legally bound to confine their activities to official crossings and rely on the border guards to bring smuggling activities along the green border to their attention.[4] Such arrangements are not necessarily the norm. In his study of the early twentieth-century border between British and French Togoland, Nugent (2002) sketches a fascinating narrative that shows how armed customs agents were charged with the task of policing the entire length of the frontier.

The relationship between a given state's border guards and customs officials is supposed to be symbiotic and cooperative. In practice, relations among the agencies are fraught with tension. As the previous chapter demonstrated, the administration of a new boundary is usually tailored to meet a young state's most-favored state-building policies. Thus, if the state puts a prime value on extraction over coercion, customs agents will have a central role in administering the border, and border guards may be subordinated to assisting in that function. In Uzbekistan, customs officials were central to policing. Along the Ottoman-Greek border, by contrast, the focus was on coercion of banditry, and the collection of duties along the border lacked priority.

---

[1] There are some variations in deployment. For a number of years, Kyrgyzstan assigned officers of its National Security Services to its official crossings while assigning the green border to the Ministry of Defense. In 2002, it unified the two. Interview with Talaibek Usulbaliev, deputy to the regional manager, Border Management Program in Central Asia (BOMCA), Bishkek, Kyrgyzstan, 21 August 2006.

[2] States or local officials may make exceptions and allow people and goods to cross along the green border. Local populations living in borderlands may be given permission to access territory on the other side without going through regular posts. The earlier Ottoman-Greek case showed that border authorities sometimes encouraged unofficial crossings in order to make border administration more efficient.

[3] Interview with Tamas Kiss, project manager for Kyrgyzstan and Kazakhstan, BOMCA, Bishkek, Kyrgyzstan, 21 August 2006.

[4] Interview with Col. Kudrat Samsakovich Karimov, Osh, Kyrgyzstan, 23 August 2006.

Another reason for intraagency tension at the local level is that in Central Asia logistical facilities are usually not shared.[5] As a result, resentment builds when the housing and working facilities of one agency are better equipped than those of the other. On Turkmenistan's side of the Dashovuz border crossing, for example, the customs office is in superior shape compared to the miserable housing facilities of the border guards.

Depending on the state and on their rank, border guards receive $15–50 a month.[6] While these salaries appear meager, it is important to put them in the context of purchasing power. Uzbek and Turkmen recruits are paid on the low end of this scale, although this is offset by large subsidies for many staples. Russian recruits from the 201st division reportedly received about $30 a month. These salaries allowed the guards along the Tajik-Afghan border, where prices for available goods were extremely low, an appreciable disposable income. International officials explain that entire villages in the border zone collapsed economically when the Russian division left in 1999 and was replaced by an ethnic Tajik division with substantially less disposable income.[7]

Although Russian border divisions remained stationed along the Kyrgyz-Chinese and Tajik-Afghan borders until the late 1990s, the guards of each republic were ethnically representative of each republic's titular nationality. Border guards could communicate across the border to their counterparts in Russian. In multiethnic areas, such as the Ferghana Valley, it is not uncommon for recruits native to the district to speak two or more Central Asian languages.[8] It is not clear whether ethnic minorities in each state were recruited to the border guard or to other sections of the army. However, Central Asian states appear to have breached many Soviet practices, including the principle of rotation. This principle deployed recruits to serve in areas outside their home districts in order to foster a broader feeling of national unity and, more importantly, to prevent a situation in which recruits might fail to use coercive force against the people of their

---

[5] Confirmed on visits to several border areas and in discussions with BOMCA officials.

[6] I have been able to make these estimates after triangulating a number of statistics and statements from officials in Uzbekistan and Kyrgyzstan. Also see Jones Luong (2003b) on the need to reform and enhance the pay of border guards.

[7] Interview with Philip Peirce, regional program manager, BOMCA, Bishkek, Kyrgyzstan, 21 August 2006.

[8] Multilingualism is common in Central Asia. Moreover, in multiethnic areas there is a higher degree of mutual intelligibility among languages in the same family.

own districts (Jones 1985). Many recruits now appear to be serving near their home districts in Kyrgyzstan and Uzbekistan.

Having established a series of uniform factors that characterize the border guards of Central Asian states, I now present three case studies on local authorities and cross-border cooperation. These cases demonstrate that substantial cooperation occurs when border guards share parameters or a common view of the objectives of border management, have access to an arena for communication, and possess the ability to monitor behavior. To establish an arena for communication, it is necessary for posts to be paired along the entire length of a particular boundary, including the green border, where most illegal crossings are likely to occur. If all three conditions are present, a boundary regime will begin to evolve. If one or more of the conditions are missing, cooperation will be highly limited. If the conditions are absent or have very low values, then conflict is likely to occur over the administration of the border. The cases considered here represent each of these three scenarios.

Durable Cooperation: The Kyrgyz-Kazakh Boundary

Along the western portion of this boundary, the landscape alternates between dry mountains and densely populated plains. Bishkek, the Kyrgyz capital, is barely 30 km from the border and flooded with cars bearing Kazakh license plates, while large towns like Tokmok sit more or less adjacent to the boundary and benefit from Kazakh patrons at their animal markets. The eastern half of this border, which is the focus here, is sparse in population and mountainous. In Karakol *oblast*– a Kyrgyz region sandwiched between a wall of mountains where the Kyrgyz, Kazakh, and Chinese borders converge – a single crumbling road is the sole connection to Kazakhstan for hundreds of miles.[9] The economy of the area is heavily based on agriculture and animal husbandry. Many Kyrgyz villages are located near the Kazakh border, which is easily accessible over dozens of unofficial passes and mountain pastures.[10]

---

[9] *Oblast* refers to territorial subdivisions found in imperial Russia, the Soviet Union, and many post-Soviet states. While Kyrgyzstan continues to refer to its regions as *oblasts*, Uzbekistan now uses *viloyat*, a word of Arabic origin.

[10] Locals in one such village, Keng-Suu, spoke of a place nearby called "Soldier's Pass." It was historically used as a site of crossing to escape invading Soviet armies.

Locals in a number of villages in the border area explain that several issues arise given their proximity to the Kazakh border. These problems include property theft and disputes over land-use rights. The border creates an incentive for animal theft. Sheep and horses are stolen from the Kyrgyz side and sold on the Kazakh side, where they fetch a substantially higher price. Kyrgyz villagers also complain that Kazakhs cross the border to feed their animals illegally on Kyrgyz pastures.[11]

While such flows may seem insignificant or unimportant to security, it is important to note two things. First, such illegalities are at the core of local security concerns. The poverty rates and subsistence economy of Karakol *oblast* means that even the theft of several animals can economically devastate an entire family. Systematic theft can impoverish entire clusters of villages. Second, such disputes over property theft and land use along other stretches of Central Asia's borders have triggered violence, increased ethnic tensions, and resulted in border closure. Kyrgyzstan's Batken *oblast* in the south is an excellent case in point to be considered later.

Above and beyond issues of theft, the Kyrgyz-Kazakh border zone is also a potential site of cross-border extremism. While officials publicly describe the border as a zone of peace and stability, privately they express concerns about the smuggling of weapons to and from Kazakhstan as well as the crossing of religious extremists. The border zone is sparsely populated and mountainous, yet located between more densely populated Kazakh and Chinese regions. This creates concern that this will be the crossing of choice for individuals intent on committing acts of political violence.

The border guard base in Karakol, the administrative capital of the region, is charged with policing a 267 km stretch of the border with Kazakhstan. Kazakh border guards were first deployed to the border in 1998 from the nearby military base at Kegen. Prior to this period, Kyrgyz border guards had taken a laissez-faire attitude toward the border; they remained at the border guard base and would periodically drive two hours to the border to check the situation.[12] After 1998, Kyrgyz guards were also deployed to three posts in the area. The deployment seems to have been largely a reaction to the administrative occupation by Kazakh guards and customs officials of a point allegedly 8 km deep in Kyrgyz territory.[13] Yet this

---

[11] The author observed animals crossing the border at three different locations.

[12] As confirmed by villagers in Keng-Suu, Kyrgyzstan.

[13] In the previous chapter I argued that the Kyrgyz state insisted on delimiting the border before deploying border guards to it. The developments along the Kazakh-Kyrgyz border

dispute did not impede working relations between Kazakh and Kyrgyz guards. Border guards constructed several posts with the capacity to interface and monitor each other's activities. In the case of the disputed crossing, Kyrgyz military officers built a border guard facility that was set back a couple of kilometers from the Kazakh post. This gave them the ability to observe and communicate with the post without causing clashes over the disputed location.[14]

Since the late 1990s several cooperative practices have begun to evolve. These practices include coordinating patrols so that the limited manpower available to each side's guard can be deployed in the most efficient way possible. For instance, border post commanders coordinate their patrols so that they can secure twice the normal length of border. Kyrgyz guards patrol one stretch of border, while the Kazakh guards patrol a 10-km stretch immediately adjacent; each side trusts the other to guard the border in both directions.[15] Second, coordinating patrols requires regular communication between border guards posted to each side. This requires only the authorization of the on-site post officer, thus making the coordination an entirely local affair.[16] While these practices may not seem terribly significant, it is important to note that they are technically in violation of Kyrgyz law. According to officials working in matters of border security, a score of laws would have to be amended in order to allow security officials to talk to one another at the local level.[17] Recently, Kyrgyz and Kazakh guards have upgraded their cooperation to joint patrols and the occasional joint use of a helicopter.[18]

Cooperation is somewhat surprising given the context of the territorial dispute, which local military officials dismissed to me as a "minor issue." By contrast, an MP recently elected from the border area defines this as a major problem and says that Kyrgyz nationals are repeatedly asked to vacate the area by Kazakh guards.[19] The disputed territory, indeed, is some

do not contradict this argument. Delimitation work on the Kyrgyz-Kazakh boundary had already begun along other stretches of the border. Thus Kyrgyz central authorities attained their most desired policy even in the context of the emerging territorial dispute.

[14] Confirmed during a visit to Karkara, Kyrgyzstan.

[15] Interview with Col. Artur Maratovich, commander of Karakol Border Guard Base, Karakol, Kyrgyzstan, 14 August 2006.

[16] Ibid.

[17] Interview with Peirce.

[18] Interview with Maratovich.

[19] Interview with Japarov Sadir Nurgojoevich, member of parliament, Bishkek, Kyrgyzstan, 27 August 2006.

of the most attractive land in the area for pasturing animals and cutting grass for feed. Despite this, locals living within sight of the post maintain that they can and do access the land so long as they avoid the area immediately adjacent to the post.[20]

Limited Cooperation: The Kyrgyz-Chinese Border

Not far from the disputed territory, the Kazakh and Kyrgyz borders meet China. From this point, the Kyrgyz-Chinese border winds in a southwesterly direction to eventually meet the Tajik boundary. Under agreements Kyrgyzstan made with the Russian Federation, the border remained in the keep of Russian forces. A government resolution in October 1992 handed combined jurisdiction of the border to Russian guards and the Kyrgyz Ministry of Interior.[21] Only in 1999, following the exit of Russian guards, did the border pass to the exclusive jurisdiction of Kyrgyz agencies.[22] The border guard base in Karakol is responsible for 362 km of this border. Col. Maratovich, the commander of the Karakol border guard base, explains that insurgency, cross-border extremism, separatism, criminality, and weapons smuggling dominate the list of joint Kyrgyz-Chinese concerns along this boundary. As discussed in a previous chapter, this stretch of border appears to be Central Asia's most cooperative and jointly pacified boundary. Chinese and Kyrgyz officials moved speedily to diffuse and resolve a long-standing dispute inherited from the Soviet period over a mountainous region known as the Uzengi-Kuush. Both states attempted to foster trade and to prevent Uighur separatists from using Kyrgyz land to launch insurgencies (Fravel 2005).

Although much was made of the high-level cooperation, it did not devolve to the local level. Direct contact between Kyrgyz and Chinese guards remains minimal. Maratovich explains that, in contrast to the Kazakh border, where guards can talk to their counterparts with the permission of the post officer, his personal permission is required for Kyrgyz border guards to speak to their Chinese counterparts.[23] In the Uzengi-Kuush area, Kyrgyz and Chinese border guards can see one another, but the

---

[20] According to villagers in Karkara.

[21] See Publication of Kyrgyz Border Law, no. 530/17, 30 October 1992 (in Russian).

[22] Russian forces began to exit the country in 1998. Most were out by 1999, and the remaining few left in 2001.

[23] Some Chinese border guards speak Kyrgyz and Uighur. This means that they can communicate with their Kyrgyz counterparts without interpreters.

mountainous terrain keeps border guards from being able to approach and interact with the other side's posts. Maratovich foresees more Kazakh-style cooperation but plays down the extent to which they will police the border jointly with the Chinese guards. Relief maps of the Chinese-Kyrgyz border demonstrate that the main impediment to cross-border cooperation is geographic. Virtually all of the 362 km of the zone under the jurisdiction of the Karakol base ranges in elevation from 4,000 to 7,000 meters. The Kyrgyz frontier lands are particularly mountainous and generally uninhabited. This is in contrast to the Chinese side, where the mountains fall off rather quickly, giving way to populated plains. This means Kyrgyz guards stationed in the area would have to be equipped with food, gas, and housing for long stretches of time. This would be expensive and perhaps unnecessary; of the thirty mountain passes in the area that may be used to cross over the border unofficially, only two are passable year round.[24] Creating interfacing posts where the Kyrgyz and Chinese guards could interact with and monitor one another is a practical impossibility along much of the border. Border guard posts further south along the border at the Torugart and Irkeshtam (Erkesh-tam) passes are the exceptions. All road traffic headed to and from China must pass through these two crossings.

In order to make up for the geographic constraints on cooperation, Kyrgyz soldiers stationed in the region attempt to forge links with local populations. In exchange for assistance in policing and for providing intelligence on people moving in and out of villages in border zones, soldiers are authorized to reward locals. Border guards of the Karkara base occasionally give locals petty cash or petrol in exchange for providing information on individuals that they suspect are engaging in separatist or violent activities.[25]

Along this stretch of the boundary, the links between border guards and local populations are more durable than those between the Kyrgyz and Chinese border services. Each side unilaterally polices the border, with little local coordination. Cross-border cooperation is limited despite the ability of some guards and captains to communicate with their foreign counterparts via technology such as wireless devices. Such technology is not a sufficient substitute for the regular face-to-face communication that occurs

---

[24] Fearon and Laitin (2003) argue that rough terrain gives rebel forces the opportunity to challenge state control and hide from state forces. However, the Kyrgyz-Chinese border suggests that there may be limits to such opportunities, particularly at extreme elevations.
[25] Interview with Maratovich.

when border posts of two sides are paired and placed near one another. There are several reasons for this. Not all border guards will have access to such devices, which may be limited to border captains or only to some posts. Communication via wireless devices also does not allow for unfettered, simultaneous, and constant communication along the entire length of the border. Geographic pairing of border posts is necessary in order for guards to have the unfettered ability to communicate with and monitor the activities of their foreign counterparts.

Tension and Escalation: The Kyrgyz-Uzbek Boundary

The situation on the Kyrgyz-Uzbek boundary is in sharp contrast to the stretches of border previously discussed. For much of the period from 1998 to the present, the border was the site of escalation and violent incidents. These incidents included violence between Uzbek and Kyrgyz border guards, violence between locals from the two sides of the border, violence between locals and border guards, and violence perpetrated by militants on locals and border guards.

Much of the Kyrgyz-Uzbek boundary snakes through the densely populated Ferghana Valley. In contrast to the surrounding arid mountains, the valley is a deep green for much of the year. Rivers, reservoirs, and canals fed by water from upstream mountains sustain the valley's cotton fields. The border that runs through the valley divides villages, fields, and markets.[26] Illegal trade, drug trafficking, and cross-border militancy dominate official concerns.

Unlike the situation at the Chinese-Kyrgyz border, there are few geographic constraints to posting guards directly on the borderline. The Uzbeks unilaterally posted guards on the Kyrgyz border in the Ferghana in the mid-1990s.[27] Kyrgyz guards were not posted to the border until 1999 and then only to official crossings.[28] Locals in many areas explain that while they would see Uzbek guards patrolling the border, Kyrgyz guards were not present. Even along some official crossings, the Kyrgyz side had not posted guards. This severely disadvantaged Kyrgyz nationals who had to

---

[26] In some cases the border passes through people's back yards. One government official grumbled that some people technically need passports to use their own toilets. Interview with Baktibek Ajibekovich Usupov, head representative of the Kyrgyz Ministry of Foreign Affairs to the South, Osh, Kyrgyzstan, 23 August 2006.

[27] Confirmed by traders at Kara-Suu and by villagers in Burgandiya, Kyrgyzstan.

[28] Interview with Col. Kudrat Samsaskovich Karimov, Osh, Kyrgyzstan, 23 August 2006.

submit to the scrutiny of Uzbek guards while ethnic Uzbeks were able to enter Kyrgyz territory without checks.[29]

Uzbekistan's unilateral militarization of the Ferghana border and the lack of Kyrgyz posts meant that there could be little coordination, much less cooperation, in policing the border. At best, border guards escalate incidents, attributing them to the indolence or deliberate provocation of the other side's guard. At worst, armed guards encounter each other in disputed territory with violent results.[30]

International officials working to train Uzbek and Kyrgyz border guards explain three tendencies among border guards: (a) an overreliance on equipment and weapons, (b) a tendency to escalate events upward, and (c) the taking of unpredictable and destabilizing decisions to open, move, or close posts by commanders in the field.[31]

These tendencies suggest that local authority has run amok. This is especially surprising on the Uzbek side, where the state has invested heavily in directly monitoring the activities of its agents along its border in order to prevent such escalation and unpredictability. Reports of disputes and events at the border usually move from the on-site location, to the border post, to the border chief, to the border detachment, to the head of the border services in Bishkek, to the Ministry of Interior, and finally to the Ministry of Foreign Affairs. The minister of foreign affairs then contacts the Uzbek ambassador, triggering a symmetric downward movement.[32] Two weeks of time are lost communicating information that the two side's border captains could convey instantly through a face-to-face meeting.

Despite the aggressive policing styles of the Uzbek military, overreaction and inefficiency characterize the border. First, Uzbek security forces routinely categorize a wide array of incidents as cases of militancy or extremism.[33] Second, Uzbek policing demonstrates elements of inefficiency. Despite the heavy manpower invested in policing the border,

---

[29] Interview with Jerome Bouyjou, director of the OSCE Osh field office, Bishkek, Kyrgyzstan, 27 August 2006.

[30] In September 2005, for example, Uzbek border troops on patrol ambushed a Kyrgyz patrol on a disputed section of the border. BBC Monitoring, 12 November 2003, "Kyrgyz-Uzbek Tension Builds Up over Disputed Border Post Near Sokh Enclave," Global News Wire, Bishkek; and 15 September 2005, "Kyrgyz, Uzbek Border Troops at Talks after Incident," AKI Press, Bishkek.

[31] Interview with Peirce.

[32] Interview with Kiss. Much of this reporting and escalation happens via cell phone.

[33] Particularly striking is the overuse of the word "terrorist" to describe those illegally crossing the border (Megoran 2005, 2006). Uzbek guards tend to profile border crossers by

between 1999 and 2004 militants demonstrated ample ability to evade the static policing tactics of the Uzbek military.[34]

Following an uprising in the summer of 2005 in Uzbekistan's Andijon province near the Kyrgyz border (Chivers 2005), a period of unusual cooperation on security issues began between the Uzbek and Kyrgyz governments.[35] This cooperation represented a sudden thaw in the otherwise tense relations between the two states. A central aspect of this cooperation has included joint security measures in the Ferghana Valley against suspected militants. Officials explain that Uzbek security services appear to have been given permission to operate in Kyrgyz territory in the Ferghana.[36] This suggests that the border is neither legitimately open nor secure. To make up for the lack of cooperation at the level of the border and for the inefficient provision of security, the Uzbek state now conducts its operations on Kyrgyz territory.

The case studies presented here provide ample support for the argument on how boundary regimes form (see Table 6.1). In order for border guards to jointly manage a boundary, three conditions are required: shared parameters of administrative tasks, an arena for communication, and the ability to monitor behavior and compliance. In the case of the Kazakh-Kyrgyz border, where all three conditions obtain, the border authorities of the two sides cooperate locally to jointly police the border. In the process, they sidestep the controversial and potentially destabilizing issue of the territorial dispute along their border. Along the Kyrgyz-Chinese border, guards hold common views of the objectives of boundary management. However, they lack the ability to communicate regularly across the border because of geographic constraints. As a result, there is little coordination of policing at the local level. Instead, cooperation is limited to the diplomatic level and to annual border guard conferences in capital cities.

---

distinguishing marks such as beards or tattoos. Strip searches to locate tattoos are not uncommon.

[34] The IMU used Tajik territory to attack Kyrgyz and Uzbek border areas in 1999. In February 1999 it is alleged to have conducted a failed assassination attempt against the Uzbek president. By 2001 IMU militants had successfully evaded Uzbek border patrols. They used Tajik territory adjacent to the border to store weapons until they could be smuggled over the border for operations. The policing style of the Uzbek military appears to have been so ineffectual that in one case IMU operatives infiltrated the border and attacked the units from behind.

[35] See *Times of Central Asia*, 17 August 2006, "Anti-Terror Crackdown May Target Uzbeks."

[36] As explained to the author by a high-level official in the Kyrgyz Ministry of Migration (name withheld).

Table 6.1. *Policing and cooperative outcomes by 2006*

Border	Policing Issues	Interaction Capacity	Policing and Cooperation	Territorial Dispute
Kyrgyz-Kazakh	Extremists; drug and weapons smuggling; animal theft	High: posts generally interface	Jointly policed locally; substantial cooperation at diplomatic level	Ongoing since 1998: Karkara dispute; delimitation not complete
Kyrgyz-Uzbek	Extremists; drug and weapons smuggling; illegal labor; smuggled cotton and petrol	Limited: some posts are paired	Unilaterally policed by each side; heaviest policing done by the Uzbek side; tension at local and diplomatic levels over border policing	Ongoing since 1999: disputes around enclaves; delimitation not complete
Kyrgyz-Chinese	Extremists and separatists; weapons smuggling; stolen scrap metal	Very limited: geography prevents pairing of posts	Unilaterally policed by Chinese side; high-level diplomatic cooperation	Resolved: Uzengi-Kuush dispute resolved in 2003; dispute dates back to nineteenth century
Kyrgyz-Tajik	Drug smuggling; extremists; illegal logging and pasturing	Very limited: posts not paired	Unilaterally policed by both sides with few Kyrgyz border guards and very few Tajik guards; tension at local and diplomatic levels	Residual, undeclared dispute: Tajik refugees and migrants encroaching on Kyrgyz land since mid-1990s; no delimitation progress

Finally, along the Uzbek-Kyrgyz border, conflict and escalation prevail over cooperation. Along this border, none of the three conditions are fully present at the local level. Border guards lack the ability to communicate with their counterparts on the other side, and they have been given divergent administrative goals by their respective states. The Kyrgyz state formed a border guard vested with the goal of promoting the movement of goods and people, while the Uzbek guards were charged with the task of restricting flows.

Although the findings provide ample evidence for the theory, it is important to be circumspect. Central Asia's states are still in the early stages of statehood, and international organizations actively fund cross-border initiatives. Such initiatives may be able to override some of the self-destructive policing practices in the region. The role of international organizations in border management will be discussed in the concluding chapter. More immediate to these cases are issues of corruption and trafficking. Such illicit activities are a prominent feature along all international borders. This is the focus of the following section.

Trafficking and Corruption

Intuitively, one would expect boundary regimes to facilitate collusion and corruption among border authorities. Such regimes place the border authorities of two states in proximity to one another. If border guards and customs officials are able to communicate regularly with the other side's local authorities in order to coordinate policing, it is possible that they may come to use such arenas of interaction to collude for profit. Two border posts may collude to protect smuggling networks or to craft a mutual agreement on the amount of goods or currency to extract from those carrying legitimate goods across the border. If state agents operate with substantial administrative autonomy, they may have the ability to hide corrupt practices from central state authorities.

Such arguments would rely on the precarious assumption that the central state has an interest in fighting trafficking and corruption. This is not the case in much of Central Asia. The previous chapter showed that Tajikistan's governing authorities have a strong interest in protecting smuggling networks to benefit the state and enhance the personal revenues of officials. The border has been crafted to allow drug networks safe passage. In Kyrgyzstan, positions in the customs service, police, and border guard are regularly bought and sold, with the profit from the sales being distributed to higher-level officials (International Crisis Group 2002b). Claims about the origin of corruption along interstate borders must therefore take into account the broader environment.

Here I will discuss five Central Asian border crossings and assess whether there is a correlation between the form of policing (joint, unilateral, cooperative) and the scale of corruption along that crossing (see Map 6.1). I attempt to gauge the scale of corruption, the types of products being smuggled, and how illicit activity affects border guard relations with their superiors. Kyrgyz border and customs officials are present at all the crossings. Otherwise, the five crossings vary on a number of criteria: neighboring state, level

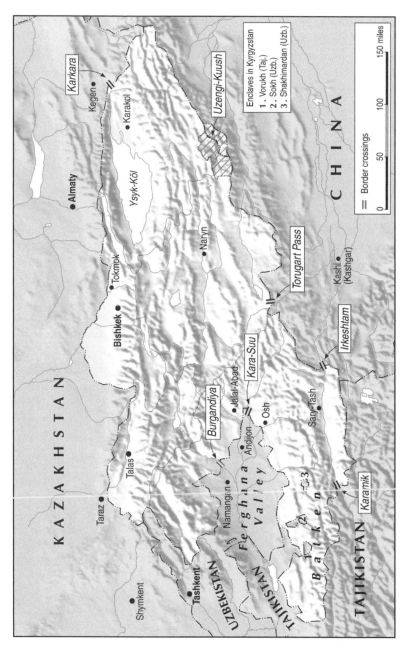

Map 6.1. Kyrgyz border crossings. *Source:* Phillip Schwartzberg, Meridian Mapping.

145

of cooperation, types of illegal and rent-seeking activities, and the official or unofficial nature of the crossing.

Irkeshtam crossing (Kyrgyz-Chinese border): Irkeshtam is one of two official crossings between Kyrgyzstan and western China. The post is open five days a week during daylight hours. It is a moderately trafficked crossing used mostly by lorries bringing cheap Chinese consumer goods into southern Kyrgyzstan and onward to the Ferghana Valley. Limited numbers of individuals truck in heavy volumes of goods. The goods headed into China are primarily animal by-products (wool and leather) but also include substantial scrap metals pilfered from sites in Kyrgyzstan and Uzbekistan.[37]

The distance between the Chinese and Kyrgyz customs posts in Irkeshtam is approximately five kilometers. There is no cooperation or regular contact between the posts. The border guard posts are closer together, yet as discussed earlier, local-level contacts between Chinese and Kyrgyz guards are rare and require high-level authorization.

The value of the Chinese-Kyrgyz border trade officially tops $100 million.[38] Truck drivers are known to pay bribes to reduce the valuation of the goods they are carrying in order to reduce their tax burdens.[39] Kyrgyz officials at the post seem to have been particularly guilty of suppressing valuation estimates. This became embarrassingly clear when a Chinese official visiting the Kara-Suu market announced the value of goods passing through Irkeshtam to be three times higher than the value Kyrgyz customs officials had declared earlier.[40]

Kara-Suu market crossing (Kyrgyz-Uzbek crossing): Consumer goods that pass through Irkeshtam eventually make it to the massive market in Kara-Suu. In Soviet times, Kara-Suu was a small farming town bisected by an

---

[37] Throughout Kyrgyzstan there is ample evidence of the illegal export of pilfered scrap metal. Manhole covers go missing, and tin and aluminum domes are often stripped from tombs. Uzbek authorities also complain about theft of metal and copper wiring.

[38] In 2000, Kyrgyz-Chinese trade was valued at $117.6 million (International Crisis Group 2001b). More recently, the value of trade at the Irkeshtam crossing was valued at just over $100 million. Interview with Col. Kudrat Samsaskovich Karimov, Osh, Kyrgyzstan, 23 August 2006.

[39] Usually at border crossings there are at least two options. Guards either let goods through with a bribe and without valuating the truckloads, or they add a bribe on top of the customs tax. The latter form of corruption raises the total price of a bribe. Traders find the former more attractive and will lobby for a higher bribe rather than a lower valuation (Schleifer and Vishny 1993).

[40] Interview with Abdimomun Joldoshev, regional director, International Business Council, Osh, Kyrgyzstan, 25 August 2006.

irrigation canal that served as the line between the Uzbek and Kyrgyz SSR. In recent years Kara-Suu market has become the largest in the region. The cost of purchasing a truck-size crate in the market for storage and retail use skyrocketed from $700 in 2001 to $20,000 in 2006.[41] The Kara-Suu market is located adjacent to the border on the Kyrgyz side. The town on the Uzbek side has the same name, but with a different spelling (Qorasuv). Uzbeks bring agricultural products such as cottonseed oil to the market and return with consumer goods and agricultural products that are scarce on the Uzbek side.[42]

Crossing the border into Kara-Suu involves traversing a footbridge over the irrigation canal. This crossing is unofficial. Uzbek locals constructed the border bridge illegally in order to have access to the Kyrgyz market. The Uzbek and Kyrgyz posts were constructed there subsequently in order to monitor traffic. It is estimated that nearly 40,000 people cross the bridge each day during daylight hours.[43] Less than fifty meters separate Uzbek and Kyrgyz border guard facilities.[44] In the summer of 2006, the bribery rate averaged five to ten Kyrgyz som per round trip crossing (ten to twenty cents).[45] Porters who shuttle numerous times across the border each day reportedly pay a flat per-day fee that is good so long as the same border guards are on shift. Locals working in the market explain that the border crossing is generally efficient despite its unofficial status. Kara-Suu is one of the few places on the border where Uzbek and Kyrgyz officials have direct and sustained unofficial contact with one another. The result is that local border authorities have developed conventions on how to monitor this unofficial post in order to balance openness with personal profit.[46]

Burgandiya crossing (Kyrgyz-Uzbek border): The Kyrgyz town of Burgandiya is a small farming community located adjacent to the border in the north Ferghana Valley. In Soviet times, the most direct means of traveling from Kara-Suu to Burgandiya was a two-hour drive over the Uzbek

---

[41] Ibid.

[42] Potatoes are sometimes in short supply on the Uzbek side of the Ferghana Valley. Reportedly the government discourages the cultivation of potatoes in the Ferghana as they harbor pests that are harmful to the more lucrative cotton crop.

[43] Interview with Jerome Bouyjou, director of OSCE Osh field office, Bishkek, Kyrgyzstan, 27 August 2006.

[44] Observed during an on-site visit.

[45] Confirmed in discussions with local traders during a visit to the border market.

[46] The volume of traffic at this post is staggering compared to the traffic at a nearby official crossing, Dostuk. Dostuk, a few miles to the south of Kara-Suu crossing, is the official road crossing between the two states. It was virtually deserted on the day of the author's visit.

SSR. The drive now takes nearly five hours via a hastily constructed bypass road that skirts the easternmost tip of Uzbekistan. Along this drive one sees makeshift piles of rubble, fences, and wire blocking roads that formerly gave open access to Uzbek territory.

Cotton farming is an important source of income along both sides of the border. However, on the Uzbek side cotton farmers are required to sell to the state at a fixed price below world market rates, while on the Kyrgyz side market prices prevail.[47] The farms on the Kyrgyz side are also at a higher elevation, which means that the picking season in Kyrgyzstan is later than the season in Uzbekistan.

Border villages such as Burgandiya are appealing destinations for Uzbek migrant laborers and cotton smugglers. During the picking and priming seasons, Uzbek laborers sneak over the border and head to the village center. A villager from Burgandiya explains that on one spring day he was sent by his father to find people to help prime the plants.[48] He showed up rather late, at 6:30 A.M., only to find 150 people waiting for work. He choose a group of workers, took them to the field, and gave them food and water. In the evening he paid them and gave them tea, bread, and water and then escorted them back to the center of the village, where money changers were waiting to convert the workers' wages into Uzbek currency.[49] Workers are paid by the kilo and can make three to four dollars a day picking cotton if productive. Cotton smugglers would also head to Burgandiya, carrying 60–70 kg of cotton on their backs and wading across the canal or ducking across the barbed wire along the border. The sale of the cotton on the Kyrgyz side was often clear profit as it was taken from state holdings.

In earlier years, when the price of gas was higher on the Kyrgyz side, villagers recall a brisk trade in smuggled petrol. Young men with three-wheeled motorcycles replaced the passenger seat in the basket with large tin drums that held 200 liters of diesel and gas. In full view of Uzbek border guards, they placed wooden planks over the narrowest point of the boundary channel and crossed over into Uzbekistan. One trip earned a profit of three

---

[47] Villagers report that at one point the son of the former president unsuccessfully tried to force farmers to sell cotton to him at depressed prices.

[48] Cotton plants are primed in the spring by clipping the tops in order to prevent the plant from growing too high.

[49] Money traders with huge bags of Uzbek currency wait in the center of the village for the workers to covert their wages before going back over the border. The bags of cash are large – not because of the amount of income earned, but rather because of the low value of the *O'zbek so'mi*. The largest banknote of 1,000 was equivalent to 80 U.S. cents in August 2006.

or four dollars. Several trips meant much more. Uzbek guards received the equivalent of twenty to fifty cents to look the other way. Locals explain that Kyrgyz border guards were deployed only to official crossings and that they were rarely deployed to the green border. This meant that the Uzbeks effectively governed the crossing regime and unilaterally determined bribery rates.

Karamik crossing (Kyrgyz-Tajik border): The Karamik posting is an official crossing on Kyrgyzstan's southern border with Tajikistan. Medirbek Sabirov, head of the Customs Office in Osh *oblast*, explains that the post is to remain open twenty-four hours a day according to an agreement reached between the Tajik and Kyrgyz governments. While the constant hours of the post are meant to facilitate the movement of goods and people, it remains one of the most remote and least-used posts in the country.[50] The Kyrgyz side of the post is poorly provisioned, and guards do not like to serve there. Officials working with international organizations claim that along posts such as Karamik, Tajik officials are less systematic about making people pay bribes to cross.[51] Part of the answer here may lie in the little-known fact that much of the Kyrgyz south was overrun by ethnic Tajiks fleeing the civil war in the 1990s. Having reached a critical mass, they run many localities and own businesses and farm land. They have developed closer relations with Tajik border guards, who are sympathetic and less willing to solicit bribes.

Officials also state that border guards in Tajikistan are instructed and paid from above to leave corridors open to the drug trade (see Chapter 5). While it is difficult to ascertain with certainty the scale and level of corruption at the Karamik post, it seems to be substantively different from that at other crossings. If Tajik guards are indeed instructed by their superiors to allow the drug routes to operate without interference, then it is highly possible that they are not systematically soliciting bribes from local populations. From the local perspective, this top-down corruption of the Tajik guards has a beneficial effect on the openness of the border. At the same time, it may explain Kyrgyz unwillingness to serve at that post if opportunities to solicit bribes from locals are unavailable.

Karkara crossing (Kyrgyz-Kazakh border): Although the Karkara border area was discussed earlier, little was said about corruption. Discussions

---

[50] Interview with Medirbek Sabirov, head of the Osh Customs Office, Osh, Kyrgyzstan, 25 August 2006. It appears that the United States government bankrolled the construction of the Kyrgyz customs post. In the summer of 2006 it was not yet in use.

[51] Interview with Bouyjou.

with border officials and locals in the area suggest that there is little or no corruption along this border posting. Yet statements about the lack of corruption are unreliable; individuals do not usually incriminate themselves or their colleagues. Thus it is important to use alternate indicators to gauge the incidence of corruption along this border.

Changes in criminal patterns in recent years are instructive. Animals used to be stolen and shuttled across the border post's area in full view with the complicity of border guards. Now it is more common that animals stolen in Kyrgyzstan are shuttled, not across the border, but to markets in other parts of the country. Kazakh buyers frequent the Kyrgyz border market in Tokmok, which is a known destination for stolen animals.[52] The border zone near Tokmok is out of the jurisdiction of the Karkara border guard base. Faced with tighter border policing, criminal networks now send stolen animals to domestic markets rather than over the border.

The case studies indicate an inconsistent relationship between the proximity of border posts and corruption dynamics. At both the Karkara post (Kyrgyz-Kazakh border) and the Kara-Suu post (Kyrgyz-Uzbek border), guards have the capacity to interact regularly with their counterparts. Yet Karkara demonstrates little obvious corruption, while bribes are ubiquitous at the Kara-Suu footbridge. What might explain this? The deployment of border guards at Kara-Suu market crossing was a rather exceptional measure. Local populations created an unauthorized international crossing when they constructed a footbridge over a canal to connect the Uzbek side to the Kyrgyz market. Uzbek (and later Kyrgyz) authorities reactively stationed guards to maintain a symbolic presence at the crossing and to monitor public security. Border officials bribed their way onto positions at those posts in order to extract revenues from the shuttle traders who operated exclusively at the footbridge on the crossing. The proximity of the Uzbek and Kyrgyz posts probably made it easier to agree on a standard for soliciting tolls.

The cases also reveal that the scale of corruption on the Uzbek side is rather incongruous with the level of control the Uzbek state exerts on its agents. Despite the oversight that the president's office and the national security services have over border administration, corruption and rent seeking prevail among Uzbek border guards.[53]

---

[52] As explained by locals using that market.

[53] Uzbek Law on the Border, no. 8820-I, 20 August 1999; also see the revised version, no. 621-II, 30 April 2004 (in Russian).

One way of accounting for this dynamic may be to look to the literature on the principal-agent problem and the dilemmas of effective monitoring. Solnick argues that state agencies and institutions are effectively composed of a chain of linked principal-agent relations (1996, 1998). Local agents and bureaucrats (including the border authorities discussed here) will abuse their authority in the absence of effective monitoring and sanctioning from above.[54] While in the Uzbek case high-level state authorities already monitor the activities of the border guard and hand down very rigid performance guidelines and policing strategies, it is possible that the monitoring channels are not sufficient to extinguish the constant opportunities for personal profit that thousands of border guards have at the local level.

Another way to account for the corruption dynamics is to argue that corruption is officially tolerated. The cabinet and the national security services may allow border guards to collect bribes that allow a petty shuttle trade to operate in consumer goods and cross-border day labor so long as guards suppress the drug trade. Evidence for this conclusion is the fact that Afghan and Tajik drug-smuggling networks prefer to bypass Uzbekistan and to traffic heroin across Kyrgyzstan. An international organization official in Kyrgyzstan explained that Tajik smugglers have found a much more willing partner on the Kyrgyz side than among Uzbek authorities; Uzbek authorities have secured steady revenues from the autarchic economy and do not require the additional revenue the drug trade would provide.[55]

The Role of Local Populations

Thus far, this chapter has discussed the factors that permit or inhibit cooperation across border authorities. Implicit in this discussion was a treatment of populations living in frontier areas either as subjects of control or as individuals engaged in illicit activities. Such consideration is incomplete. Earlier chapters on the Ottoman-Greek boundary demonstrated that frontier populations may develop symbiotic relationships with border authorities. Along the Ottoman-Greek boundary, frontier villagers contributed to the

---

[54] For more on the principal-agent problem and solutions for effective monitoring, see Bac (1996), Laitin and Fearon (2003), Ross (2004), and Olsen and Torsvik (1998). For alternatives to and criticisms of top-down monitoring, see Ostrom (1990), Anechiarico and Jacobs (1996), De Sardan (1999), and Acemoğlu and Verdier (2000).

[55] Interview, name withheld. The official also proposed that Uzbek authorities probably do not wish to allow well-organized drug smuggling networks to organize and operate in their territory. This would increase criminal activity and potentially rival state authority.

administration of the border by monitoring the activities of border posts located near their villages, providing housing and sustenance for guards when it was necessary, complaining to authorities if guards were indolent in policing and providing for security, and participating in special patrols alongside border guards when the security situation called for it.

Two factors cajoled locals into playing such a supporting role. Along both sides of the boundary, the states enacted a series of laws requiring the assistance of border populations in security matters. Yet legal obligations may not explain the activities of populations at the border, especially if these laws go unenforced. In the Ottoman-Greek case study, I demonstrated that legal obligations had only a small effect on the obligations and service of locals in monitoring the border. More important are the cooperative networks that Ottoman and Greek guards shared across the line. The stronger the ties and cooperation across border authorities, the more likely frontier localities were to participate in the administration of the boundary and to monitor its security affairs. Prior chapters have presented examples of villages contributing to border security by helping Ottoman and Greek border guards chase down bandits. Such local contributions were more likely to take place where guards had a strong dynamic of cross-border cooperation.[56] This has resulted in a balance between the needs of local populations to have the border open for vital crossings and the needs of border authorities to secure the frontier against lawlessness and violence.

Much as in the Ottoman case, Central Asian states have laws on border protection that include explicit provisions on the obligations of local populations. While Kyrgyzstan's legal regulations are generally negative and outline restrictions on local activities in border zones,[57] the Uzbek law on borders is specific regarding the obligations of citizens in border zones. Statutes 36–38 of Uzbekistan's border law vest citizens with responsibility for contributing intelligence, material, and labor for the upkeep and policing of the state border.[58] However, such legal directives are rarely enforced.

---

[56] Yet the Ottoman-Greek case also demonstrates how segments of the population may also destabilize cooperation. Locals at the Sourbe crossing routinely manipulated Ottoman and Greek border guards in order to have unfettered access to the other side. In another instance, locals in the Ottoman Empire petitioned the sultan to invest substantial sums in border infrastructure in their vicinity and exaggerated the insecurity of the area. This was a rather ironic turn of events. The border had become more secure because of cross-border cooperation, yet some local populations did not want to lose state investment.

[57] Law of the State Border of the Kyrgyz Republic, 18 February 1999 (in Russian).

[58] Uzbek Law on the Border, 20 August 1999 and 30 April 2004.

Instead, the spatial positioning of border authorities and the extent to which they interact with their counterparts affects how local populations contribute to the administration of the boundary. At the high-traffic Kara-Suu market crossing, where Uzbek and Kyrgyz guards operate in close proximity, an instructive event took place. Uzbek border guards attempted to stop a woman with her goods on their side of the border.[59] The argument degenerated into a tussle between the woman and several guards. The guards injured the woman's arm and attracted the attention of a group of Uzbek porters shuttling through the boundary. The porters accused the guards of violating proper behavior and began to pelt them with stones. Though well armed, the guards did not fire warning shots or threaten the porters with their weapons; instead, they retreated to a safe position and retaliated by throwing stones back at the porters.

This anecdote demonstrates the informal yet distinct role that locals may play as monitors and enforcers of the border regime. Locals censured the guards in response to an infraction of common procedure. Both sides operated with restraint that allowed the quick restoration of order. The border crossing was closed for less than twenty minutes and reopened once the woman was carried off to a local clinic. This example indicates (a) the willingness of Uzbek locals employed on the boundary to sanction their own state's authorities, (b) the capping of violence short of lethal force, and (c) the power relations between impoverished shuttle traders and the Uzbek and Kyrgyz guards who collude to exact tolls at this unofficial crossing.

The role of local populations is channeled in a fundamentally different direction further west along this boundary, where the posts of Uzbek and Kyrgyz guards are not paired. In May 2006, Kyrgyz guards reportedly roughed up two young Uzbek nationals they caught on the Kyrgyz side and booted them back over the border. Taking matters into their own hands, 200 villagers from the Uzbek village of Kushyar invaded the Kyrgyz side, smashing cars and property in retaliation for the border guards' behavior.[60]

Even further to the west, along the boundaries of Kyrgyzstan's Batken region, ethnic Tajiks kidnapped three Kyrgyz border guards from their

---

[59] This incident was recounted to the author by a trader at the Kara-Suu market. I confirmed this incident later with a journalist of *Vercherniy Bishkek* in Osh, Kyrgyzstan. Their names have been withheld.

[60] The same journalist described this incident. For a similar incident, see BBC Monitoring International Reports, 29 September 2004, "Kyrgyz Border Guards Stoned by Uzbek Residents," Asia Africa Intelligence Wire, Osh.

posts and spirited them deep inside Tajikistan. Locals organized the kidnapping in order to punish the border guards for killing a Tajik national. The individual had been killed inside Kyrgyz territory while collecting wood with friends. The Kyrgyz border guards claimed that they had only fired warning shots.[61] The incident raced up the chain of local and regional administration, drawing into the conflict the Tajik and Kyrgyz Ministries of Foreign Affairs. While local Tajik officials offered to speedily return the border guards, Kyrgyz officials preferred to let the guards languish in a Tajik prison for several weeks in order to complete the proper paperwork and avoid giving a precedent for future kidnappings or other extra-territorial dispensation of justice.

These examples should not be seen as motivated by ethnic tensions. Much as in the first example involving the Kara-Suu porters, economic scarcity and survival frame the actions of local populations. Unlike the Kara-Suu porters, locals in the last two examples demonstrated (a) a willingness to sanction the other side's boundary authorities, (b) an inclination for unrestrained force, and (c) a shift in the scale of the conflict that strategically brought in other locals to overwhelm boundary authorities. In these examples, the lack of contact across Kyrgyz and Tajik authorities permitted local populations to impose their own preference for an unrestricted border.

Given the absence of cooperation across border guard agencies and the anemic diplomatic ties between the Tajik, Uzbek, and Kyrgyz Foreign Ministries, local and regional authorities have attempted to cultivate cross-border links with their counterparts in order to resolve border-related conflicts. Village elders in border communities meet to discuss problems of proximity to the border and will occasionally adjudicate and punish those from their communities who commit illegal acts on the other side. Fearon and Laitin (1996) argue that such intracommunal activities may prevent local incidents from spiraling into broader ethnic conflict. Following the disturbance in Kushyar village discussed earlier, the Uzbek and Kyrgyz governors of the two bordering districts met and pledged to cooperate. One agreement determined that flocks of animals and those tending them may cross the border for grazing so long as they follow the rules and regulations of local pasture schedules and pay nominal local tariffs. While such agreements are mostly an ad hoc reaction to particular incidents, they serve as

---

[61] See *The Times of Central Asia*, 16 June 2005, "Captured Border Guards to be Returned to the Motherland."

The View from Below

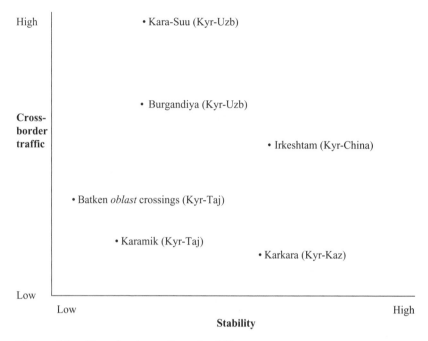

Figure 6.1. Cross-border traffic and stability.

an alternative way of managing the border in the absence of credible state authority.

Conclusions

Figure 6.1 summarizes the findings of the chapter. It locates particular segments and crossings of Kyrgyzstan's borders relative to two indicators. The *x*-axis indicates the stability of the boundary. Stability here does not imply the fixity of the border; rather, it refers to the incidence of violence and escalation and to the predictability of regulations governing crossing along that border point. Irkeshtam, along the Kyrgyz-Chinese border, registered no incidents of escalation or conflict among border authorities and functions at reliable and predictable hours even though the requirements for clearing customs remain vague. It thus measures high in stability. The *y*-axis measures the volume of cross-border traffic in terms of the number of crossings performed on a daily basis. Tens of thousands of crossings take place on busy market days at the Kara-Suu footbridge, while crossings along sections of the Kyrgyz-Tajik border in the Batken *oblast* and Karkara can be measured in mere scores.

The figure contains two implications. First, instability does not necessarily suppress cross-border traffic. The reverse may be true. Even low volumes of traffic may be sufficient to destabilize a boundary when there is a lack of local cooperation between border authorities. Along the remote Kyrgyz-Tajik border, the attempts of small rural communities to access scarce resources on the other side have led to violent escalation. The lack of regular contact between Kyrgyz and Tajik guards means that incidents of animal theft, foraging, and illegal use of pastures cannot be resolved locally. Such events have disproportionate effects on Kyrgyz-Tajik diplomatic relations. Second, the figure highlights the distinct dynamics of the local and macro levels of border organization. If the previous chapter demonstrated that the states used economic motives to standardize the functioning and administration of their borders, this chapter demonstrates how those policies were frustrated at the local level. Kyrgyz state preferences for a border that would be open to trade and managed cooperatively found willing partners in Kazakhstan and China. But these policies proved disastrous along the Tajik border, where Tajik officials left the border undelimited and unpoliced, exposing limited numbers of Kyrgyz guards to hostile Tajik locals. The figure shows a similar tension for Uzbek policies. The Uzbek state tailored its border organization to the needs of its autarchic economic policies yet failed to suppress the flow of goods and people across its borders. At Burgandiya, Uzbekistan lost control of its guards, who allowed illegal trade in petrol and cotton in exchange for slim bribes. On its side of the Kara-Suu crossing (Qorasuv), the Uzbek state lost control of the local level in a different way. Although Kara-Suu today appears as a formal crossing with a heavy presence of armed Uzbek guards, it is perhaps the best example of how local dynamics can frustrate official, high-level policies. Kara-Suu was established as an unofficial crossing by local traders in defiance of state border control policies. In legalizing the crossing, the Uzbek state established its presence but also admitted the defeat of its border control directives at the hands of locals.

7

Implications and Interventions

In its simplest form, my argument maintains that border security depends on institutional design and not on a state's wealth or military capacity. If many borders in troubled states do not succeed in keeping out insurgents, trapping smugglers, or deterring bandits, this failure can be attributed to the way border control institutions are conceived and constructed at the micro and macro levels. These levels reveal a paradox: on the one hand, states micromanage their borders in order to enhance their authority. On the other hand, the surrender of authority to local boundary administrators ultimately leaves states more secure.

In this chapter, I recap my argument at each level while referring to a number of examples from my cases. I discuss the implications of this argument for the future study of boundaries and for policy makers. The findings of the prior chapters are particularly important given the growing involvement of the United States, the European Union, and the United Nations in assisting new or troubled states with border security. Here I discuss a number of these programs, explain how they attempt to target the micro- and macro-level dimensions of border control, and assess their emergent outcomes. Finally, I conclude with a discussion of present-day Afghanistan and its borders. This discussion illustrates a potential extension of the theory and serves as an early warning for the limits of policy intervention.

The Argument Revisited

Locally embedded boundary regimes are critical to securing borders that are affected by insurgencies, banditry, weapons smuggling, and cross-border terrorism. In boundary regimes, administrative autonomy and unfettered access to their foreign counterparts allows border guards, border captains, and customs officers to pool their resources in policing a border. Several micro-level conditions are necessary to create a boundary regime. Border guards must have an arena for communicating with their foreign counterparts and monitoring one another. I have argued that border guards also need to have a broad shared understanding of the problems that plague a given border. Along the nineteenth-century Ottoman-Greek boundary, former brigands were sent to the border with only a general directive to suppress cross-border banditry. Within these general parameters, Ottoman and Greek guards took advantage of the geographic proximity of their posts to devise joint policing efforts to make the border more secure. The evolution of this cooperative boundary regime was gradual. Interactions regarding border policing were at times contentious and tense. Yet the local conditions and shared view of the problem allowed the guards to develop an innovative boundary regime that was insulated from the belligerent diplomacy that characterized high-level Ottoman-Greek relations.

A border cannot be jointly managed in the absence of devolution and local arenas for communicating and monitoring. This absence affects an international boundary where posts are set back substantially, where border walls and dead zones separate border guards, or where the posts are not paired with those on the other side. Along the twenty-first-century Kyrgyz-Chinese boundary, for example, the extreme mountains and high elevation of the line prevented border posts from being paired. Despite being able to communicate with one another by radio and wireless, the Kyrgyz and Chinese guards do not have unfettered access to the posts of the other side to regularly discuss policing procedures or to monitor one another's activities. As a result, cross-border cooperation along the Chinese-Kyrgyz border is slight, despite mutual policing problems. The border is unilaterally managed despite cooperative diplomatic relations.

High degrees of top-down intervention also impede boundary regimes. The cases showed that there is a zero-sum relationship between top-down intervention and cross-border cooperation. That is, the greater the degree of state intervention, the lower the ability of border authorities to cooperate across a boundary, even when neighboring states face a mutual threat and agree on the stakes in border policing. When state agencies micromanage the affairs of their guards and intervene often in border incidents, they restrict the extent to which guards can cooperate with their foreign counterparts. Such intervention creates a vicious cycle of greater centralization:

the more states monitor and manage the affairs of their local agents, the less able agents are to cope with emerging threats. In turn, the more states try to attenuate the failings of border control, the more likely they are to militarize their borders.

This has transpired along both nineteenth- and twenty-first-century state borders. For instance, the Greek state's centralizing reforms in the second half of the nineteenth century decimated the well-functioning boundary regime. In their attempt to regulate the boundary regime, Greek officials rolled back innovative gains that Greek and Ottoman border guards had achieved. One such strategy was that of hot pursuit. Greek and Ottoman border guards had reciprocally allowed their counterparts the right to enter sovereign territory while chasing bandits and fugitives along any point of the remote boundary. Greek state officials restricted the right of hot pursuit along the boundary in order to monitor the activities of foreign guards. As a consequence, they hobbled border control, and bandits learned to avoid crossing along officially designated points. In the twenty-first-century, Uzbekistan's tightly centralized border control methods ensure that boundary incidents escalate rapidly to the capital city, giving border guards little opportunity to resolve incidents locally. High-level Uzbek officials, in turn, interpret the events as evidence of Kyrgyz incompetence and hostile intent. This high degree of intervention has foreclosed cross-border cooperation despite mutual concerns with extremist violence in frontier regions. Uzbek policing methods are now wholly unilateral and aggressively militarized; along some segments of the boundary, Uzbek military units have occupied Kyrgyz territory and are policing the line on both sides.

While these cases demonstrate the nefarious effects of high-level intervention in order they are silent about the content of intervention. In the Greek case, intervention did not come from the very top of the border guard hierarchy but from the Greek Parliament, which passed restrictive laws governing the administration of the boundary. In the Uzbek case, intervention emanated wholly from the executive. Military headquarters monitored the activities of units along the border, and the Uzbek national security services gave Uzbek guards rigid policing repertoires. Such scrutiny did not prevent large-scale corruption. Instead, it promoted escalation with neighboring states over policing methods. The cases considered show that intervention from any high-level state institution is sufficient to foreclose cross-border cooperation and promote conflict. Future research may usefully focus on different types of top-down intervention in order to differentiate their relative effects.

It would not be surprising to observe unilateral border policing in cases where diplomatic relations are fragile and tenuous. However, the cases presented here have shown that such harmful macro-level intervention transpires even in situations where a mutual threat would lead us to expect cooperation and coordination across the border. Why has this been the case?

The answer to this question lies in state building. The state-building paths that new states pursue determine border control strategies. In their initial years of existence, states face a crisis of authority and struggle to build institutions of rule across inherited territory. An examination of state-building modes pursued in capital cities has allowed me to predict subsequent border control strategies. Surprisingly, state builders did not design their border control strategies to respond to emerging threats at their borders. New states tailored border control either to strengthen their policing ability or to shore up their dominant mode of extracting revenues in order to perpetuate rule. The cases reflected the trade-off between extractive and coercive policies. Despite the miserable economic foundation of the Greek state, Greek state builders were most concerned with creating a border that would deter cross-border banditry. Indeed, the Ottoman and Greek states shared this goal, and they opted not to use their border as a site for collecting lucrative customs duties. A similar trade-off was observed in the contemporary Central Asian cases. Extraction and revenue generating strategies of state building took precedence over coercive strategies. Each Central Asian state designed border control to promote its unique economic trajectory, a choice that came at the expense of deterring cross-border extremism.

The dynamics in Central Asia highlight how divergent state-building strategies can result in the implementation of incompatible policies of border control. Such implementation has deleterious effects on cooperation and security even in cases where neighboring states face a mutual cross-border threat. Uzbekistan pursued an autarchic mode of state building that required a closed economic border that would prevent subsidized gas, cotton, and consumer goods from leaking to lucrative free markets in neighboring states. Kyrgyzstan pursued a trader mode of state building. This necessitated open borders that would enable a brisk trade and lure international investment and foreign credit. Tajik state builders were satisfied with a smuggling path of state formation that allowed the state to survive with revenues from drug-smuggling transit networks. When the unilateral state-building paths of these neighboring states met at their common borders, conflict and escalation were the result. They came near the brink of fighting over the stationing of customs authorities, trade flows, and border laws, while doing little to prevent cross-border militancy.

Implications

This book has three crucial implications for scholars and policy makers. The first implication concerns the field of international relations. State-building strategies have a strong effect on conflict and cooperation among new states and their neighbors. The cases have demonstrated that state formation determines how new states perceive threats and how they prioritize security strategies. Individual state-building paths trigger specific strategies of border security, which then determine the extent to which states will cooperate with neighboring states in securing their frontiers. This book thus joins the ranks of a growing group of works concerned with the effects of state-building processes on international security and cooperation (Lake 1996; Herbst 2000; Gavrilis 2004; Atzili 2006; Goemans 2006; Cooley 2008). Investigating state-building practices reveals state preferences, preferences that structure how states approach conflict and cooperation. This approach may explain international outcomes that scholars have failed to explain or that they treat as outliers. State-building approaches may also explain why states do not cooperate more often with their neighbors in matters other than border control.

A second implication of the argument concerns ethnic conflict and the logic of partition. Prominent strands of the literature on ethnic conflict suggest that multiethnic border regions may be prone to violence and secession, especially in cases where one ethnic group has the potential to break away and join a neighboring state of co-ethnics (Kaufmann 1996; Mearsheimer and Van Evera 1999).[1] This project has demonstrated that boundary regimes have the capacity to provide adequate levels of security even along multiethnic frontiers. Along the Ottoman-Greek boundary, Greek-speaking villagers on both sides of the boundary monitored the

---

[1] For counterarguments to partition, variations on the logic of ethnic conflict and secessionism, and a discussion of the optimality of boundaries, see Kumar (1997), Easterly and Levine (1997), Alesina and Spolaore (1997), Posen (1993), Ratner (1993), Schaeffer (1990), Sambanis (2000), Sluga (2001), Toft (2003), Fearon and Laitin (2003), and Walter (2003, 2006). Also see Lustick (1996) on the internal dynamics of homelands and boundaries.

activities of border guards and even served as willing volunteers in helping the guards chase down criminal elements. Their contribution to border policing indicates that local interests in security may trump ethnic allegiance. Violence along the Kyrgyz-Tajik border appeared to be ethnically motivated. Ethnic Tajiks on both sides of the border engaged in violent confrontations with Kyrgyz guards. Such attacks coincided with ethnic divisions but were not motivated by them. Ethnic Tajiks attacked Kyrgyz border guards in protest and retribution for the ad hoc restrictions that Kyrgyz guards had placed on their cross-border movement. Whom borders divide matters less than how they divide. While this project has established that intermingled and hostile ethnic groups may contribute to border control, I have not systematically investigated the conditions under which local populations will support or undermine the activities of border guards. This may prove a fruitful avenue of future research.

A third implication concerns intervention. Intervention in matters of border security is not new. However, the claims defended here present scholars and policy makers with tools to assess the likelihood that international interventions along insecure borders will succeed or fail. In the nineteenth century and for much of the twentieth, great powers such as England, France, and Russia were active in moving old borders, crafting new ones, and designing guards and customs officials in order to manage the frontiers of their colonial possessions (Curzon of Keddleston 1908; Ronaldshay 1927; Nichols 1995; Black 1997: 138; Nugent 2002). In the present day, intervention in border control involves a host of states great and small, international organizations, nongovernmental organizations, and even private security firms. As the security and movement of a substantial part of the world's population is consequently at risk, this book would not be complete without a discussion of the current state of intervention as it affects troubled peripheries. In the following section I discuss the dynamics and likely fate of contemporary interventions in Central and South Asia that aim to enhance border security. I then discuss the twenty-first-century boundaries of Afghanistan, currently the site of a multilateral state-building experiment whose success or failure holds critical implications for global security.

Contemporary Interventions

With a budget of 50 million Euros, the Border Management Program for Central Asia (BOMCA) has been conducting a fascinating experiment in professionalizing and training border guards.[2] BOMCA's goal is to assist Central Asian states in establishing open and secure borders. BOMCA is funded by the European Union, operates under the mandate of the United Nations Development Program, and is staffed by international officials and Central Asian advisors. Its headquarters are located in a rented house on a central Bishkek backstreet. The program has regional offices in the capital cities of Uzbekistan, Turkmenistan, Kazakhstan, and Tajikistan.

Officials at BOMCA hope to train and transform Central Asian border authorities with a limited budget and in an environment that they perceive to be corrupt. BOMCA officials believe that their mission is complicated by the perniciousness of the Soviet legacy. As BOMCA sees it, the Soviet experience gave Central Asian officials a static understanding of the border where "the idea of facilitating movement is alien to the system."

BOMCA's multiphase plan seeks to implement "integrated border management" – a style of border policing particular to Europe where border authorities of two or more states manage their border jointly and cooperatively. BOMCA is in an early phase of the project. The current phase involves taking steps to build confidence between Central Asian governments, setting up new border posts and mobile units to handle both legal and illegal crossings, and experimenting with cross-border meetings of post commanders. Future phases will involve more ambitious cooperative goals such as regular meetings between border post commanders and the joint operation of select border crossings. BOMCA officials also want greater involvement of civilian populations. They hope to promote community-based policing involving civilians who live in border areas. Intelligence gathered from local communities can serve as an early-warning mechanism for emerging border security issues. Most ambitiously, BOMCA hopes that border authorities will eventually share intelligence and lists of suspects in order to prevent the entry or exit of wanted individuals. All of the measures are part of a plan to embed Central Asian authorities in an interdependent web of cooperation.

BOMCA's initiatives will facilitate the micro-level conditions that this project has argued are necessary for the creation of open and secure boundaries. BOMCA's attempt to promote regular meetings between border guards may create arenas of interaction that border captains and guards

---

[2] The information in this section is based on a number of interviews with BOMCA officials conducted by the author in Kyrgyzstan and Uzbekistan during the summer of 2006. A list of interviews conducted can be found in the References section.

of the two sides will use in order to discuss border control problems and pose potential cooperative solutions. Likewise, BOMCA's attempt to ensure that border posts are consistently paired with those of the other side means that guards will have the capacity to monitor the activities of the other side. BOMCA officials report that border guards and captains have enthusiastically reacted to experimental cross-border meetings, even along the Uzbek-Kyrgyz boundary, where conflict and escalation have been prevalent.

However, high-level state officials have been less enthusiastic about such initiatives. Local border officials have complained privately to BOMCA officials that they do not have the political mandate to make substantive changes in policing. BOMCA consequently has chosen the Akyol crossing – located on the relatively more cooperative Kazakh-Kyrgyz border – as the site of an experimental integrated management post. In the coming years, BOMCA will build an integrated border guard and customs facility that will be operated jointly by the services of both sides. This will facilitate crossing, minimize processing time, and reduce the number of checks people and goods have to clear. More importantly, it is intended to demonstrate to regional elites the benefit of adopting an integrated model of border control.

However, BOMCA faces two critical dilemmas that may limit its ability to achieve its goals. First, part of BOMCA's mandate involves assisting Central Asian border authorities with infrastructural and equipment needs. Such equipment runs the gamut from refrigerators to keep food from spoiling in remote posts to motion sensors that detect movement at unmanned and unofficial crossings. Host governments have placed substantial pressure on BOMCA to provide technology and infrastructure. This lobbying may distract from the program's training mission and may also harm the program's relations with host governments when their expectations for equipment and infrastructure upgrades are not met. A former manager of BOMCA pledged to provide much more technology and infrastructure than the organization's budget could sustain.[3]

Second, while BOMCA is clearly in step with the micro-level dynamics of border security, its greatest challenge lies in overcoming macro-level dynamics. The program does not address the macro-level sources of border

---

[3] To give another example, during my interview the representative of the Kyrgyz Ministry of Foreign Affairs in South Kyrgyzstan requested that I ask BOMCA officials in Bishkek exactly when they plan to construct the promised border crossing in the Osh area.

security strategies. In the case of Central Asia, it was shown that state-building dynamics have resulted in divergent border security strategies that are inflexible and often incompatible with those of the other side. BOMCA may do much to facilitate boundary regimes in cases where state-building dynamics along both sides are compatible, but may have little effect elsewhere.

A host of United States government agencies are also investing substantial resources and energies in helping states cope with insurgencies, trafficking, and cross-border extremism in their frontier areas. Unlike BOMCA's technocratic initiatives, which emphasize professional training and joint border control, American interventions are based on boosting military capacity and unilateral control. In Iraq, the U.S. military is currently using marine divisions to train Iraqi soldiers for service in the border guard. The Department of Defense runs training and equipment programs in the Horn of Africa, where it suspects terror groups will try to take advantage of weak state authority and porous borders. In much of the former Soviet Union, the Department of Homeland Security has been building high-tech, multi-million-dollar customs facilities at designated points of entry in former Soviet states. The customs facilities include six-lane roadways, inspector booths, cargo inspection areas, closed-circuit remote television cameras, computers, communication systems, and air-conditioned buildings that include sleeping quarters and detention cells (Langewiesce 2006). Such facilities are intended to assist host states in detecting illegal trade in nuclear material. Much of the recent multibillion-dollar military aid package to Pakistan is slated to go to anti-Taliban operations along the Afghan-Pakistan border and to the construction of a border fence.[4]

While host states are usually enthusiastic about the military assistance and technology the United States provides, this may undermine border security in the long run. Poor states may not be able to maintain expensive, high-tech policing equipment in the absence of long-term aid commitments. The deployment of military units may temporarily increase a state's ability to police its border, but it can also trigger escalation and conflict with a neighbor that feels threatened by a large-scale military deployment. Moreover, military aid may enable states to pursue border control unilaterally rather than seeking cooperative strategies with neighbors.

---

[4] However, officials at NATO headquarters in Brussels explained to the author that they oppose such a fencing policy as inefficient and hopelessly unilateral.

The Limits of Intervention: Afghanistan in the Twenty-First Century

This book has established a durable and inescapable link between state building and border control strategies in new states. Yet the argument also has immediate implications for the boundaries of states recovering from collapse.[5] When states fail, institutions of border control likewise fail. After all, borders are political institutions whose function depends on national authorities, state policies, and local agents. In both Iraq and Afghanistan, U.S.-led invasions catalyzed the collapse of authority through physical destruction of public infrastructure and government property, a widespread purging of bureaucrats, and the decommissioning or suppression of military and paramilitary forces (Marten 2004). When the state ceased to exist, agents responsible for the border abandoned their posts, and the boundary became little more than a line on a map. Given such dynamics, border security institutions in states recovering from collapse have a newness to them that places them within the scope of the argument.[6]

Given the substantial efforts the international community is investing in rebuilding authority both in the center and at the margins of failed states, it is important to consider how such interventions may affect borders. This book concludes with a discussion of state building, border control, and intervention in Afghanistan. This discussion extends the argument and makes critical observations for policy makers, whose rebuilding efforts in Afghanistan will have consequences for international security throughout the twenty-first century.

In Afghanistan's modern history there has been no single, central state in the typical sense of the word. At different moments in its history, its territory has included dozens of ethnic groups and languages, multiple sovereigns, small-scale local chiefs, tribal confederations, and warlords (Qureshi 1966; Allen 2003; Rubin 2007). It has experienced British, Russian, and Soviet invasions and has seen only brief periods of superficial central rule. This lack of central rule benefited warlords, who survived by dominating politics

---

[5] For debates, definitions, and effects of state failure and collapse, see *Foreign Policy* (2007), Reno (1998), and O'Leary, Lustick, and Callaghy (2001).

[6] In 2006, the Iraq Study Group underscored the importance of border control on the successful recovery of state authority. Border security was mentioned twenty-eight times throughout its report, which urgently recommended that the United States train Iraqi border guards and prod them to cooperate with the border authorities of surrounding states, including Iran and Syria (Baker and Hamilton 2006).

and the economy in their areas and by pursuing independent foreign policies across Afghan borderlands (Marten 2007). Some warlords flourished to the extent that they began to mint their own coins (Goodhand 2005). One challenge to this decentralized system developed in the 1990s in the form of the Taliban. These extremist Muslim rebels emerged in 1994 with Pakistan's support, built their support base among Afghanistan's ethnic Pashtuns, and used profits from the illicit economy to acquire weapons (Khalilzad and Byman 2000). The Taliban were so successful in setting up a rival government that by 1996 they controlled nearly 90 percent of the country. While the expansion was partially due to their military tactics, the early success of the Taliban was likely due to their ability to extract revenues and control the economy. Goodhand (2005) estimates that the Taliban effectively taxed cross-border trade to generate $75 million in annual tax revenues. Briefly tolerant of the opium trade, Taliban authorities issued a religious directive against the cultivation of opium. This measure left warlords without a source of income and made them dependent on the Taliban. Taliban rule came to a quick end in 2001 with a U.S.-led military intervention in the wake of the 9/11 terror attacks. There followed a multilateral nation-building effort designed to create a stable governing structure and develop the Afghan economy.[7]

Years after the intervention, the Afghan state was at a critical juncture. The United States had shifted its focus and energies to stabilizing Iraq, leaving NATO's International Security Assistance Force (ISAF) to take up the slack. The Taliban had seen a steady resurgence in a number of southern provinces, and warlords dominated politics and the economy in outlying areas (Anderson 2007; Rubin 2007). Afghan state revenues depended on international aid and grants, while much of the economy was dependent on opium cultivation and smuggling. According to the United Nations Office of Drug Control, in 2006 the total export value of Afghan opium rose to $3.1 billion, and gross profits to traffickers was estimated to be $2.34 billion. Afghanistan was estimated to cultivate 82 percent of the global opium crop, which amounted to a staggering 46 percent of gross domestic product (UNODC 2006).

In this critical context, border control became a central concern of states and international agencies assisting the Afghan government. Afghanistan had not implemented a regular and comprehensive border control policy,

---

[7] Given the aims, the intervention would best be labeled a "state-building" mission.

and it had not yet trained or deployed a sufficient number of border guards. Drug smuggling across Afghanistan's borders boomed. Racketeers and smugglers, often protected by warlords in frontier regions, used the thinly policed borders to evade customs controls. Suicide bombers found their way into Afghanistan across the mountainous border with Pakistan (Neumann 2007). Disputes over the location of the boundary and resources along the frontier threatened to trigger cross-border violence on a regular basis. The uncontrolled border was undermining security and threatening the international community's vision of an Afghanistan that would have a licit, expanding economy and stable authority.

A number of initiatives sponsored by international agencies and donor states are directly or indirectly involved in the process of creating secure borders for Afghanistan. The UNODC has set up eighty-seven patrols on the Afghan side of the border to fight drug smuggling.[8] NATO forces and Provincial Reconstruction Teams (PRTs) are deployed throughout Afghanistan, where they provide security, rebuild infrastructure, and monitor progress (Dziedzic and Seidl 2005). In 2007, the U.S. State Department donated $900 million to fight the cross-border drug trade.[9] Moreover, the German government has sponsored a series of programs to train Afghan forces and border guards. China, Iran, and Pakistan have pledged to assist in Afghan border control with equipment and training.[10] The military trilateral involving the United States, Pakistan, and Afghanistan has met over a dozen times to discuss border control issues, coordinate policies, and propose and implement solutions (Neumann 2007). The U.S. Department of Defense and BOMCA are also in charge of security initiatives along their respective stretches of the Tajik-Afghan border.

Despite their abundance and generous funding, such interventions are likely to fail given Afghanistan's state-building path, which indicates a clear preference for open and unpoliced borders. Why is this so? International financial support aside, the post-Taliban state survives through two principal strategies: co-optation and protection of smuggling networks. State builders in Kabul have pursued state building by co-opting warlords into the political process. Warlords are given wide latitude in their own provinces in

---

[8] BBC Monitoring International Reports, 21 November 2004, "Iran's Border with Afghanistan 'Well Protected' – UN Official," IRNA, Tehran.

[9] In January 2007 I attended a briefing at NATO headquarters in Brussels. The briefing discussed the dilemmas of NATO's mission in Afghanistan.

[10] Interview with George Katsirdakis, head of the Defense Cooperation, Defense Policy and Planning Division, NATO, Brussels, Belgium, 15 January 2007.

exchange for not fighting the government in Kabul, not supporting those who fight it, occasionally participating in political processes and meetings in Kabul, and turning over a portion of the revenues extracted from provinces.[11] As a result, licit extraction of government revenues is minimal, and tax collection is negotiated with powerful warlords rather than regularized through central government offices and their subsidiary regional offices (Marten 2007).

The second strategy involves protecting lucrative smuggling networks. This strategy is both direct and indirect. It occurs directly when central state officials, such as those in the Ministry of Interior, extract huge bribes from traffickers who ferry opium and other goods across the border. It also takes place when police posts are sold by state officials to the highest bidders. According to Rubin (2007), in poppy growing districts police posts that earn monthly salaries under $100 are sold for $100,000. The process occurs indirectly when central state authorities grant warlords, militia leaders, or tribal heads permission to control a smuggling route. Such an unwritten contracting relation usually results in the payment of a tribute or a percentage of the profits to central authorities.

Afghan state-building policies of co-optation and smuggling consequently rely on an open, unpoliced border. Border policing would curtail drug smuggling operations that directly and indirectly accrue revenues to the Afghan state. Moreover, border policing via a professionalized border guard would violate the co-optation policies that govern Kabul's relations with outlying elites. Cross-border transit is often controlled by local militia leaders who exact customs and tolls.[12] Effective border policing would, paradoxically, make central state authorities less rather than more secure.

Afghanistan's state-building trajectories create a permissive environment for cross-border violence and diplomatic crisis. In neighboring Iran, the drug trade has long been considered a primary security issue. Iran's authorities aim to prevent the entry of drug smugglers and opiates into

---

[11] The author owes much of this information to conversations with diplomats and Afghan officials that took place in the summer of 2007. These discussions took place under a nonattribution agreement.

[12] In this respect, present-day Afghanistan bears a resemblance to the Ottoman Empire, discussed in prior chapters. In the Ottoman Empire, state officials would contract local armed men (organized into *derbent*) to exact customs and tolls at critical roads, bridges, and crossings. The state would receive only a portion of the revenues in exchange for an obligation on the part of *derbent* officials to keep a relative peace in outlying areas.

their territory. A representative of the United Nations Drug Control Program (UNDCP) points out that Iran moved to eradicate its opium crop in 1979 and that it has invested substantial funds and manpower to fight the drug trade.[13] Iran's preferences are incompatible with those of Afghan state builders, whose security depends on the successful transit of narcotics. The preference for an open border will also do little to prevent the entry of suicide bombers and the cross-border movement of extremists. While the security of the Afghan state or of particular officials may depend on limiting the Taliban or keeping suicide bombers trained in Pakistan from entering the country, it is the open border that keeps the state afloat and the overall political order intact.

Given such incompatible preferences along Afghanistan's boundaries, it is no surprise that neighboring states are resorting to aggressive and unilateral policing efforts. A substantial portion of Iran's military is currently stationed along the long border with Afghanistan. Iranian officials have reported thousands of military, police, and civilian casualties resulting from attempts to fight the drug trade. The Iranian government intends to build a series of fences and walls along segments of the border (Gouvernour 2002; Gall 2005). Pakistan likewise has stationed a large military presence along the border and has made plans for a fence and mine fields along the boundary (Ramesh 2005; Gall 2006). At many places, border markers and posts have been moved, and Pakistani military units now police the border from well within the territory of Afghanistan (Wrong 2003).

The cases examined in this book suggest a pessimistic trajectory for Afghanistan and its relations with neighboring states. If the international initiatives discussed here fail to alter the course of Afghanistan's border strategies, its borders may increasingly become havens for insurgents and extremists and may become objects of violent escalation with neighboring states (Barfield and Hawthorne 2007).

A solution to the dilemma is not easy, and Afghanistan's borders serve as a warning of the limits of intervention. Third-party states, international organizations, and aid agencies may be able to do little to promote border security if a well-controlled border contradicts the very foundations of state formation. There are realistic and unrealistic solutions. An unrealistic

---

[13] In recent years, Iran has spent billions of dollars on border fortifications. As of 2002, it had lost 3,000 men in fighting the cross-border drug trade (Gouverneur 2002). In the 1990s, its parliament approved a budget for digging channels to stop border trafficking, and in 2000 it voted yet another series of measures to upgrade the border with electronic equipment.

solution would be to expect Afghanistan to voluntarily change its state-building path. It is also beyond the realm of possibility for the international community to reimburse Afghan officials and cultivators indefinitely for the loss of revenues from opium cultivation and smuggling. A more realistic approach would begin modestly by first coordinating the initiatives discussed here, which directly or indirectly affect border security in Afghanistan. These initiatives do not pool their resources, nor do they share vital information regarding their field experience. A coordinated effort would do well to concentrate the initiatives in a single region of Afghanistan to serve as a pilot program. Such a program would deploy both the micro- and macro-level strategies discussed in this book.

At the local level, cross-border tribal militias could be given duties and lucrative salaries as border guards. Commissioning locals with security tasks has had successful precedents. In the case of the Ottoman-Greek boundary, former bandits were hired to police the border. They had great knowledge of the border area and were also well versed in local criminality, experience that they used to suppress remaining bandits. Naturally, such a program would have to take place along both sides of the boundary. Afghanistan's boundaries are home to numerous cross-border ethnic and tribal groups that could be good candidates for such an initiative. This would take place along with a congruent effort to buy out warlords and militias in that area who benefit from an uncontrolled border. Given Afghanistan's uncentralized state structure, it would be possible to attempt this initiative along a single section of the frontier without altering the sum total of Afghan state building. While isolated to a particular stretch of boundary, such a program could serve as a learning experience for the international community and a demonstration for Afghan state builders in Kabul of the alternatives to state formation. Much easier and cheaper than reimbursing and eradicating opium cultivation, such an intervention would still require complicated coordination and patience among international technocrats for the long haul.

This book has argued that how states intervene and design their border control institutions matters much more than their capacity or wealth. Getting the institutions right has been an enduring and illusive dilemma for states. Technocratic and administrative solutions to border security problems are often subject to broader political dynamics and constraints. Cooperative, efficient boundary regimes are in short supply in part because of the macro dynamics of state building. These dynamics restrict the efforts of border authorities at the local level and prevent states from crafting open and secure borders. State builders will tend to win out over border guards. To reverse this tendency and to better understand the dynamics of interstate borders, historians, social scientists, and policy makers would do well to search for boundary regimes that quietly exist today and to rediscover those that history has gradually swept away.

Bibliography

Archival Documents

The Archives of the Prime Ministry, Istanbul, Turkey

BBA – Başbakanlık Arşivi (Osmanlı Arşivi)

A.MKT.NZD: Sadaret Defterleri, Bab-ı Ali Evrak Odası
A.MKT.UM: Sadaret Defeterleri, Umumi
Ayniyat Defterleri, Tırhala
Cevdet Tasnifi: Hariciye, Askeriye, Zaptiye
Harita Kataloğu
Hatt-ı Hümayun Tasnifi
HR.MKT: Hariciye Nezareti, Mektubi Kalemi
HR.SYS: Hariciye Nezareti, Siyasi Kısmı
İrade Dahiliye
İrade Yunanistan Defteri
Yıldız Tasnifi, Sadaret Hususi Maruzat Evrakı

The Historical Archives of the Foreign Ministry, Athens, Greece

AYE – Istorikon Archeion tou Ipourgeiou Eksoterikon

3/1: Sunoriaka
4/1: Sunoriaka
4/2: Lestrika
4/3, 4: Orothetika
78/1: Peri Charton

Public Record Office, London, UK

FO – Foreign Office Files

FO 32: Political and Other Departments: General Correspondence before 1906, Greece

FO 78: Political and Other Departments: General Correspondence before 1906, Ottoman Empire

FO 195: Embassy and Consulates, Turkey (formerly Ottoman Empire): General Correspondence

Greek Periodicals

Aion, Athens, 1851–53
Anatole, Athens, 1852–67
Aneksartesia, Larisa, 1882–85
Faros tes Othruos, Lamia, 1856–60, 1874–77
Fone ton Methorion, Lamia, 1860–61

Interviews

Interviewees who requested anonymity are not identified here.

Antheunissens, Pierre-Paul. Interviewed September 4, 2006. Project manager for Turkmenistan and Uzbekistan, Border Management Programme for Central Asia (BOMCA), Tashkent, Uzbekistan.

Bouyjou, Jerome. Interviewed August 27, 2006. Director of Osh Field Office, Organization for Security and Cooperation in Europe (OSCE), Bishkek, Kyrgyzstan.

Joldoshev, Abdimomun. Interviewed August 25, 2006. Regional director, International Business Council, Osh, Kyrgyzstan.

Karimov, Kudrat Samsakovich. Interviewed August 23, 2006. Former police colonel, Osh.

Katsirdakis, George. Interviewed January 15, 2007. Head, Defense Cooperation, Defense Policy and Planning Division, NATO, Brussels, Belgium.

Kiss, Tamas. Interviewed August 21, 2006. Project manager for Kazakhstan and Kyrgyzstan, BOMCA, Bishkek.

Maratovich, Temirov Artur. Interviewed, August 14, 2006. Commander of border guard base, Karakol, Kyrgyzstan.

Nurgojoevich, Japarov Sadir. Interviewed August 27, 2006. Deputy, Kyrgyz Parliament, Bishkek.

Peirce, Philip. Interviewed August 21, 2006. Regional program manager, BOMCA, Bishkek.

Sabirov, Medirbek. Interviewed August 25, 2006. Head of Osh Customs Office, Osh.

Bibliography

Usubaliev, Talaibek. Interviewed August 21, 2006. Deputy to regional manager, BOMCA, Bishkek.
Usupov, Baktibek Ajibekovich. Interviewed August 23, 2006. Representative of the Ministry of Foreign Affairs to the South, Osh.

Laws and Treaties

Convention on the Suppression of Brigandage, 1856, signed by Greece and the Ottoman Empire (renewed in 1865) (in Greek and French).
Law of the State Border of the Kyrgyz Republic, February 18, 1999, drafted by the Kyrgyz Parliament (signed by President Akayev, March 19, 1999) (in Russian).
Publication of Kyrgyz Border Law, Government Resolution no. 530/17, October 30, 1992 (in Russian).
Secure Fence Act of 2006, H.R. 6061, 109th Congress, Second Session, Washington, D.C.
Uzbek Law on the Border, no. 8820–1, August 20, 1999, signed by President Karimov (revised April 30, 2004) (in Russian).

Newswires

Agence France Presse
AFX News
BBC Monitoring, Central Asia Unit
BBC Monitoring, International Reports
BBC News World Edition
BBC Uzbek
Current Digest of the Soviet Press
Current Digest of the Post-Soviet Press
Financial Times Information
ITAR-TASS
United Press International

Books, Articles, and Chapters

Abazov, Rafis. 1999. "Policy of Economic Transition in Kyrgyzstan." *Central Asian Survey* 18, no. 2: 197–223.
Abbott, Andrew. 1995. "Things of Boundaries." *Social Research* 62, no. 4: 857–882.
Abou-El-Haj, Rifa'at Ali. 1969. "The Formal Closure of the Ottoman Frontier in Europe, 1699–1703." *Journal of the American Oriental Society* 89: 460–497.
About, Edmond. 1855. *Greece and the Greeks of the Present Day*. Edinburgh: Thomas Constable and Co.
Acemoğlu, Daron, and Thierry Verdier. 2000. "The Choice between Market Failures and Corruption." *The American Economic Review* 90, no. 1 (March): 194–211.

Adamson, Fiona B. 2006. "Crossing Borders: International Migration and National Security." *International Security* 31, no. 1 (Summer): 165–199.

Adler, Emanuel, and Michael Barnett, eds. 1998. *Security Communities*. New York: Cambridge University Press.

Agrawal, Arun, and Jesse Ribot. 1999. "Accountability in Decentralization: A Framework with South Asian and West African Cases." *Journal of Developing Areas* 33, no. 4 (Summer): 473–502.

Albert, Mathias. 1998. "On Boundaries, Territoriality and Postmodernity: An International Relations Perspective." *Geopolitics* 3, no. 1: 53–68.

Alesina, Alberto, and Enrico Spolaore. 1997. "On the Number and Size of Nations." *The Quarterly Journal of Economics* 112, no. 4 (November): 1027–1056.

Allan, Nigel J. R. 2003. "Rethinking Governance in Afghanistan." *Journal of International Affairs* 56, no. 2 (Spring): 193–202.

Alymkulov, Emil, and Marat Kulatov. 2001. "Local Government in the Kyrgyz Republic." In Igor Munteanu and Victor Popa, eds., *Developing New Rules in the Old Environment*. Budapest: Open Society Institute, pp. 522–600.

Amer, Ramses. 1997. "Border Conflicts between Cambodia and Vietnam." *IBRU Boundary and Security Bulletin* 5, no. 2 (Summer): 80–91.

Anderson, John. 1997. *The International Politics of Central Asia*. Manchester: Manchester University Press.

Anderson, John Lee. 2007. "The Taliban's Opium War." *The New Yorker* (July 9 and 16): 60–71.

Anderson, M. S. 1966. *The Eastern Question, 1774–1923: A Study in International Relations*. London: Macmillan.

Anderson, Malcom. 1997. *Frontiers: Territory and State Formation in the Modern World*. Cambridge: Polity Press.

Andreas, Peter. 2000. *Border Games: Policing the U.S.-Mexico Divide*. Ithaca, NY: Cornell University Press.

2003. "Redrawing the Line: Borders and Security in the Twenty-first Century." *International Security* 28, no. 2 (Fall): 78–111.

Anechiarico, Frank, and James B. Jacobs. 1996. *The Pursuit of Absolute Integrity: How Corruption Control Makes Government Ineffective*. Chicago: University of Chicago Press.

Ardant, Gabriel. 1972. *Histoire de l'impôt. Livre II: Du XVIIIe au XXe siècle*. Paris: Fayard.

Asiwaju, Anthony I. 1994. "Borders and Borderlands as Linchpins for Regional Integration in Africa: Lessons of the European Experience." In Clive H. Schofield, ed., *Global Boundaries: Vol. 1. World Boundaries*. London: Routledge, pp. 57–75.

Atzili, Boaz. 2007. "When Good Fences Make Bad Neighbors: Fixed Borders, State Weakness, and International Conflict." *International Security* 31, no. 3 (Winter): 139–173.

Axelrod, Robert M. 1983. *The Evolution of Cooperation*. New York: Basic Books.

1997. *The Complexity of Cooperation: Agent Based Models of Competition and Cooperation*. Princeton, NJ: Princeton University Press.

Bibliography

Bac, Mehmet. 1996. "Corruption, Supervision, and the Structure of Hierarchies." *Journal of Law, Economics, and Organization* 12, no. 2 (October): 277–298.

Badykova, Najia. 2006. "Regional Cooperation in Central Asia: A View from Turkmenistan." *Problems of Economic Transition* 48, no. 8 (December): 62–95.

Bailey, Frank Edgar. 1970. *British Policy and the Turkish Reform Movement: A Study in Anglo-Turkish Relations, 1826–53*. New York: H. Fertig.

Baker, James A. III, and Lee H. Hamilton, cochairs. 2006. *The Iraq Study Group Report: The Way Forward*. Washington, DC: United States Institute of Peace.

Barfield, Thomas, and Amy Hawthorne. 2007. "The Durand Line: History, Consequences, and Future." Report of a conference organized by the American Institute of Afghanistan Studies and the Hollings Center in Istanbul, Turkey.

Barkey, Karen. 1994. *Bandits and Bureaucrats: The Ottoman Route to State Centralization*. Ithaca, NY: Cornell University Press.

——— 2008. *Empire of Difference*. New York: Cambridge University Press.

Barkey, Karen, and Mark Von Hagen, eds. 1997. *After Empire: Multiethnic Societies and Nation-Building: The Soviet Union and Russian, Ottoman, and Hapsburg Empires*. Boulder, CO: Westview Press.

Barnett, Michael. 1992. *Confronting the Costs of War: Military Power, State, and Society in Egypt and Israel*. Princeton, NJ: Princeton University Press.

——— 1998. *Dialogues in Arab Politics: Negotiations in Regional Order*. New York: Columbia University Press.

Bates, Robert H. 1981. *Markets and States in Tropical Africa: The Political Basis of Agricultural Policies*. Berkeley: University of California Press.

Beissinger, Mark R. 2002. *Nationalist Mobilization and the Collapse of the Soviet State*. New York: Cambridge University Press.

Beissinger, Mark R., and Crawford Young. 2002. "Convergence to Crisis: Pre-Independence State Legacies and Post-Independence State Breakdown in Africa and Eurasia." In Mark R. Beissinger and Crawford Young, eds., *Beyond State Crisis? Postcolonial Africa and Post-Soviet Eurasia in Comparative Perspective*. Washington, DC: Woodrow Wilson Center Press.

Biggs, Michael. 1999. "Putting the State on the Map: Cartography, Territory, and European State Formation." *Comparative Studies in Society and History* 41, no. 2 (April): 374–405.

Bigham, Clive. 1897. *With the Turkish Army in Thessaly*. London: Macmillan.

Black, Jeremy. 1997. *Maps and History: Constructing Images of the Past*. New Haven, CT: Yale University Press.

Blake, Gerald H. 1998. "The Objectives of Land Boundary Management." *IBRU Boundary and Security Bulletin* 6, no. 3: 55–59.

Blok, Anton. 2001. *Honour and Violence*. Cambridge, UK: Polity.

Blumi, Isa. 2003. "Contesting the Edges of the Ottoman Empire: Rethinking Ethnic and Sectarian Boundaries in the Malësore, 1878–1912." *International Journal of Middle East Studies* 35, no. 2 (May): 237–256.

Boehm, Christopher. 1984. *Blood Revenge: The Anthropology of Feuding in Montenegro and Other Tribal Societies*. Lawrence: University of Kansas Press.

Boone, Catherine. 2003. *Political Topographies of the African State: Territorial Authority and Institutional Choice*. New York: Cambridge University Press.

Brubaker, Rogers. 1996. *Nationalism Reframed: Nationhood and the National Question in the New Europe*. Cambridge: Cambridge University Press.

Bueno de Mesquita, Bruce. 2006. "Game Theory, Political Economy, and the Evolving Study of War and Peace." *American Political Science Review* 100, no. 4 (November): 637–642.

Bueno de Mesquita, Bruce, Alistair Smith, Randolph M. Siverson, and James D. Morrow. 2003. *The Logic of Political Survival*. Cambridge, MA: MIT Press.

Bunce, Valerie. 1999. *Subversive Institutions: The Design and the Destruction of Socialism and the State*. New York: Cambridge University Press.

Byrd, William, and Martin Raiser with Anton Dobronogov and Alexander Kitain. 2006. "Economic Cooperation in the Wider Central Asia Region." Working Paper 75. Washington, DC: The World Bank.

Çadırcı, Musa. 1988. "Renovations in the Ottoman Army, 1792–1869." *Revue Internationale d'Histoire Militaire* 67: 87–102.

———. 1989. "Türkiye'de kaza yönetimi (1840–1876)." *Belleten* 53, no. 206: 237–257.

———. 1997. *Tanzimat Döneminde Anadolu Kentleri'nin Sosyal ve Ekonomik Yapısı*. Ankara: Türk Tarih Kurumu.

Caporaso, James A. 2000. "Changes in the Westphalian Order: Territory, Public Authority and Sovereignty." *International Studies Review* 2, no. 2: 1–28.

Carter, David B., and H. E. Goemans. 2006. "The Making of the Territorial Order: How Borders are Drawn." Unpublished manuscript.

Chandler, Andrea. 1998. *Institutions of Isolation: Border Controls in the Soviet Union and Its Successor States, 1917–1993*. Montreal: McGill-Queens University Press.

Chaudry, Kiren Aziz. 1989. "The Price of Wealth: Business and State in Labor Remittance and Oil Economies." *International Organization* 43, no. 1 (Winter): 101–145.

Cherikov, Sadyrbek. 2005. "Who Is in Charge of Border Security?" *The Times of Central Asia* (June 17), p. 1.

Chirot, Daniel, and Karen Barkey. 1983. "States in Search of Legitimacy: Was There Nationalism in the Balkans of the Early Nineteenth Century?" *International Journal of Comparative Sociology* 24, no. 1–2: 30–46.

Chivers, C. J. 2005. "Uzbek Government Retakes Border Town." *New York Times* (May 20), p. 4.

Chrestos, Thanases. 1999. *Ta Sinora tou Hellenikou kratous kai hoi diethneis sinthekes (1830–1947)*. Athens: Demiourgia.

Cohen, Paul A. 1997. *History in Three Keys: The Boxers as Event, Experience, and Myth*. New York: Columbia University Press.

Commission Europèenne pour la délimitation Turco-Greque. 1883. Constantinople: Imprimerie de Ministère de la Guerre.

Cooley, Alexander. 2005. *Logics of Hierarchy: The Organization of Empires, States, and Military Occupations*. Ithaca, NY: Cornell University Press.

———. 2008. *Base Politics: Democratic Change and the US Military Overseas*. Ithaca, NY: Cornell University Press.

Bibliography

Cornell, Svante E. 1999. "The Devaluation of the Concept of Autonomy: National Minorities in the Former Soviet Union." *Central Asian Survey* 18, no. 2: 185–196.

Curzon of Kedleston, Lord. 1908. *Frontiers,* 2nd ed. The Romanes Lecture: delivered in the Sheldonian Theatre, Oxford (Nov 2, 1907). Oxford: Clarendon Press.

Dakin, Douglas. 1972. *The Unification of Greece, 1770–1923.* New York: St. Martin's Press.

Darden, Keith Alexander. 2008. *Economic Liberalism and Its Rivals: The Formation of International Institutions among the Post-Soviet States.* New York: Columbia University Press.

David, Stephen R. 1991. "Explaining Third World Alignment." *World Politics* 43, no. 2 (January): 233–256.

Davison, Roderic H. 1963. *Reform in the Ottoman Empire, 1856–1876.* Princeton, NJ: Princeton University Press.

——— 1978. "Ottoman Diplomacy at the Congress of Paris (1856) and the Question of Reforms." In *VII. Türk Tarih Kongresi, Kongreye Sunulan Bildiriler.* Ankara: Türk Tarih Kurumu, pp. 580–586.

——— 1983. "The Ottoman-Greek Frontier Question, 1876–1882, from Ottoman Records." In his *Nineteenth Century Ottoman Diplomacy and Reforms.* Istanbul: The Isis Press, pp. 239–256.

——— 1992. "Britain, the International Spectrum and the Eastern Question, 1827–1841." *New Perspectives on Turkey* 7: 15–35.

——— 1999. "The Ottoman Empire and the Congress of Berlin." In his *Nineteenth Century Ottoman Diplomacy and Reforms.* Istanbul: The Isis Press, pp. 175–196.

De Sardan, Olivier J. P. 1999. "A Moral Economy of Corruption in Africa?" *The Journal of Modern African Studies* 37, no. 1 (March): 25–52.

Desch, Michael C. 1996. "War and Strong States, Peace and Weak States?" *International Organization* 50, no. 2 (Spring): 237–268.

Diehl, Paul, ed. 1999. *A Road Map to War.* Nashville, TN: Vanderbilt University Press.

Diez, Thomas, Stephan Stetter, and Mathias Albert. 2006. "The European Union and Border Conflicts: The Transformative Power of Integration." *International Organization* 60 (Summer): 563–593.

Domna-Visvizi, Donta. 1972. "The Great Powers and the Greek Insurrectionary Movements in Epirus, Thessaly, and Macedonia, 1853–1854." *ACTES du IIe congres international des etudes de sud-est europeen,* vol 3. Athens, pp. 3–16.

Driault, Edouard, and Michel Lheriter. 1925. *Histoire Diplomatique de la Grece de 1821 a nos jours.* 3 vols. Paris: Les Presses Universitaires de France.

Dziedzic, Michael J., and Michael K. Seidl. 2005. "Provincial Reconstruction Teams." United States Institute of Peace, Special Report 147.

Easterly, William, and Ross Levine. 1997. "Africa's Growth Tragedy: Policies and Ethnic Divisions." *Quarterly Journal of Economics* 122, no. 4 (November): 1203–1251.

Economist Intelligence Unit. 2001. *Country Report, Uzbekistan* (March).

Elman, Colin, and Miriam Fendius Elman. 2001. *Progress in International Relations Theory: Appraising the Field.* Cambridge, MA: MIT Press.

Farley, James Lewis. 1862. *The Resources of Turkey Considered with Especial Reference to the Profitable Investment of Capital in the Ottoman Empire.* London: Longman, Green, Longman, and Roberts.

Fazal, Tanisha. 2007. *State Death: The Politics and Geography of Conquest, Occupation, and Annexation.* Princeton, NJ: Princeton University Press.

Fearon, James D. 1995. "Rationalist Explanations for War." *International Organization* 49, no. 3 (February): 379–414.

——— 1997. "Signaling Foreign Policy Interests: Tying Hands versus Sinking Costs." *Journal of Conflict Resolution* 41, no. 1: 68–90.

Fearon, James D., and David D. Laitin. 1996. "Explaining Interethnic Cooperation." *American Political Science Review* 90, no. 4: 715–735.

Fearon, James D., and David D. Laitin. 2003. "Ethnicity, Insurgency, and Civil War." *American Political Science Review* 97, no. 1 (February): 75–90.

Fierke, Karen M. 2000. "Logics of Force and Dialogue: The Iraq/UNSCOM Crisis as Social Interaction." *European Journal of International Relations* 6, no. 3: 335–371.

Findley, Carter. 1970. "The Legacy of Tradition to Reform: Origins of the Ottoman Foreign Ministry." *International Journal of Middle East Studies* 1, no. 4: 334–357.

——— 1980. *Bureaucratic Reform in the Ottoman Empire: The Sublime Port, 1789–1922.* Princeton, NJ: Princeton University Press.

Fletcher, Joseph F., and Boris Sergeyev. 2002. "Islam and Intolerance in Central Asia: The Case of Kyrgyzstan." *Europe-Asia Studies* 54, no. 2: 252–275.

Foreign Policy. 2007. "The Failed States Index." *Foreign Policy* 161 (July/August): 54–63.

Fortna, Benjamin C. 2005. "Change in the School Maps of the Late Ottoman Empire." *Imago Mundi* 57, no. 1: 23–34.

Fravel, Taylor M. 2005. "Regime Insecurity and International Cooperation: Explaining China's Compromises in Territorial Disputes." *International Security* 30, no. 2 (Fall): 46–83.

——— 2008. *Strong Borders, Secure Nation: Cooperation and Conflict in China's Territorial Disputes.* Princeton, NJ: Princeton University Press.

Fuller, Graham E. 1992. *Central Asia: The New Geopolitics.* Santa Monica, CA: RAND.

Furlong, Kathryn, Nils Petter Gleditsch, and Håvard Hegre. 2006. "Geographic Opportunity and Neomalthusian Willingness: Boundaries, Shared Rivers, and Conflict." *International Interactions* 32, no. 1 (January–March): 79–108.

Gall, Carlotta. 2005. "Armed and Elusive, Afghan Drug Dealers Roam Free." *New York Times* (January 2), p. 3.

——— 2006. "Afghan Angry at Pakistan's Plan for Mines and Fence on Border." *New York Times* (December 29), p. 6.

Gartzke, Eric. 2007. "The Capitalist Peace." *American Journal of Political Science* 51, no. 1 (January): 166–191.

Bibliography

Gavrilis, George. 2004. "Sharon's Endgame for the Barrier." *The Washington Quarterly* 27, no. 4: 7–20.

2006. "The Forgotten West Bank." *Foreign Affairs* 85 (January/February): 66–76.

2009. "Boundary Making and Border Disputes." In George T. Kurian, ed., *International Encyclopedia of Political Science*. Washington DC: CQ Press.

Georges, Giorgos. 1996. *He Prote Makrochronia Hellenotourkike Dienekse: To Zetema tes Ethnikotetas, 1830–1869*. Athens: Ekdoseis Kastaniote.

Gibson, Edward L. 2005. "Boundary Control: Subnational Authoritarianism in Democratic Countries." *World Politics* 58 (October): 101–132.

Gilpin, Robert. 1981. *War and Change in World Politics*. Cambridge: Cambridge University Press.

Gleason, Gregory. 2001a. "Foreign Policy and Domestic Reform in Central Asia." *Central Asian Survey* 20, no. 2: 167–182.

2001b. "Inter-State Cooperation in Central Asia from the CIS to the Shanghai Forum." *Europe-Asia Studies* 53, no. 7: 1077–1095.

2003. *Markets and Politics in Central Asia: Structural Reform and Political Change*. London: Routledge.

Goemans, Hein E. 2006. "Bounded Communities: Territoriality, Territorial Attachment, and Conflict." In Miles Kahler and Barbara F. Walter, eds., *Territoriality and Conflict in an Era of Globalization*. New York: Cambridge University Press, pp. 25–61.

Goertz, Gary, and Paul F. Diehl. 1992. *Territorial Changes and International Conflict*. London: Routledge.

Goff, Patricia M. 2000. "Invisible Borders: Economic Liberalization and National Identity." *International Studies Quarterly* 44: 533–562.

Goodhand, Jonathan. 2005. "Frontiers and Wars: The Opium Economy in Afghanistan." *Journal of Agrarian Change* 5, no. 2 (April): 191–216.

Gould, Roger V. 1993. "Collective Action and Network Structure." *American Sociological Review* 58, no. 2 (April): 182–196.

1995. *Insurgent Identities: Class, Community, and Protest in Paris from 1848 to the Commune*. Chicago: University of Chicago Press.

Gouverneur, Cedric. 2002. "Iran Loses Its Drugs War." *Le Monde Diplomatique* (March) [translated by Harry Forester].

Griffiths, Iewan. 1996. "Permeable Boundaries in Africa." In Paul Nugent and A. I. Asiwaju, eds., *African Boundaries: Barriers, Conduits and Opportunities*. London: Pinter, pp. 68–86.

Haghayeghi, Mehrdad. 1995. *Islam and Politics in Central Asia*. New York: St. Martin's Press.

Halavart, İsmail. 1973. "1878 Berlin Kogresinden Sonra Osmanlı Devleti ile Yunistan'ın Hudut Tashihi Meselesi." M.A. thesis, Department of History, Istanbul University.

Hanks, Reuel R. 2000. "Emerging Spatial Patterns of the Demographics, Labour Force and FDI in Uzbekistan." *Central Asian Survey* 19, no. 3: 351–366.

Harari, Maurice. 1958. "The Turco-Persian Boundary: A Case Study in the Politics of Boundary-making in the Near and Middle East." Ph.D. thesis, Department of Political Science, Columbia University, New York.

Hardin, Garrett. 1968. "The Tragedy of the Commons." *Science* 162: 1243–1248.

Hassner, Ron. 2006. "The Path to Intractability: Time and the Entrenchment of Territorial Disputes." *International Security* 31, no. 3 (Winter): 107–138.

Hatipoğlu, M. Murat. 1998. *Yunanistan'daki Gelişmelerin Işığında Türk-Yunan İlişkilerin 101. Yılı.* Ankara: Türk Kültürünü Araştırma Enstitüsü.

Hechter, Michael. 2000. *Containing Nationalism.* Oxford: Oxford University Press.

Helleiner, Eric. 2003. *The Making of National Money: Territorial Currencies in Historical Perspective.* Ithaca, NY: Cornell University Press.

Henrikson, Alan K. 2000. "Facing Across Borders: The Diplomacy of Bon Voisinage." *International Political Science Review* 21, no. 2: 121–147.

Hensel, Paul R. 2001. "Contentious Issues and World Politics: The Management of Territorial Claims in the Americas, 1816–1992." *International Studies Quarterly* 45, no. 1 (March): 81–109.

Heper, Metin. 1980. "Center and Periphery in the Ottoman Empire: With Special Reference to the Nineteenth Century." *International Political Science Review* 1, no. 1: 81–105.

Herbst, Jeffrey. 1989. "The Creation and Maintenance of National Boundaries in Africa." *International Organization* 43, no. 4: 673–692.

    2000. *States and Power in Africa: Comparative Lessons in Authority and Control.* Princeton, NJ: Princeton University Press.

Herzfeld, Michael. 1986. *Ours Once More: Folklore, Ideology, and the Making of Modern Greece.* New York: Pella.

Hiro, Dilip. 1995. *Between Marx and Muhammad: The Changing Face of Central Asia.* London: HarperCollins.

Hirschman, Albert O. 1978. "Exit, Voice, and the State." *World Politics* 31, no. 1 (October): 90–107.

Hoover, Glenn E. 1930. "Our Mexican Immigrants." *Foreign Affairs* 8: 99–107.

Horsman, Stuart. 1999. "Uzbekistan's Involvement in the Tajik Civil War, 1992–97: Domestic Considerations." *Central Asian Survey* 18, no. 1: 37–48.

Horton, Thomas Galland. 1854. *Turkey: The People, Country, and Government.* London: Mason and Co.

Hui, Victoria Tin-bor. 2005. *War and State Formation in Ancient China and Early Modern Europe.* New York: Cambridge University Press.

Huntington, Samuel P. 1993. "The Clash of Civilizations?" *Foreign Affairs* 72, no. 3 (Summer): 22–49.

Huth, Paul. 1996. *Standing Your Ground: Territorial Disputes and International Conflict.* Ann Arbor: University of Michigan Press.

İnalcık, Halil. 1973. "Application of the Tanzimat and Its Social Effects." *Archivum Ottomanicum* 5: 97–128.

Bibliography

Ingram, Paul, and Crist Inman. 1996. "Institutions, Intergroup Competition, and the Evolution of Hotel Populations around Niagara Falls." *Administrative Science Quarterly* 41, no. 4 (December): 629–658.

International Crisis Group (ICG). 2001a. "Central Asia: Islamist Mobilization and Regional Security." Asia Report 14 (March 1).

———. 2001b. "Central Asia: Fault Lines in the New Security Map." Asia Report 20 (July 4).

———. 2001c. "Central Asia: Drugs and Conflict." Asia Report 25 (November 26).

———. 2002a. "Central Asia: Border Disputes and Conflict Potential." Asia Report 33 (April 4).

———. 2002b. "Central Asia: The Politics of Police Reform." Asia Report 42 (December 10).

———. 2003a. "Tajikistan: A Roadmap for Development." Asia Report 51 (April 24).

———. 2003b. "Radical Islam in Central Asia: Responding to Hizb ut-Tahrir." Asia Report 58 (June 30).

———. 2003c. "Central Asia: Islam and the State." Asia Report 59 (July 10).

———. 2004a. "The Failure of Reform in Uzbekistan: Ways Forward for the International Community." Asia Report 76 (March 11).

———. 2004b. "Northern Uganda: Understanding and Solving the Conflict." Africa Report 77 (April 14).

———. 2005a. "Uzbekistan: The Andijon Uprising." Asia Briefing 38 (May 25).

———. 2005b. "Kyrgyzstan: A Faltering State." Asia Report 109 (December 16).

———. 2005c. "Ethiopia and Eritrea: Preventing War." Africa Report 101 (December 22).

———. 2006a. "Uzbekistan: In for the Long Haul." Asia Briefing 45 (February 16).

———. 2006b. "Central Asia: What Role for the European Union?" Asia Report 113 (April 10).

International Monetary Fund. 1996a. "Republic of Tajikistan: Recent Economic Developments." IMF Staff Country Report no. 96/55 (June).

———. 1996b. "Republic of Kyrgyzstan: Recent Economic Developments." IMF Staff Country Report no. 96/98 (September).

———. 2000. "Republic of Uzbekistan: Recent Economic Developments." IMF Staff Country Report no. 00/36 (March).

Ioannidou-Bitsiadou, Georgia. 1993. "The Bavarian Loans and Chancellor Bismarck's Intervention in the Greek-Turkish Dispute over Greece's Borders (1878–1881)." *Balkan Studies* 34, no. 1: 73–83.

Ishiyama, John. 2002. "Neopatrimonialism and the Prospects for Democratization in the Central Asian Republics." In Sally N. Cummings, ed., *Power and Change in Central Asia*. London: Routledge, 42–58.

Issawi, Charles. 1980. *The Economic History of Turkey: 1800–1914*. Chicago: University of Chicago Press.

Jackson, Nicole J. 2005. "The Trafficking of Narcotics, Arms and Humans in Post-Soviet Central Asia: (Mis)perceptions, Policies and Realities." *Central Asian Survey* 24, no. 1 (March): 39–52.

Jackson, Robert H., and Carl G. Rosberg. 1986. "Why Africa's Weak States Persist: The Empirical and Juridical in Statehood." In Atul Kohli, ed., *The State and Development in the Third World.* Princeton, NJ: Princeton University Press, pp. 259–82.

Johansson, Rune. 1982. "Boundary Conflict in a Comparative Perspective: A Theoretical Framework." In Raimondo Strassoldo and Giovanni Delli Zotti, eds., *Cooperation and Conflict in Border Areas.* Milan: Franco Angeli Editore, pp. 179–214.

Jones, Ellen. 1985. *Red Army and Society: A Sociology of the Soviet Military.* Boston: Allen and Unwin.

Jones, Stephen B. 1945. *Boundary-making: A Handbook for Statesmen, Treaty Editors, and Boundary Commissioners.* Washington: Carnegie Endowment for International Peace, Division of International Law.

Jones Luong, Pauline. 2000. "After the Break-up: Institutional Design in Transitional States." *Comparative Political Studies* 33, no. 5 (June): 563–592.

   2002. *Institutional Change and Political Continuity in Post-Soviet Central Asia: Power, Perceptions, and Pacts.* New York: Cambridge University Press.

   2003. "Political Obstacles to Economic Reform in Uzbekistan, Kyrgyzstan, and Tajikistan: Strategies to Move Ahead." World Bank Report prepared for the Lucerne Conference of the CIS-7 Initiative (January 20–22).

Kafadar, Cemal. 1994. *Between Two Worlds: The Construction of the Ottoman State.* Berkeley: University of California Press.

Kahler, Miles, and Barbara F. Walter, eds. 2006. *Territoriality and Conflict in an Era of Globalization.* New York: Cambridge University Press.

Kalyvas, Stathis N. 1999. "Wanton and Senseless? The Logic of Massacres in Algeria." *Rationality and Society* 11, no. 3: 243–285.

Kang, David C. 2002. *Crony Capitalism: Corruption and Development in South Korea and the Philippines.* New York: Cambridge University Press.

Kapil, Rari L. 1966. "On the Conflict Potential of Inherited Boundaries in Africa." *World Politics* 18, no. 4: 656–673.

Karimov, I. A. 1995. *Vatan Sazhdagoh Kabi Muqaddasdir: Ma'ruzalar, Nutqlar, Suhbatlar.* Toshkent: O'zbekiston.

   1997. *Uzbekistan: On the Threshold of the Twenty-first Century.* Surrey: Curzon.

Karpat, Kemal H. 1982. "Millets and Nationality: The Roots of the Incongruity of Nation and State in the Post-Ottoman Era." In Benjamin Braudie and Bernard Lewis, eds., *Christians and Jews in the Ottoman Empire: The Functioning of a Plural Society.* New York: Holmes and Meier, pp. 142–168.

Kasaba, Reşat. 1988. *The Ottoman Empire and the World Economy: The Nineteenth Century.* Albany: State University of New York Press.

Kaser, Michael, and Santosh Mehtotra. 1996. "The Central Asian Economies after Independence." In Roy Allison, ed., *Challenges for the Former Soviet South.* Washington DC: Brookings, pp. 217–305.

Katzenstein, Peter, ed. 1996. *The Culture of National Security: Norms and Identity in World Politics.* New York: Columbia University Press.

Bibliography

Kaufman, Herbert. 1960. *The Forest Ranger: A Study in Administrative Behavior*. Baltimore: Johns Hopkins University Press.

Kaufmann, Chaim. 1996. "Possible and Impossible Solutions to Ethnic Civil Wars." *International Security* 20, no. 4: 136–175.

Kazemi, Laila. 2003. "Domestic Sources of Uzbekistan's Foreign Policy, 1991 to the Present." *Journal of International Affairs* 56, no. 2 (Spring): 205–216.

Keohane, Robert O. 1984. *After Hegemony: Conflict and Cooperation in the World Political Economy*. Princeton, NJ: Princeton University Press.

Keohane, Robert O., Andrew Moravcsik, and Anne-Marie Slaughter. 2000. "Legalized Dispute Resolution: Interstate and Transnational." *International Organization* 54, no. 3: 457–488.

Khalilzad, Zalmay, and Daniel Byman. 2000. "Afghanistan: The Consolidation of a Rogue State." *The Washington Quarterly* 23, no. 1 (Winter): 65–78.

Khoury, Dina. 2001. "Tribe and Ethnicity in the Mapping of Ottoman Frontiers: Classifying Tribal Populations on the Eastern Frontier, 1550s-1850s." Paper presented at the annual meeting of the American Historical Association (January).

Kier, Elizabeth. 1997. *Imagining War: French and British Military Doctrine between the Wars*. Princeton, NJ: Princeton University Press.

Kodaman, Bayram, ed. 1993. *1897 Türk-Yunan Savaşı: Tesalya Tarihi*. Ankara: Türk Tarihi Kurumu Basımevi.

Kofos, Evangelos. 1975. *Greece and the Eastern Crisis, 1875–1878*. Thessaloniki: Institute for Balkan Studies.

Koichiev, Arslan. 2003. "Ethno-territorial Claims in the Ferghana Valley during the Process of National Delimitation, 1924–7." In Tom Everett-Heath, ed., *Central Asia: Aspects of Transition*. New York: Routledge, pp. 45–56.

Köksal, Yonca. 2002. *Local Intermediaries and Ottoman State Centralization: The Tanzimat Reforms in the Provinces of Edirne and Ankara*. Ph.D. dissertation, Sociology Department, Columbia University, New York.

⸺ 2006. "Coercion and Mediation: Centralization and Sedentarization of Tribes in the Ottoman Empire." *Middle Eastern Studies* 42, no 3 (May): 469–491.

Koliopoulos, Giannes. 1987. *Brigands with a Cause: Brigandage and Irredentism in Modern Greece, 1821–1912*. Oxford: Clarendon Press.

⸺ 1999. "Brigandage and Insurgency in the Greek Domains of the Ottoman Empire, 1853–1908." In Dimitri Gondicas and Charles Issawi, eds., *Ottoman Greeks in the Age of Nationalism: Politics, Economy and Society in the Nineteenth Century*. Princeton, NJ: The Darwin Press, pp. 143–150.

Krasner, Stephen. 1999. *Sovereignty: Organized Hypocrisy*. Princeton, NJ: Princeton University Press.

Kratochwil, Friedrich. 1986. "Of Systems, Boundaries and Territoriality: An Inquiry into the Formation of the State System." *World Politics* 39, no. 1: 27–52.

Kreps, David M. 1990. *Game Theory and Economic Modeling*. Oxford: Clarendon Press.

Kristof, Ladis K. D. 1959. "The Nature of Frontiers and Boundaries." *Annals of the Association of American Geographers* 49, no. 3: 269–282.

Kumar, Radha. 1997. "The Troubled History of Partition." *Foreign Affairs* 73 (January/February): 22–34.

Kwiatkowska, Barbara. 2000. "The Eritrea/Yemen Arbitration: Landmark Progress in the Acquisition of Territorial Sovereignty and Equitable Maritime Boundary Delimitation." *IBRU Boundary and Security Bulletin* 8, no. 1 (Spring): 66–86.

Kydd, Andrew. 1997. "Game Theory and the Spiral Model." *World Politics* 49 (April): 371–400.

Laitin, David D. 1986. *Hegemony and Culture: Politics and Religious Change among the Yoruba.* Chicago: University of Chicago Press.

    1998. *Identity in Formation: The Russian-speaking Populations in the Near Abroad.* Ithaca, NY: Cornell University Press.

Lake, David A. 1996. "Anarchy, Hierarchy, and the Variety of International Relations." *International Organization* 50, no. 1: 1–33.

Lamont, Michele, and Virga Molnar. 2002. "The Study of Boundaries in the Social Sciences." *Annual Review of Sociology* 28: 167–195.

Langewiesche, William. 2006. "How to Get a Nuclear Bomb." *The Atlantic* (December): 80–98.

Lattimore, Owen. 1962. *Studies in Frontier History: Collected Papers, 1928–1958.* London: Oxford University Press.

Leake, W. M. 1835. *Travels in Northern Greece*, vol. 1. Amsterdam: Adolf M. Hakkert (reprint of London 1835 edition).

Legro, Jeffrey W. 1996. "Culture and Preferences in the International Cooperation Two-Step." *The American Political Science Review* 90, no. 1: 118–137.

Levi, Margaret. 1988. *Of Rule and Revenue.* Berkeley: University of California Press.

Linington, G. 1997. "Zimbabwean-South African Border Relations." In Solomon Nkiwane, ed., *Zimbabwe's International Borders: A Study in National and Regional Development in Southern Africa*, vol 1. Harare: University of Zimbabwe Press.

Lubin, Nancy. 2003. "Who's Watching the Watchdogs?" *Journal of International Affairs* 56, no. 2 (Spring): 43–56.

Luhman, Niklas. 1982. "Territorial Borders as System Boundaries." In Raimondo Strassoldo and Giovanni Delli Zotti, eds., *Cooperation and Conflict in Border Areas*. Milan: Franco Angeli Editore, pp. 235–245.

Lukin, Alexandr. 2004. "Shanghai Cooperation Organization: Problems and Prospects." *International Affairs* (Moscow) 50, no. 3 (June): 31–40.

Lustick, Ian S. 1993. *Unsettled States, Disputed Lands: Britain and Ireland, France and Algeria, Israel and the West Bank-Gaza.* Ithaca, NY: Cornell University Press.

    1996. "History, Historiography, and Political Science: Multiple Historical Sources and the Problem of Selection Bias." *American Political Science Review* 90, no. 3 (September): 605–618.

Macfie, A. L. 1996. *The Eastern Question, 1774–1923.* London: Longman.

Malmberg, Torsten. 1980. *Human Territoriality: A Survey of Behavioural Territories in Man with Preliminary Analysis and Discussion of Meaning.* New York: Mouton.

Mandel, Robert. 1980. "Roots of the Modern Interstate Border Dispute." *Journal of Conflict Resolution* 24, no. 3 (September): 427–454.

Bibliography

Manski, Charles F. 2000. "Economic Analysis of Social Interactions." *Journal of Economic Perspectives* 14, no. 3 (Summer): 115–136.

March, James G., and Johan P. Olsen. 1998. "The Institutional Dynamics of International Political Orders." *International Organization* 52, no. 4 (Autumn): 943–969.

Marek, Angie C. 2005. "Border Wars." *U.S. News and World Report* (November 28): 48–56.

Marten, Kimberly. 2004. *Enforcing the Peace: Learning from the Imperial Past.* New York: Columbia University Press.

2007. "Warlordism in Comparative Perspective." *International Security* 31, no. 3 (Winter): 41–73.

Martinez, Oscar J. 1994. "The Dynamics of Border Interaction: New Approaches to Border Analysis." In Clive H. Schofield, ed., *Global Boundaries: Vol. 1; World Boundaries.* London: Routledge, pp. 1–15.

McAdam, Doug, Sidney Tarrow, and Charles Tilly. 2001. *Dynamics of Contention.* New York: Cambridge University Press.

Mearsheimer, John. 2001a. *The Tragedy of Great Power Politics.* New York: Norton.

2001b. "The Impossible Partition." *New York Times* (January 11), p. 31.

Mearsheimer, John, and Robert Pape. 1993. "A Partition Plan for Bosnia – The Answer." *New Republic* 208: 24–32.

Mearsheimer, John, and Stephen Van Evera. 1999. "Redraw the Map, Stop the Killing." *New York Times* (April 4), p. 23.

Mega, Georgiou A. 1946. *Thessalikai Oikeseis.* Athens: Yfupourgeio Anoikodomeseos.

Megoran, Nick. 2005. "The Critical Geopolitics of Danger in Uzbekistan and Kyrgyzstan." *Environment and Planning D: Society and Space* 23: 555–580.

2006. "For Ethnography in Political Geography: Experiencing and Re-Imagining Ferghana Valley Boundary Closures." *Political Geography* 25: 622–640.

Megoran, Nick, Gael Raballand, and Jerome Bouyjou. 2005. "Performance, Representation and the Economics of Border Control in Uzbekistan." *Geopolitics* 10: 712–740.

Menon, Rajan, and Hendrik Spruyt. 1999. "The Limits of Neorealism: Understanding Security in Central Asia." *Review of International Studies* 25: 87–105.

Migdal, Joel S. 1994. "The State in Society: An Approach to Struggles for Domination." In Joel S. Migdal, Atul Kohli, and Vivienne Shue, eds., *State Power and Social Forces: Domination and Transformation in the Third World.* New York: Cambridge University Press, pp. 7–34.

2001. *State in Society: Studying How States and Societies Transform and Constitute One Another.* New York: Cambridge University Press.

ed. 2004. *Boundaries and Belonging: States and Societies in the Struggle to Shape Identities and Local Practices.* New York: Cambridge University Press.

Mitzen, Jennifer. 2001. "Toward a Visible Hand: The International Public Sphere in Theory and Practice." Ph.D. dissertation, University of Chicago.

2005. "Reading Habermas in Anarchy: Multilateral Diplomacy and Global Public Spheres." *American Political Science Review* 99, no. 3 (August): 401–417.

Moravcsik, Andrew. 1997. "Taking Preferences Seriously: A Liberal Theory of International Politics." *International Organization* 51, no. 4 (Autumn): 513–553.

Munro, R. 1994. "China's Waxing Spheres of Influence." *Orbis* 38, no. 4: 585.

Naim, Moses. 2005a. "Broken Borders." *Newsweek* [International Edition] (October 24): 57.

2005b. "It's the Illicit Economy, Stupid." *Foreign Policy* 151 (November/December): 96.

2006. "Borderline; It's Not about Maps." *The Washington Post* (May 28), p. B1.

Neumann, Ronald. 2007. "Borderline Insanity: Thinking Big about Afghanistan." *The American Interest* 3, no. 2 (November/December), pp. 52–58.

Newman, David. 1994. "The Functional Presence of an 'Erased' Boundary: The Re-emergence of the Green Line." In Clive H. Schofield and Richard N. Schofield, eds., *The Middle East and North Africa: World Boundaries*, vol. 2. London: Routledge, p. 71–98.

ed. 1999. *Boundaries, Territory, and Post-Modernity*. London: Frank Cass.

2006. "Borders and Bordering: Towards an Interdisciplinary Perspective." *European Journal of Social Theory* 9, no. 2: 171–186.

Nichols, Robert. 1995. *The Frontier Tribal Areas, 1840–1990*. Occasional Paper 34. New York: Afghanistan Forum.

Noori, Neema. 2005. "Delegating Coercion: Linking Decentralization to State Coercion in Uzbekistan." Ph.D. dissertation, Department of Sociology, Columbia University, New York.

North, Douglass C. 1990. *Institutions, Institutional Change and Economic Performance*. New York: Cambridge University Press.

Nourzhanov, Kirill. 2005. "Saviours of the Nation or Robber Barons? Warlord Politics in Tajikistan." *Central Asian Survey* 24, no. 2 (June): 109–130.

Nugent, Paul. 2002. *Smugglers, Secessionists and Loyal Citizens on the Ghana-Togo Frontier: The Lie of the Borderlands since 1914*. Athens: Ohio University Press.

Olcott, Martha Brill. 1993. "Central Asia's Political Crisis." In Dale F. Eickelman, ed., *Russia's Muslim Frontiers: New Directions in Cross-Cultural Analysis*. Bloomington: Indiana University Press, pp. 49–62.

1995. *Central Asia's New States: Independence, Foreign Policy, and Regional Security*. Washington, DC: United States Institute of Peace Press.

2005. *Central Asia's Second Chance*. Washington, DC: Carnegie Endowment for International Peace.

O'Leary, Brendan, Ian S. Lustick, and Thomas Callaghy, eds. 2001. *Right-sizing the State: The Politics of Moving Borders*. Oxford: Oxford University Press.

Olsen, Trond E., and Gaute Torsvik. 1998. "Collusion and Renegotiation in Hierarchies: A Case of Beneficial Corruption." *International Economic Review* 39, no. 2 (May): 413–438.

Ong, Russell. 2005. "China's Security Interests in Central Asia." *Central Asian Survey* 24, no. 4 (December): 425–439.

Orhonlu, Cengiz. 1990. *Osmanlı İmperatorluğunda Derbend Teşkilatı*. İstanbul: İstanbul Üniversitesi Edebiyat Fakültesi Yayınları.

Ortaylı, İlber. 1985. *Tanzimat'tan Cumhuriyet'e Yerel Yönetim Geleneği*. İstanbul: Hil Yayın.

——— 1994. "Ioannina and Its Port-town Preveza in the Late Ottoman Empire (1865–1895)." In his *Studies in Ottoman Transformation*. Istanbul: Isis Press.

Ostrom, Elinor. 1990. *Governing the Commons: The Evolution of Institutions for Collective Action*. New York: Cambridge University Press.

——— 2000. "Collective Action and the Evolution of Social Norms." *Journal of Economic Perspectives* 14, no. 3: 137–158.

Ostrom, Elinor, James Walker, and Roy Gardner. 1992. "Covenants with and without a Sword: Self Governance Is Possible." *American Political Science Review* 86, no. 2: 404–417.

Oye, Kenneth A. 1986. "Explaining Cooperation under Anarchy: Hypotheses and Strategies." In Kenneth A. Oye, ed., *Cooperation under Anarchy*. Princeton, NJ: Princeton University Press, pp. 1–24.

Paasi, Anssi. 1996. *Territories, Boundaries, and Consciousness: The Changing Geographies of the Finnish-Russian Boundary*. New York: Wiley and Sons.

——— 1998. "Boundaries as Social Processes: Territoriality in the World of Flows." *Geopolitics* 3, no. 1: 69–88.

Paganele, Spuridonos K. 1882. *Odoiporikai Semeioseis: B', He stratiotike katalepsis Artes kai Thessalias*. Athens: Enoseos.

Paparregopoulos, Konstantinos. 1932. *Historia tou Hellenikou Ethnous apo ton archaiotaton chronon mechri tou 1930*. Athens: Eleutheroudakes.

Parks, Michael. 1990. "Soviet Region Declares State of Emergency; Uzbekistan Fears Spillover of Violence." *Washington Post* (June 9), p. A18.

Peckham, Robert Shannan. 2001. *National Histories, Natural States: Nationalism and the Politics of Place in Greece*. London: I. B. Tauris.

Petropoulos, John Anthony. 1968. *Politics and Statecraft in the Kingdom of Greece, 1833–1843*. Princeton, NJ: Princeton University Press

Polat, Necati. 2002. *Boundary Issues in Central Asia*. Adrsley, NY: Transnational Publishers.

Pomfret, Richard. 1995. *The Economies of Central Asia*. Princeton, NJ: Princeton University Press.

Posen, Barry R. 1993. "The Security Dilemma and Ethnic Conflict." In Michael E. Brown, ed., *Ethnic Conflict and International Security*. Princeton, NJ: Princeton University Press, pp. 103–124.

Prescott, John R. V. 1987. *Political Frontiers and Boundaries*. London: Allen and Unwin.

Quataert, Donald. 2003. "Recent Writings in Late Ottoman History." *International Journal of Middle East Studies* 35, no. 1 (February): 133–139.

Qureshi, S. M. M. 1966. "Pakhtunistan: The Frontier Dispute between Afghanistan and Pakistan." *Pacific Affairs* 39, no. 1/2 (Spring/Summer): 99–114.

Raczka, W. 1998. "Xinjiang and Its Central Asian Borderlands." *Central Asian Survey* 17, no. 3: 373–407.

Ramesh, Randeep. 2005. "US Backs Pakistani-Afghan Border Fence." *The Guardian* (September 14): 22.

Rashid, Ahmed. 1994. *The Resurgence of Central Asia: Islam or Nationalism?* Karachi: Oxford University Press.

2002. *Taliban: Islam, Oil and the New Great Game in Central Asia.* London: I. B. Tauris.

Ratner, Steven R. 1996. "Drawing a Better Line: Uti Possidetis and the Borders of New States." *American Journal of International Law* 90, no. 4: 590–624.

Reno, William. 1998. *Warlord Politics and African States.* Boulder, CO: Lynne Rienner.

Rodden, Jonathan, and Susan Rose-Ackerman. 1997. "Does Federalism Preserve Markets?" *Virginia Law Review* 83, no. 7 (October): 1521–1572.

Roebuck, Julian, and Thomas Barker. 1974. "A Typology of Police Corruption." *Social Problems* 21, no. 3: 423–437.

Rogan, Eugene L. 1999. *Frontiers of the State in the Late Ottoman Empire: Transjordan, 1850–1921.* Cambridge: Cambridge University Press.

Ron, James. 2000a. "Boundaries and Violence: Repertoires of State Action along the Bosnia/Yugoslavia Divide." *Theory and Society* 29, no. 5: 609–647.

2000b. "Savage Restraint: Israel, Palestine and the Dialectics of Legal Repression." *Social Problems* 47, no. 4 (November): 445–472.

2003. *Frontiers and Ghettos: State Violence in Serbia and Israel.* Berkeley: University of California Press.

Ronaldshay, Earl of. 1927. *The Life of Lord Curzon*, vol. 1. London: Ernest Benn.

Rosecrance, Richard. 1996. "The Rise of the Virtual State." *Foreign Affairs* 75, no. 4 (July/August): 45–61.

Rosenberg, Christoph B., and Maarten De Zeeuw. 2001. "Welfare Effects of Uzbekistan's Foreign Exchange Regime." *IMF Staff Papers* 48, no. 1: 160–178.

Ross, Michael. 2004. "How Does Natural Resource Wealth Influence Civil Wars?" *International Organization* 58, no. 1 (Winter): 35–67.

Rothchild, Donald. 2002. "The Effects of State Crisis on African Interstate Relations (and Comparisons with Post-Soviet Eurasia)." In Mark R. Beissinger and Crawford Young, eds., *Beyond State Crisis? Postcolonial Africa and Post-Soviet Eurasia in Comparative Perspective.* Washington, DC: Woodrow Wilson Center Press, pp. 189–215.

Rubin, Barnett. 1993. "The Fragmentation of Tajikistan." *Survival* 35, no. 4 (Winter): 71–91.

2007. "Saving Afghanistan." *Foreign Affairs* 86, no. 1 (January/February): 57–78.

Ruggie, John Gerard. 1993. "Territoriality and Beyond: Problematizing Modernity in International Relations." *International Organization* 47, no. 1: 139–174.

Rumer, Boris Z. 2005. "Central Asia: At the End of the Transition." In Boris Rumer, ed., *Central Asia at the End of the Transition.* London: M. E. Sharpe, pp. 3–70.

Rumley, Dennis, and Julian V. Minghi, eds. 1991. *The Geography of Border Landscapes.* London: Routledge.

Rushworth, Dennis. 1997. "Mapping in Support of Frontier Arbitration: Boundary Definition: Boundary Disclaimer Notes; Toponymy." *Boundary and Security Bulletin* 7, no. 1: 61–66.

Bibliography

Sack, Robert. 1986. *Human Territoriality: Its Theory and History*. Cambridge: Cambridge University Press.

Sahlins, Peter. 1990. "Natural Frontiers Revisited: France's Boundaries since the Seventeenth Century." *American Historical Review* 95, no. 5: 1423–1451.

1991. *Boundaries: The Making of France and Spain in the Pyrenees*. Berkeley: University of California Press.

Sambanis, Nicholas. 2000. "Partition as a Solution to Ethnic War." *World Politics* 52: 437–483.

Schaeffer, Robert. 1990. *Warpaths: The Politics of Partition*. New York: Hill and Wang.

Schelling, Thomas C. 1980. *The Strategy of Conflict*. Cambridge, MA: Harvard University Press.

Schina, Nikolaou Th. 1886. *Odoiporikai semeioseis Makedonias, Epeirou, neas orothetikes grammes kai Thessalias*, vol. 4. Athens: Messager d'Athenes.

Schleifer, Andrei, and Robert W. Vishny. 1993. "Corruption." *The Quarterly Journal of Economics* 108, no. 3 (August): 599–617.

Schroeder, Paul W. 1986. "The 19th Century International System: Changes in the Structure." *World Politics* 39, no. 1: 1–26.

Schwedler, Jillian. *Faith in Moderation: Islamist Parties in Jordan and Yemen*. New York: Cambridge University Press.

Scott, James C. 1998. *Seeing Like a State: How Certain Schemes to Improve the Human Condition Have Failed*. New Haven, CT: Yale University Press.

Sergeant, Lewis. 1897. *Greece in the Nineteenth Century: A Record of Hellenic Emancipation and Progress: 1821–1897*. London: T. Fisher Unwin.

Seton-Watson, R. W. 1955. *Britain in Europe, 1789–1914: A Survey of Foreign Policy*. Cambridge: Cambridge University Press.

Sfeka-Theodosiou, Aggelike. 1989. *He prosartese tes Thessalias. He prote fase sten ensomatose mias Hellenikes eparchias sto Helleniko kratos (1881–85)*. Ph.D. thesis, Aristoteleion University, Thessalonike.

Shaw, Stanford J., and Ezel Kural Shaw. 1977. *History of the Ottoman Empire and Modern Turkey*, vol. 2: *Reform, Revolution, and Republic: The Rise of Modern Turkey*. Cambridge: Cambridge University Press.

Sherman, Lawrence W. 1980. "Three Models of Organizational Corruption." *Social Problems* 27, no. 4 (April): 478–491.

Simmons, Beth A. 2006. "Trade and Territorial Conflict in Latin America: International Borders as Institutions." In Miles Kahler and Barbara Walters, eds., *Territoriality and Conflict in an Era of Globalization*. New York: Cambridge University Press, pp. 251–287.

Siverson, Randolph, and Harvey, Starr. 1990. "Opportunity, Willingness and the Diffusion of War." *American Political Science Review* 84, no. 1: 47–67.

Sluga, Glenda. 2001. *The Problem of Trieste and the Italo-Yugoslav Border: Difference, Identity, and Sovereignty in Twentieth Century Europe*. Albany: State University of New York Press.

Snidal, Duncan. 1985. "Coordination versus Prisoners' Dilemma: Implications for International Cooperation and Regimes." *The American Political Science Review* 79, no. 4 (December): 923–942.

Solnick, Steven L. 1996. "The Breakdown of Hierarchies in the Soviet Union and China: A Neoinstitutional Perspective." *World Politics* 48, no. 2: 209–238.

1998. *Stealing the State: Control and Collapse in Soviet Institutions*. New York: Cambridge University Press.

Squatriti, Paolo. 2002. "Digging Ditches in Early Medieval Europe." *Past and Present* 176 (August): 11–65.

Stamatake, I. D. 1846. *Pinaks Chorographikos tes Hellados*. Athens: Blassaridou.

Starr, Harvey, and G. Dale Thomas. 2002. "The 'Nature' of Contiguous Borders: Ease of Interaction, Salience, and the Analysis of Crisis." *International Interactions* 28: 213–235.

Stein, Arthur A. 1982. "Coordination and Collaboration: Regimes in an Anarchic World." *International Organization* 36, no. 2 (Spring): 299–324.

Steinmo, Sven, Kathleen Thelen, and Frank Longstreth, eds. 1995. *Structuring Politics: Historical Institutionalism in Comparative Analysis*. Cambridge: Cambridge University Press.

Strong, Frederick. 1842. *Greece as a Kingdom; or a Statistical Description of that Country*. London: Longman, Brown, Green and Longmans.

Tatsios, Theodore George. 1984. *The Megali Idea and the Greek-Turkish War of 1897: The Impact of the Cretan Problem on Greek Irredentism, 1866–1897*. Boulder, CO: East European Monographs.

Thelen, Kathleen. 2003. "How Institutions Evolve: Insights from Comparative Historical Analysis." In James Mahoney and Dietrich Rueschemeyer, eds., *Comparative Historical Analysis in the Social Sciences*. New York: Cambridge University Press, pp. 208–240.

Thies, Cameron G. 2002. "A Pragmatic Guide to Qualitative Historical Analysis in the Study of International Relations." *International Studies Perspectives* 3: 351–372.

2004. "State Building, Interstate and Intrastate Rivalry: A Study of Post-Colonial Developing Country Extractive Efforts, 1975–2000." *International Studies Quarterly* 48: 53–72.

2006. "Public Violence and State Building in Central America." *Comparative Political Studies* 39, no. 10 (December): 1263–1282.

Thomson, Janice E. 1994. *Mercenaries, Pirates, and Sovereigns: State-Building and Extraterritorial Violence in Early Modern Europe*. Princeton, NJ: Princeton University Press.

Tilly, Charles. 1992. *Coercion, Capital, and European States, AD 990–1992*. Cambridge, MA: Blackwell.

1998. "International Communities, Secure or Otherwise." In Emanuel Adler and Michael Barnett, eds., *Security Communities*. New York: Cambridge University Press, pp. 397–412.

1999. "Survey Article: Power – Top Down and Bottom Up." *The Journal of Political Philosophy* 7, no. 3: 330–352.

2000. "Historical Analysis of Political Processes." In Jonathan H. Turner, ed., *Handbook of Sociological Theory*. New York: Plenum, pp. 567–588.

2005a. *Trust and Rule*. New York: Cambridge University Press.

2005b. *Identity, Boundaries and Social Ties*. Boulder, CO: Paradigm.

2007. "Contentious Performances." Unpublished manuscript, Columbia University.

Tilly, Charles, and Sid Tarrow. 2007. *Contentious Politics*. Boulder, CO: Paradigm.

Tishkov, Valery. 1995. "'Don't Kill Me, I'm a Kyrgyz!': An Anthropological Analysis of Violence in the Osh Ethnic Conflict." *Journal of Peace Research* 32, no. 2 (May): 133–149.

1997. *Ethnicity, Nationalism and Conflict in and after the Soviet Union: The Mind Aflame*. London: Sage.

Toft, Monica Duffy. 2003. *The Geography of Ethnic Violence: Identity, Interests, and the Indivisibility of Territory*. Princeton, NJ: Princeton University Press.

Trisko, Jessica N. 2005. "Coping with the Islamist Threat: Analyzing Repression in Kazakhstan, Kyrgyzstan and Uzbekistan." *Central Asian Survey* 24, no. 4 (December): 373–389.

Tronvoll, Kjetil. 1999. "Borders of Violence – Boundaries of Identity: Demarcating the Eritrean Nation-State." *Ethnic and Racial Studies* 22, no. 6 (November): 1037–1060.

Türkgeldi, Ali Fuat. 1957. *Mesail-i Mühimme-i Siyasiyye*, vol. 2. Ankara: Türk Tarih Kurumu.

Üçyol, Rıfat. 1988. "The Border Dispute between the Ottoman Empire and Greece: Rearranging the Border according to the Berlin Treaty of 1878 and Giving Land to Greece (1878–1881)." *Revue Internationale d'Histoire Militaire* 67: 119–139.

Ülkekul, Cevat. 1998. *Cumhuriyet Dönemi Türk Haritacılık Tarihi*. Istanbul: Dönence.

United Nations Development Programme (UNDP). 2005. "Bringing Down Barriers: Regional Cooperation for Human Development and Security." Humanitarian Development Report.

United Nations Office of Drugs and Crime (UNODC). 2006. "Afghanistan Opium Survey."

United States Department of State. 2002. *World Military Expenditures and Arms Transfers, 1999–2000*. Washington, DC: Bureau of Verification and Compliance.

Van Evera, Stephen. 1994. "Hypotheses on Nationalism and War." *International Security* 18, no. 4 (Spring): 5–39.

Varshney, Ashutosh. 2001. "Ethnic Conflict and Civil Society: India and Beyond." *World Politics* 53 (April): 362–398.

Vasquez, John. 1993. *The War Puzzle*. New York: Cambridge University Press.

1995. "Why Do Neighbors Fight? Proximity, Interaction, or Territoriality." *Journal of Peace Research* 32, no. 3 (August): 277–293.

Veremis, Thanos. 1990. "From the National State to the Stateless Nation, 1821–1910." In Martin Blinkhorn and Thanos Veremis, eds., *Modern Greece: Nationalism and Nationality*. Athens: Sage-Eliamep, pp. 9–22.

Wagner, R. Harrison. 2007. *War and the State: The Theory of International Politics*. Ann Arbor: University of Michigan Press.

Waldron, Arthur. 1990. *The Great Wall of China: From History to Myth*. Cambridge: Cambridge University Press.

Walker, R. B. J. 1993. *Inside/Outside: International Relations as Political Theory*. Cambridge: Cambridge University Press.

Walsh, Declan. 2006. "G2: The Wild Frontier." *The Guardian* (January 31): 6.

Walter, Barbara F. 2003. "Explaining the Intractability of Territorial Conflict." *International Studies Review* 5, no. 4 (December): 137–153.

    2006. "Building Reputation: Why Governments Fight Some Separatists but Not Others." *American Journal of Political Science* 50, no. 2: 313–330.

Walters, William. 2002. "Mapping Schengenland: Denaturalizing the Border." *Environment and Planning D: Society and Space* 20: 561–580.

Weber, Cynthia. 1995. *Simulating Sovereignty: Intervention, the State and Symbolic Exchange*. Cambridge: Cambridge University Press.

Weber, Eugen. 1976. *Peasants into Frenchmen: The Modernization of Rural France, 1870–1914*. Stanford, CA: Stanford University Press.

Weinthal, Erika. 2002. *State Making and Environmental Cooperation: Linking Domestic and International Politics in Central Asia*. Cambridge, MA: MIT Press.

Wendt, Alexander. 1999. *Social Theory of International Politics*. New York: Cambridge University Press.

Wiener, Myron. 1971. "The Macedonian Syndrome: An Historical Model of International Relations and Political Development." *World Politics* 23, no. 4: 665–683.

Wood, William B. 2000. "GIS as a Tool for Territorial Negotiations." *IBRU Boundary and Security Bulletin* 8, no. 3: 72–79.

Wrong, Michela. 2003. "Peacekeepers on Guard as Frontier Feud Brews Again." *Financial Times* (12 July).

Yasamee, F. A. K. 1996. *Ottoman Diplomacy: Abdulhamid and the Great Powers, 1878–1888*. Istanbul: Isis Press.

Yıldız, Hakkı Dursun. 1992. *150. Yılında Tanzimat*. Ankara: Türk Tarih Kurumu.

Zegin, Cahide. 1978. "Yunanistan 'Tashih-i Hudud' Mes'elesiyle ilgili Türk ve Avrupa Hariciyye Nezaretleri Yazışmaları." M.A. thesis, History Department, Istanbul University.

Index

Index